G. WILLIAM DOMHOFF,
the author of this book,
is Assistant Professor of Psychology,
and Fellow of Cowell College,
at the University of California
at Santa Cruz. He has published
numerous articles on the new
dream research and essays on
psychoanalytic theory.

Who
Rules America?

G. WILLIAM DOMHOFF

A SPECTRUM BOOK

PRENTICE-HALL, INC.

ENGLEWOOD CLIFFS, NEW JERSEY

To Judy

Current printing (last digit):

20 19 18 17 16 15 14

Preface . . . . .

My special thanks to the following social scientists who read all or parts of early drafts of this manuscript: political scientists Hoyt Ballard, Karl Lamb, Robert Simmons, and Benjamin Smith; sociologists E. Digby Baltzell, Frank Lindenfeld, Charles H. Page, and Erwin O. Smigel; psychologists Calvin S. Hall, Henry Minton, Jerry Phelan, and Edward Simmel; anthropologist James Downs; and economist Paul M. Sweezy. I think the value of their criticisms can be found in the fact they are unlikely to recognize many parts of the revised manuscript that appears as this book.

Several students participated in the research that underlies this book. Where their work has been a significant contribution to the documentation of one part of the thesis I have expressed my appreciation with a specific citation in the main text or in the reference notes.

I also want to extend my gratitude to those of the library and secretarial staffs at the University of California, Santa Cruz, for all the help and patience they afforded me. I want to thank especially Charlotte Cassidy, Becky Dilts, Sonné Lemke, and Happy Hunter, who shared in the final typing. Thanks also to Paul Molfino and Marc Sproule of the duplication department for running off and putting together several dozen copies of the first draft.

But my biggest and most special thanks go to my wife, Judy, who understood when my mind drifted from the topic of the moment and smiled knowingly when I hurried away to polish a phrase or add a paragraph. Most of all, she tolerated my late arrival at dinner and entertained Lynne (4½), Lori (3½), and Bill (1½) during my many hours at the typewriter.

I have expressed my appreciation to all those close intellectual friends and interested students who might rightfully wish to identify themselves with all or part of this enterprise by using the editorial "we" throughout the main narrative.

Finally, I have tried to make it unnecessary to continually skip to the reference notes in the back of the book by including more than the usual number of authors and book titles in the main text. However, there are still several hundred reference notes for the interested specialist. The casual reader can begin with the first chapter—the critical scholar or serious student is advised to begin with the Introduction.

Santa Cruz, California   G.W.D.

Contents

Contents

Introduction . . . . .

This book is inspired by the ideas of four very different men—E. Digby Baltzell, C. Wright Mills, Paul M. Sweezy, and Robert A. Dahl. Many other scholars contributed documentation and minor theoretical points, and a considerable amount of data was gathered by myself and my students, but the basic ideas which guided this study were developed in an attempt to ground Mills's "power elite" in Baltzell's "American business aristocracy" (Sweezy's "ruling class"), and to show that Dahl's finding of "pluralism" on the local level is not incompatible with the idea of a national upper class that is a governing class.

E. Digby Baltzell, the author of *An American Business Aristocracy*[1] and *The Protestant Establishment,* is a sociologist who is also a hereditary member of the Philadelphia branch of the American upper class. He combines his insider's knowledge with a Columbia University doctorate in sociology to present the historical and institutional background of a social class whose exploration has been left, with certain notable exceptions, to novelists and society-page journalists. Baltzell believes that this American upper class is a governing class, or "establishment," in his terms, and that its development coincided with the growth of the national corporate economy in the late nineteenth and early twentieth centuries. In this limited theoretical sense he agrees with Marxian theory, but his values are very different from those of Marxists. Baltzell holds to "aristocratic," or "Tocquevillean" values, favoring an open-class system, based on business enterprise, over a classless socialism. With certain exceptions, such as the failure of private schools to produce the quantity and quality of statesmen trained by their like number in England, and the failure of prejudiced elements of the upper class to assimilate the twentieth-century ethnic rich, Baltzell approves of the American Way. Although he would probably consider himself a conservative—for that is how he classifies such upper-class Presidents as Theodore Roosevelt, Franklin D. Roosevelt, and John F. Kennedy—he would most likely be considered a "liberal" within the context of present-day American politics.

The late C. Wright Mills was also a sociologist, but unlike Baltzell he was an angry middle-class Texan who held to radical ideas. He had little use for the American Way.[2] However, by talking in terms of "elites" and "institutions" rather than "classes," and by rejecting the revolutionary role claimed for the working class as a "labor metaphysic," he threw consternation into the ranks of orthodox radicalism.[3] Mills's perspective was sarcastic and biting, and it has been compared unfavorably with that of Baltzell by one of the leading authorities on the sociology of politics, Seymour Martin Lipset.[4] Be that as it may, Mills broke new ground when he reopened the discussion of the American power structure with his justly famous *The Power Elite.*

Paul M. Sweezy, author of "Interest Groups in the American Economy," "The American Ruling Class," *The Theory of Capitalist Development,* and *Monopoly Capital* (with Paul Baran), is what C. Wright Mills liked to call a "plain Marxist." [5] This means that Sweezy applies Marxist methodology to the changing American reality rather than trying to graft on conclusions drawn from Marxist studies of different countries or earlier epochs. It also means that his conclusions are as likely as not to be in disagreement with those of the Soviet Union or Red China. An economist, Sweezy received his Ph.D. at Harvard.

Robert A. Dahl, finally, is a Yale University political scientist who has made well-taken critical comments on previous studies of national political power ("A Critique of the Ruling Elite Model") as well as having produced a prototype of what such studies should be at the local level (*Who Governs?*). While convinced of "pluralism" as opposed to "elitism" for most local politics, he believes that the evidence for a ruling elite model at the national level never has been adequately assessed.

Any book which attempts to demonstrate that American society is controlled from its highest levels also must deal with the fact that the country is a democracy. This study will not imply otherwise. Instead, it will attempt to support a concept of democracy that is casually buried in *Southern Politics,* a fact-filled book by one of America's great political scientists, the late Harvard empiricist V. O. Key:

The operation of democracy may depend on competition among conflicting sections of the "better element" for the support of the masses of voters. Hence, the workings of democracy require a considerable degree of disagreement within the upper classes.[6]

By emphasizing disagreement within the American upper class, it is possible to agree with the great number of observers who see the United States as a society in which politics is often based upon shifting coalitions and in which the blue-collar and white-collar classes sometimes gain a measure of influence. However, even after agreeing that the American upper class is neither monolithic nor omnipotent, let alone omniscient, it is still possible to demonstrate the fundamental fact that the American upper class is a governing class. The shifting coalitions are dominated, as we shall see, by members of the American upper class.

The sociological study which follows is concerned with the years 1932 through 1964. It is beholden to no theory about the dynamics of history or the structure of society or the future of man. In fact, it is because "ruling class" is a term that implies a Marxist view of history that the more neutral term "governing class" is employed. However, it must be stressed that the term "governing class" as used in this book is in no way related to the incorrect usage of that term by the Italian social theorist Vilfredo Pareto. Pareto was talking about "governing elites," with little or no concern for socioeconomic classes.[7]

We have used a great many names and a great many citations from the popular press to exemplify our thesis. However, the validity of the argument is not based upon the examples. Rather, it is based upon the systematic data that are presented throughout each chapter. This has to be emphasized because the use of examples can often give the impression that one is "selecting" evidence. The use of a great many illustrations from the mass media is in keeping with Mills's belief that what is going on in the world is revealed most directly and organically in the daily press.[8] It also serves to dispel any notion that the "real" rulers of America are somehow behind the scenes rather than before the public each and every day.

Because our topic is a controverisal one on which misunderstandings can easily occur, we will use this introduction for explicit definitions of such key terms as "social class," "co-optation," "governing class," and "power elite." We will also explain and briefly defend the methodology we will use in trying to determine whether or not the American upper class is a governing class. We will return to many of these topics at greater length in the final chapter.

According to Mills, in a controversial footnote in the twelfth chapter of *The Power Elite*, "class" is an economic term.[9] However, this is not necessarily the case. "Class" can also refer to a group of families with similar aspirations and values, to families who perceive each other as equals and freely intermarry. Baltzell quotes the following definition with approval:

A "Social Class" is the largest group of people whose members have intimate access to one another. A class is composed of families and social cliques. The interrelationships between these families and cliques, in such informal activities as dancing, visiting, receptions, teas, and larger informal affairs, constitute the function of the social class.[10]

We can be satisfied that this brief definition of social class is a generally acceptable one, for it does not differ materially from those presented by the Marxist Sweezy, the sociologist Joseph Kahl, and the political scientist Dahl. "A social class, then," says Sweezy, "is made up of freely inter-marrying families." [11] Kahl notes, "If a large group of families are approximately equal to each other and clearly differentiated from other families, we call them a *social class*," [12] while Dahl defines equal "social standing" in terms of

the extent to which members of that circle would be willing—disregarding personal and idiosyncratic factors—to accord the conventional privileges of social intercourse and acceptance among equals; marks of social acceptability include willingness to dine together, to mingle freely in intimate social events, to accept membership in the same clubs, to use forms of courtesy considered appropriate among social equals, to intermarry, and so on.[13]

Our starting point, then, must be the demonstration of an observable, differentiated, interacting social group with more or less definite boundaries. In other words, does an identifiable social upper class exist in the United States? This question is closely related to a second empirical question which interests us in the light of Mills's objection that "class" is an economic term: Does this social upper class overlap in membership with any particular economic "class"? The answer to both of these questions, as will be seen in the first two chapters, is "Yes," thus making Mills's point primarily a semantic one. It will be shown that there is a national upper class made up of rich businessmen and their families, an "American business aristocracy," as Baltzell calls it. Although this national upper class has its ethnic, religious, and new-rich–old-rich antagonisms, it is nonetheless closely knit by such institutions as stock ownership, trust funds, intermarriages, private schools, exclusive city clubs, exclusive summer resorts, debutante parties, foxhunts, charity drives, and, last but not least, corporation boards. This information, when fully elaborated, can be considered a direct answer to sociologist William Kornhauser, who claims that one of the main weaknesses of Mills's work was that he did not sufficiently demonstrate the interaction of the various cliques making up his "power elite." [14] If such a weakness existed, it was in Mills's presentation and not in a lack of such interaction.

In addition to demonstrating the reality of a national upper class, we will emphasize that this social group, whether its members are aware of it or not, has well-established ways of "training" and "preparing" new members. This point must be stressed because it is certainly the case that people are moving into (not to mention out of) this group all the time. "Social mobility" is a distinct reality, and this study will document its occurrence at the highest levels of society as well as at the middle levels where it is usually studied.[15] Social mobility can be looked at from many points of view and in terms of many different questions, but the important thing to keep in mind in understanding this phenomenon in a sociological study of the upper class is the process of "co-optation." * For our purposes, we will mean by co-optation the processes whereby individuals are assimilated and committed to the institutions and values of the dominant socioeconomic group.[17] In studying co-optation we want to know which institutions select and prepare those who are assimilated, as well as the ideas and values that make a person acceptable. To anticipate somewhat, the co-optation of bright young men into the American upper class occurs through education at private schools, elite universities, and elite law schools; through success as a corporation executive; through membership in exclusive gentlemen's clubs; and through participation in exclusive charities.

Is this social upper class, with its several institutional focal points and its several means of assimilating new members, also a "governing class"? It is with this question that new ground must be broken, for systematic data are lacking. To begin with, "governing class" must be defined. Our definition is as follows:

A "governing class" is a social upper class which owns a disproportionate amount of a country's wealth, receives a disproportionate amount of a country's yearly income, and contributes a disproportionate number of its members to the controlling institutions and key decision-making groups of the country.

Disproportionate wealth and income are important in this definition because they imply that the upper class has interests that are at least somewhat different from those of other socioeconomic groups. As we will see, members of the upper class have different sources of income as well as more income than persons of other income levels. By the same token, a disproportionate number of leaders is important because it implies control of these institutions and decision-making groups. We will argue in some detail in the final chapter that these criteria, while not infallible, are at least as good as those used in other approaches to this difficult question. And if, as Dahl says of the decision-making methodology, a group is more or less a ruling elite depending upon how many decisions it controls, we

---

* As an example of another way of looking at social mobility, Baltzell stresses its importance in quenching "the Marxian dreams of revolution." He quotes Marx as saying that "the more a ruling class is able to assimilate the most prominent men of the dominated classes, the more stable and dangerous its rule." [16]

can say that a social upper class is more or less a governing class depending upon the percentage of wealth it possesses, the income it receives, and the leaders it contributes.[18] Finally, we would stress that our minimum definition is valuable because it can be related to empirical data.

Although our definition may not be acceptable to everyone, it does meet Dahl's stricture that the hypothesis contained in such a definition must be capable of disproof as well as support. In fact, the methods we will use in testing the hypothesis are similar to those used by Dahl in his study of New Haven, Connecticut. Since Dahl and one of his former students, Nelson Polsby, have been the most articulate critics of previous studies of the American power structure, we have followed their criticisms and comments with some care. We do not wish to have it pointed out to us, as Dahl did to Mills and Polsby did to Baltzell, that we did not test our hypothesis.[19] Dahl relied primarily on three methods to determine who governed in New Haven. He described them as follows:

1. To study changes in the socioeconomic characteristics of incumbents in city offices in order to determine whether any rather large historical changes may have occurred in the sources of leadership.

2. To isolate a particular socioeconomic category and then determine the nature and extent of participation in local affairs by persons in this category.

3. To examine a set of "decisions" in different "issue-areas" in order to determine what kinds of persons were the most influential according to one operational measure of relative influence, and to determine patterns of influence.[20]

Dahl's first two methods are aspects of what we will call the "sociology-of-leadership" methodology.[21] The essence of this methodology is the study of the sociological composition of leadership groups in order to determine whether or not the leaders come from any given socioeconomic class, ethnic group, or religious group. Dahl used this method in the first six chapters of *Who Governs?* With it he showed quite conclusively that members of the middle class had taken over the decision-making roles he studied in New Haven. Dahl's third method focuses on the decision-making process. With it he showed that different members of the middle class in New Haven were influential in different issue-areas. There was no one "ruling elite" that made decisions on a wide variety of issues.

Unfortunately, the decision-making method is difficult to apply because the "operational measure" of influence is the frequency with which a person "successfully initiates an important policy over the opposition of others, or vetoes policies initiated by others, or initiates a policy where no opposition appears." [22] Inferences about who initiates and who vetoes must be made after "reconstructing" the decision "by means of interviews with participants, the presence of an observer, records, documents, and newspapers." [23] However, we believe with Baltzell and Raymond Bauer, an expert in the study of policy formation, that even when the information with which to reconstruct a specific decision seems to be available, it is a very risky and tricky business.[24] Many aspects of the situation may remain secret, the participants themselves may not be able to correctly assess the roles of the various members, the "real" interests of the participants are complex and often impossible for even them to determine, and the larger context within which the issue arises may be as important in understanding the eventual decision as the decision-making process itself. Thus, we have relied on Dahl's third method somewhat less than on his first two. At the same time we have tried to remain faithful to Dahl's concern with specific issue-areas by studying the sociological backgrounds of members of decision-making groups and by studying institutions and associations which are known to have a great amount of influence in specific issue-areas. Polsby seems to be recommending our approach when he says:

If there exist high degrees of overlap among issue-areas in decision-making personnel, or of institutionalization in the bases of power in specified issue-areas, or of regularity in the procedures of decision making, then the empirical conclusion is justified that some sort of "power structure" exists.* [25]

However, since studying decision-making groups and institutional personnel is not the same thing as studying the decision-making process itself, it is very important in using this method to state explicitly the scope and limits of the powers of the given institution, association, or decision-making group. (One of the main criticisms of Mills's thesis was that he did not spell out the powers of his power elite.) The kind and limits of the powers of the groups and institutions which concern us will be noted as each one is studied, and they will be summarized in the final chapter when the problems of methodology are dealt with in greater detail.

From the information to be presented in the following chapters, it will be quite clear that the less than 1 per cent of the population comprising the American upper class, if it is a governing class, does not rule alone.† Thus,

---

* In a later version of this statement, Polsby changed the words "is justified" to read "could conceivably justify." [26]

† We use the phrase "less than 1 per cent" because we do not know the exact size of the American upper class. According to Harold M. Hodges' *Peninsula People*, listees in the *Social Register* comprise 0.2 per cent of the population of the San Francisco area, while Dixon Wecter estimated in the 1930's that 0.4 per cent of the New York population was in that city's *Social Register*.[27] Assuming that the American

it will be necessary to demonstrate that most of the non-upper-class leaders are selected and trained by members of the upper class (co-opted), or to say the same thing differently, that the advancement of these non-upper-class leaders is dependent upon their attaining goals that are shared by members of the upper class. This leads to a discussion of our concept of the "power elite," a term borrowed from Mills but defined in a slightly different manner. We agree with Mills in defining the power elite as those who have a superior amount of power due to the institutional hierarchies they command, but we deviate from Mills by restricting the term to persons who are in command positions in institutional hierarchies controlled by members of the American upper class, or, in the case of members of the federal government, to persons who come to the government from the upper class or from high positions in institutions controlled by members of the upper class.* By this definition, any particular member of the power elite may or may not be a member of the upper class. It not only allows for co-optation and for control through hired employees, but it agrees that some members of the upper class—what Baltzell calls the functionless genteel— may not be members of the power elite.[28] This definition of the power elite is very similar to Baltzell's concept of an "establishment":

The upper class, in other words, will be a ruling class or, as I should prefer to say, its leaders will form an *establishment*. . . . In a free society, while an establishment will always be dominated by upper-class members, it also must be constantly rejuvenated by new members of the elite who are in the process of acquiring upper-class status.[29]

While our definition of the power elite is somewhat different from that given by Mills, the final result of our research will show that our power elite is very similar to his. This difference lies in the fact that (1) we have

---

upper class is somewhat larger than the *Social Register* percentages would indicate, for reasons which will be given in Chapter 1, and supplementing this information with income-distribution and wealth-distribution statistics, we would estimate that the American upper class encompasses, at most, about 0.5 per cent of the population of the United States. This means that as of the early 1960's there were nearly 1 million persons in the American upper class. We will use this percentage, 0.5 per cent, in determining the amount of overrepresentation of members of the upper class in various institutions.

* We do not demand that the upper-class person in the federal government be from an institution controlled by members of the upper class in order to be considered a member of the power elite, because some important upper-class members of the federal government go directly into government work. A case in point would be the late Joseph Clark Grew, a cousin of the financier J. P. Morgan. Grew was ambassador to Japan during the 1930's and an important member of the State Department during the 1940's. According to Gar Alperovitz' *Atomic Diplomacy,* Grew was one of the key actors in the decision to drop the atomic bomb. We have no hesitation in calling him a member of a power elite grounded in the American upper class.

not assumed *a priori* that any group is part of the power elite as Mills did in so designating the corporate leaders, military leaders, and political leaders; and (2) we have grounded the power elite in the upper class. Putting it another way, we will attempt to show that Mills's power elite has its roots in Baltzell's "American business aristocracy" and serves its interests. In the case of each institution hypothesized to be a basis of the power elite, control by members of the upper class must be demonstrated empirically. Thus, when we arrive at the crucial institution in this study—the federal government—we will be in a position to show just which parts of it can be considered aspects of a power elite that is the operating arm of the American upper (governing) class. We will not assume, as Mills did, that the Executive branch of the federal government is part of a power elite, but will instead show that its leaders are either members of the upper class or former employees of institutions controlled by members of the upper class. Perhaps several examples from recent Democratic administrations will make this final point clear. Franklin D. Roosevelt, John F. Kennedy, Adlai Stevenson, Dean Acheson, Averell Harriman, Douglas Dillon, McGeorge Bundy, and Nicholas Katzenbach were hereditary members of the upper class, while Robert McNamara was president of the Ford Motor Company, Dean Rusk was president of the Rockefeller Foundation, and John Gardner was president of the Carnegie Corporation. We consider all of these men to be members of the power elite, for they are either old-line members of the American business aristocracy or former high-level employees of institutions controlled by members of that social group. We are quite aware of the humble origins of McNamara and Rusk, whose children may or may not become members of the upper class depending upon the stock accumulations of their fathers, the schools they attend, and the persons they marry.* However, we think that the nature of McNamara's and Rusk's previous employment, and the consequent status and income this afforded them, is what is important in understanding their appointment to government.†

We believe that the relationship between the concepts of "governing class" and "power elite" is quite straightforward, but it is also true that there can be confusion unless the two are compared and contrasted. To repeat, "governing class" refers to a social upper class which owns a disproportionate amount of the country's wealth, receives a disproportionate amount of the country's yearly income, and contributes a disproportionate number of its members to positions of leadership. However, some of the

---

* McNamara's son attended St. Paul's, one of the most exclusive private schools in the country.

† According to Rusk's testimony to the Senate, he continued to draw "severance pay" from the Rockefeller Foundation while he was Secretary of State.[30]

members of this social group may not be involved in anything more relevant than raising horses, riding to the hounds, or hobnobbing with the international "jet set." The "power elite," on the other hand, encompasses all those who are in command positions in institutions controlled by members of the upper (governing) class. Any given member of the power elite may or may not be a member of the upper class. The important thing is whether or not the institution he serves is controlled by members of the upper class. Thus, if we can show that members of the upper class control the corporations through stock ownership and corporate directorships, the military through the Department of Defense, and the corporate law profession through large corporate law firms and major law schools, we will have gone a long way toward demonstrating that the aims of the American power elite, as defined by either Mills or this book, are necessarily those of members of the upper class.

Perhaps the relationship between "governing class" and "power elite" can be made even clearer by outlining the steps that we will follow in attempting to answer the question: Is the American upper class a governing class?

First, we will show the existence of a national upper class that meets generally accepted definitions of social class.

Second, we will show that this upper class owns a disproportionate amount of the country's wealth and receives a disproportionate amount of its yearly income, and that members of the American upper class control the major banks and corporations, which in turn are known to dominate the American economy.

Third, we will show that members of the American upper class and their high-level corporation executives control the foundations, the elite universities, the largest of the mass media, and such important opinion-molding associations as the Council on Foreign Relations, the Foreign Policy Association, the Committee for Economic Development, the Business Advisory Council, and the National Advertising Council.

Fourth, we will show that the power elite (members of the American upper class and their high-level employees in the above institutions) control the Executive branch of the federal government.

Fifth, we will show that the power elite controls regulatory agencies, the federal judiciary, the military, the CIA, and the FBI through its control of the Executive branch of the federal government. It will be shown also that this control by the Executive branch is supplemented by other lines of control in the case of each of these branches or agencies of the government.

After it has been shown that the power elite does not control but merely influences (1) the Legislative branch of the federal government, (2) most state governments, and (3) most city governments, it will be argued that its control of corporations, foundations, elite universities, the Presidency, the federal judiciary, the military, and the CIA qualifies the American upper class as a "governing class," especially in the light of the wealth owned and the income received by members of that exclusive social group.

It should be added that by "control," we mean to imply dominance, the exercise of "power" (ability to act) from a position of "authority" (the right to exercise power by virtue of some office or legal mandate). Synonyms for control would be rule, govern, guide, and direct. "Influence," for us, is a weaker term, implying that a person can sometimes sway, persuade, or otherwise have an effect upon those who control from a position of authority. Since these vague terms can be the subject of much debate, let us once again make clear that we will try to show that members of the upper class dominate major corporations, foundations, universities, and the Executive branch of the federal government, while they merely have influence in Congress, most state governments, and most local governments. This does not mean that they are never influenced in areas where they have control, nor does it mean that they never get their way where they merely exert influence. However, the interesting thing about "control" and "influence" in a country where the concept of a governing class calls forth notions of sinister men lurking behind the throne, is that members of the American governing class in fact serve their interests from positions of authority. Authority-based control, rather than covert influence, is their dominant mode.

Chapter One . . . .
The American Upper Class

The American upper class of today is not like that of yesterday. Nor is the American upper class like that of any other country, for it alone grew up within a middle-class framework of representative government and egalitarian ideology, unhampered by feudal lords, kings, priests, or mercenary armies. Only the American upper class is made up exclusively of the descendants of successful businessmen and corporation lawyers—whatever their pretensions, few families are "old" enough or rich enough to forget this overriding fact. For all of these reasons it is often concluded by those who use other societies as their standard that an American upper class does not exist. The purpose of this chapter will be to show that one does exist, and that it is very noticeable when we know how and where to look for it. Our exposition will draw heavily on the writings of Baltzell and secondarily on high-society historians and chroniclers such as Dixon Wecter (*The Saga of American Society*), Cleveland Amory (*The Proper Bostonians*), and Lucy Kavaler (*The Private World of High Society*).

Briefly, the American upper class became national in scope in the last half of the nineteenth century, coincident with the rise of the national corporate economy which was its economic base and the national transportation–communication network which made its cohesiveness possible. Not that an upper class had never existed before in American history. Indeed it had, but it was more local in nature, an adding together of the upper classes of major cities and regions. Contributing to its local nature was the fact that the social upper classes were based upon economic foundations that were often in conflict. As is well known, the most important of these conflicts concerned Southern plantations and Northern industries. Thus, as Wecter points out, with a few notable exceptions the 1000 pre-Civil War plantation families who shared a $50-million-a-year income seldom intermarried with the Northern rich.[1] Nor was the upper class of the past as wealthy as is today's; the word "millionaire" was first coined in the 1840's, and the first serious multimillionaires appeared after the Civil War. In fact, each generation of new business wealth in the early years of this country was a little richer than the previous one, which forced the assimilation process. The "old" rich either intermarried with the new money, put their wealth into corporate stock, or fell by the wayside. Perhaps the height of the confusion was the assimilation that took place at the turn of the century, when the ostentation was so great that it led Thorstein Veblen to write of the "conspicuous consumption" of the "leisure class." Today, the fully assimilated descendants of these wealthy family founders are quiet, tasteful, and elegant when they are not being plain people at the discothèque. If this change is not due to the shock of two world wars, a depression, and the rise of the Communist world, as we suspect it is, perhaps it can be attributed to Ivy Lee and the other public relations experts hired by a few rich families in the first decades of this century:

Few phenomena in mass opinion are so amazing as the way in which these gifts —under the wise direction of the late Ivy L. Lee, pioneer "public relations counsel" to the rich—succeeded in transforming the senior Rockefeller from a hated pirate . . . into a sagely benevolent oracle of Pocantico Hills, smiling on small children and struggling young photographers and rounding the century mark to the applause of a nation.[2]

THE SOCIAL REGISTER

If there is one best guide to the membership of the national upper class, it is a set of black and orange volumes that were begun as a business venture in 1888. Termed the *Social Register,* these volumes are now published for 12 major cities—Boston, New York, Buffalo, Philadelphia–Wilmington, Baltimore, Washington, Pittsburgh, Cleveland, Cincinnati–Dayton, Chicago, St. Louis, and San Francisco. They contain at least 38,000 families and about 108,000 names. Despite the fact that the *Social Register* is a commercial venture, and that for many years one's acceptance or rejection was in the hands of the owner's low-born secretary, it can be demonstrated that it is an excellent index. First, the more general but less important considerations: (1) The owners are members of the upper class; this assures some acquaintance with their subject matter. (2) Letters from three to five persons presently listed (opinion varies as to the exact number) are necessary for being listed; this insures continuity and gradual assimilation. (3) Many members of the upper class accept the *Social Register* as an index— at least this was the case according to a study of Chicago society in the 1920's and a study of New York society in the 1950's.[3] Baltzell summarizes as follows:

On the one hand, new families are added to the *Social Register* as a result of their making a formal application to the Social Register Association in New York. In other words, a family having personal and more or less intimate social relations (in business, church, school, club, or neighborhood activities) with the various members of certain families who are members of the upper class and listed in the *Social Register* reaches a point where inclusion within the register seems expedient; someone listed in the *Social Register*, presumably a friend of the "new" family, obtains an application blank which in turn is filled out by the new family (usually by the wife) and returned to the Social Register Association in New York along with several endorsements by present upper-class members as to the social acceptability of the new family; after payment of a nominal fee, the next issue of the *Social Register*, including all pertinent information on the new family, will arrive the following November.[4]

However, these are not the most important considerations. The validity of the *Social Register* as an index of the social upper class can be demonstrated by studying the works of such students of the upper class as Wecter, Amory, and Kavaler. Such a study by this author showed that, save for the exceptions to be noted below, representatives of almost every family mentioned in their books can be found in the 1965 *Social Register Locater*, which lists the names of all persons appearing in the 12 city editions.[5] The overlap of the upper class and the *Social Register* can be documented in another way, by studying the society pages of major newspapers. For example, of 31 girls presented at San Francisco's most exclusive debutante cotillion in 1964, 27 were in the *Social Register*.

It was Baltzell who first systematically documented that the members of the social upper class and the *Social Register* are also rich businessmen and their descendants; he focused on the city of Philadelphia for his most detailed demonstration of this overlap. In addition to showing the value of the *Social Register* in identifying the Philadelphia branch of the upper class, Baltzell gave evidence for its value in other cities as well. On a national scale, Baltzell showed (1) that descendants of nine of the ten financiers studied in Frederick Allen's *The Lords of Creation* were in the *Social Register* (the tenth was Jewish); (2) that well over 75 per cent of the wealthy families in Ferdinand Lundberg's *America's Sixty Families* had easily traceable descendants (the same given names and surnames as the family founder) in the *Social Register;* and (3) that 87 of the wealthy men in Gustavus Myers' *History of the Great American Fortunes* had descendants in the *Social Register*.[6] Supplementing this, Mills noted that at least one-half of the 90 richest men of 1900 had descendants in the *Social Register*.[7] It can be concluded from the work of Baltzell and Mills that these volumes are a good index of an American upper class of rich businessmen, or more exactly, of rich businessmen and their descendants, for many of these people, financially secure due to stock ownership and trust funds, have entered the professions, pursued politics, or expended their energies on charitable and cultural projects.

As valuable as the *Social Register* is as an index to membership in the American upper class, it has five drawbacks to its use as the sole criterion. First, it is published for only 12 cities, so it is severely circumscribed geographically. It has little or no value for the South or Southwest, although some people from these areas list in the Washington and New York registers. Along this same line, only San Francisco is represented on the West Coast. Second, the *Social Register* is unlikely to list "ethnic" rich, such as Irish Catholics and Jews. While this certainly reflects an important antagonism within the upper class, there is reason to believe from intermarriage and private school attendance that this barrier is breaking down somewhat faster than the *Social Register* would indicate. Third, the *Social Register* for Washington automatically lists the President, the Vice-President, the Cabinet, the Senate, the Supreme Court, and some ambassadors. In short, a listing in the Washington *Social Register* cannot be taken as evidence for upper-class membership. This point is especially important when considering whether or not members of the upper class control the federal government. Using the Washington *Social Register* as a criterion would be a circular argument, for it is an index of the "political elite" as much as it is an index of the social upper class. This is not the case with other cities, however, nor is a listing in the Washington *Social Register* automatically transferred to another city when the non-upper-class person leaves his political office. Fourth, in considering the limitations of the *Social Register* as a sole criterion of upper-class membership, one must take into account that it seems to drop names for quite arbitrary reasons, such as scandal, divorce, marrying outside one's social class, marrying a movie star, and so forth. These instances are the occasion for much speculation about the *Social Register* and its membership criteria, but no pattern is readily apparent. Finally, no one has to be listed in the *Social Register,* and many choose not to be included. Such was the case with illustrious names like John Hay Whitney and Cornelius Vanderbilt, for example. More recently, one of Nelson Rockefeller's daughters decided to withdraw her name by the simple method of not returning a change-of-address form. Speculation that she was dropped because her minister husband was a Freedom Rider led the embarrassed owners of the *Social Register* to grant a rare and extensive interview to *The New York Times,* during which the nonlisting of Ann Clark Rockefeller Pierson was laid at her own doorstep.[8] Perhaps other members of the upper class will be withdrawing their names from an "in-group" telephone book which discriminates against the ethnic rich with whom they are interacting and intermarrying. For this reason alone, it would be necessary to find other criteria for upper-class membership. Such criteria are forthcoming from a consideration of the social institutions that underlie and interlace the American upper class.*

THE SOCIAL INSTITUTIONS OF THE UPPER CLASS

Underlying the American upper class are a set of social institutions which are its backbone—private schools, elite universities, the "right" fraternities and sororities, gentlemen's clubs, debutante balls, summer resorts, charitable and cultural organizations, and such recreational activities as foxhunts, polo matches, and yachting.† The private school is an excellent starting point, for its rise to importance was coincident with the late-nineteenth-century development of the national upper class. Baltzell emphasizes that at that time the proper school replaced the family as the chief socializing agent of the upper class: "The New England boarding school and the fashionable Eastern university became upper-class surrogate families on almost a national scale." [9] Educating the big-city rich from all over the country is only one of the functions of the private schools. They serve several other purposes as well. First, they are a proving ground where new-rich–old-rich antagonisms are smoothed over and the children of the new rich are gracefully assimilated. Then too, they are the main avenue by which upper-class children from smaller towns become acquainted with their counterparts from all over the country. Perhaps equally important is the fact that the schools assimilate the brightest members of other classes, for such assimilation is important to social stability. Sweezy calls the private schools "recruiters for the ruling class, sucking upwards the ablest elements of the lower classes and performing the double function of infusing new brains into the ruling class and weakening the political leadership of the working class." ‡ Indeed, many private schools employ persons to search out talented members of the lower classes.

* There are other social directories besides the *Social Register,* but they are not useful as indexes of upper-class membership because there is no systematic evidence to show that they really reflect a social upper class in the areas they serve. Studies such as those undertaken by Baltzell are necessary before these blue books, green books, and registers can be of value in studying the American upper class.

† However, these are by no means the only institutions which are the basis of the American upper class. Such financial and economic institutions as corporate stock and corporation boards, which are its economic basis, will be discussed in the next chapter. Intermarriage, the all-important institution that is the result of interaction in the above-noted institutions, will be discussed shortly as part of the evidence that the upper class is nationwide in its scope.

‡ After quoting Sweezy at length on this matter, Baltzell comments: "What a Marxian finds so dangerous, Tocqueville found desirable." Baltzell believes that the Marxists "rightly see the opportunitarian ideal as the worst enemy of their ideals of equality of conditions." [10]

The most prestigious of the private schools for boys are probably Groton, St. Paul's, and St. Mark's, but Choate, Hotchkiss, and St. Andrew's are not far behind. Descendants of 65 of the 87 great American fortunes studied by Myers attended either Groton, St. Paul's, or St. Mark's between 1890 and 1940. The best known of the schools, however, are Phillips Exeter and Phillips Andover, which have a greater number of scholarship students and a sizable minority of rich Jewish students. Other leading schools for boys include St. George's, Kent, Taft, Middlesex, and Deerfield in New England; Lawrenceville in New Jersey; Hill in Pennsylvania; Shattuck in Minnesota; and Episcopal High and Woodberry Forest in Virginia.

There are necessarily more than just a handful of these schools, some more intellectually challenging, some more liberal, than others. A study by Kavaler based upon interviews with upper-class women from all over the country led to a list of 130 private schools for young men and young ladies of the upper class. While this list is not perfect, leaving off such important schools as Berkshire, Salisbury, and Scarborough, it is valuable in conjunction with other considerations, such as family background and club memberships.

It is perhaps needless to add that most of these students go on to college. Kavaler estimates that 90 per cent of private school graduates attend college, while a spokesman for an association of private schools claims that 99 per cent of the female graduates of such schools now continue their education.[11] It is also needless to add that these well-prepared students attend the finest colleges and universities in the country. For example, the 1965 graduates of Lawrenceville went on to the following schools in large numbers: Harvard, 14; Princeton, 10; Yale, 8; Georgetown, 7; University of North Carolina, 7; Brown, 5; Cornell, 5; University of California, Berkeley, 5; Columbia, 4; Bucknell, 4; Penn, 4; Stanford, 4; Vanderbilt, 4; and Wesleyan, 4.[12]

Twenty-five years ago the importance of an Ivy League education could not be overestimated in studying the American upper class, and the chances were excellent that an Ivy League graduate could be so indexed. From 1900 to 1940, Harvard, Yale, Princeton, and several other select Eastern colleges brought together the rich from all over the country, superseding in importance the local universities, such as the University of Virginia, which had trained members of the upper class of their regions for so many generations. The pattern varied only slightly from city to city. Bostonians preferred Harvard, New Yorkers preferred Yale, and St. Louis and Baltimore were Princeton towns. Only two *Social Register* cities continued to favor local schools by a small margin—Philadelphia remained loyal to Penn, San Francisco to Stanford and the University of California at Berkeley. However, with the Second World War, the pattern of concentration at a few Eastern schools began to alter. Population pressures, the GI bill, stiffer entrance requirements, more scholarships for the bright but needy, and the rise in respectability of other universities were all factors in this change, but so were the experiences of the war, which did so much to shake the attitudes and prejudices of many insulated sons of the upper class. Data documenting the importance of the Ivy League schools in the development of a national upper class can be found in the historical studies by Baltzell; data revealing the change in the role of these universities have been compiled more recently by Gene Hawes.[13] His study of the New York *Social Register* showed that 67 per cent of the adult men who had attended college had received degrees from Harvard, Yale, or Princeton. In contrast, 45 per cent of those currently attending a university were at one of the Big Three. On the graduate and professional school level, Harvard and Columbia were the most important, with Yale a distant third. It will be interesting to note in future studies whether or not Harvard, Columbia, and Yale retain their pre-eminence in graduate training, for these schools have been absolutely essential in the training of the lawyers, physicians, and intellectuals of the upper class. These Ivy League schools, as Baltzell notes, also have been essential in the training of American Presidents:

In the first half of the twentieth century, five of our eight Presidents were graduates of Harvard, Yale, Princeton, and Amherst. A sixth came from Stanford, "the western Harvard," where the social system most resembled that in the East.[14]

It is not only Presidents who are trained at these elite universities. Mills's study of 513 higher politicians—men who between 1789 and 1953 served as President, Vice-President, Speaker of the House, Cabinet Member, or Supreme Court Justice—revealed that 22 per cent of them had attended Harvard, Yale, or Princeton. "If one includes such famous schools as Dartmouth and Amherst, then one-third of all the higher politicians, and 44 per cent of those who ever spent any time in college, went to top-notch Eastern schools."[15] The same pattern holds true in the business world. For example, in a study of 476 top executives who went to college, "86 per cent had received their undergraduate training at Yale, Harvard, and Princeton alone. . . ."[16] A study of all directors in Poor's *Register of Corporations, Directors, and Executives* revealed that 4135 of the directors were from Harvard. Harvard was followed in numerical representation by Yale, Princeton, and the University of Pennsylvania.[17]

There have been changes in the exclusive gentlemen's clubs that are present in every major city, but they remain, as Max Weber said, the essential proof that one is a gentleman.[18] Among these changes is the fact that women have been known to enter the clubroom on occasion, an unheard-of event in the "old days." Then too, being a member of scores of such clubs is no longer the fashion, although some few persons belong to a half-dozen or more. Finally, many clubs have fallen into bad odor because of their anti-Semitism, which has led to public resignations by prominent members of the upper class. Most shocking, many successful executives have become members, leading to the claim by the more hidebound of the hereditary rich that clubdom is going to the dogs, letting "everybody" into its august portals. For all of these revolutions, the functions of the clubs remain very similar. They provide an informal atmosphere in which new members of the upper class can be initiated into the mores that govern gentlemanly behavior. They also provide a place in which the groundwork for major business deals can be laid, and a place in which economic and political differences can be smoothed over in a friendly manner. Then, too, the clubs are a haven for the traveling businessman where he gets to know his compatriots from other localities, and a tie to the national upper class for the first families of small cities. Baltzell is most convincing when he shows that the "upper uppers" of the small cities studied by sociologists a generation ago are members of one or more of these clubs, if not graduates of the most exclusive private schools.

There are too many of these clubs to be named here. The better known include the California in Los Angeles, the Pacific Union in San Francisco, the Duquesne in Pittsburgh, the Links and the Knickerbocker in New York, the Somerset in Boston, and the Piedmont Driving Club in Atlanta. However, among the most important are the Harvard, Princeton, and Yale Clubs of New York and other major cities. The New York branches of these clubs are especially important, for they provide a place for out-of-town businessmen to see old college friends, and

. . . in addition, countless small-town boys at Princeton, Harvard, or Yale live at their respective graduate clubs during their first years out of college if they happen to be among that large group of Ivy alumni who seek their fortunes each year among the caverns of Wall Street, or, in more recent years, along Madison Avenue.[19]

These alumni clubs are also important because they are not as anti-Semitic and anti-Catholic as their more stuffy counterparts. Then too, they are more likely to continue the assimilation of bright members of other classes which was begun at the private school and/or the Ivy League college.

Resort living is not what it used to be either, although its functions also remain the same. First, huge, ostentatious "cottages" are no longer the rule. Furthermore, the "in" resorts change slightly over the years, and the style of life at various resorts may vary from "roughing it" to Victorian splendor. Also, foreign resorts have become an integral part of the circuit, and the Georgia and Florida coasts have replaced the Virginia resorts that were the Southern playgrounds of yesteryear. All this said, the resorts continue to be a fertile stamping ground for intercity marriages.

Debutante balls serve the function of corraling the democratic inclinations of libidinal impulses. Or, as Baltzell puts it, ". . . the democratic whims of romantic love often play havoc with class solidarity." [20] These coming-out parties announce that the girl is now available for marriage, preferably to the type of lad tendered an invitation. When the whirl of debutante dances and parties does not achieve its function, which is more than likely in an age when four years of college are ahead for girls as well as boys, the corraling function is taken over by the "right" sororities and fraternities, or such young adult clubs as the Bachelors and Spinsters of San Francisco, Los Angeles, and other major cities. It should be emphasized that discussions of the lavishness and frivolity of such occasions as debutante balls do not do justice to the important function they serve, for a considerable amount of intermarriage is at the crux of a well-knit social class.

To the competitive, hard-working members of the American upper class, the life of the feudal landlord apparently seems almost idyllic. In fact, one of the first acts of many newly arrived members of the upper class is to attempt to achieve the wonderful dreams of landlordism by returning to the land. They buy a farm or ranch, raise cattle or horses, and ride to the hounds. There are scores of hunts in the United States, some more exclusive than others, and so strong is the urge that the foxless Coloradans of Arapahoe gracefully substitute the coyote. The horse also figures in another major diversion for some members of the upper class. It is no mere coincidence that horse racing is called "the sport of kings," and it can be revealed that jockey clubs are not for jockeys—they house members of the upper class. This proclivity on the part of some members of the upper class for raising, riding, and racing horses helps cement the tie between the East, where riding has been a sport for some time; the border states of Maryland and Kentucky, where horses are bred and raised; and the West and Southwest, where riding is a symbol of the rugged frontier existence so recently and totally erased. Horses are also necessary for the game of polo, one sport not likely to join golf, tennis, and bridge in a complete skid to middle-class levels. For example, a handful of rich men from all over the country occasionally fly their horses to the Kleberg family's King Ranch in Kingsville, Texas, to enjoy a weekend of polo, and then return to more worldly pursuits thousands of miles away come Monday morning.* Sporting members of the upper class do not spend all of their spare time on horseback, however. There is also the water, where sailing and yachting are still the pastimes of gentlemen. Indeed, sailing gave rise to one of the most famous aphorisms of the upper class, which is repeated in just about every chronicle of high society: "You can do business with anyone," said J. P. Morgan, "but only sail with a gentleman." This is apparently the way aristocrat Franklin D. Roosevelt felt about it, for "he preferred to relax with what Jim Farley, with a touch of resentment, once called the 'Hasty Pudding Cabinet' as he watched them sail away for a brief vacation with the President on Vincent Astor's yacht." [22]

Members of the American upper class participate in a great many charitable and cultural organizations. In fact, they control most of these organizations, and the evidence for this is so ubiquitous in the daily press and the works of Baltzell and Kavaler that no attempt will be made to provide systematic documentation. A few examples will suffice:

Architect Nathaniel A. Owings [SR, SF] † has accepted the post as Chairman of the President's Council on Pennsylvania Avenue, aimed at sprucing up the nation's Capitol.[23]

Somehow they ["the New Elegants"] find time for charity work, church functions, community projects, and college alumni drives.[24]

Pittsburgh financier Andrew Mellon, a *Social Register* listee, built Washington's $15,000,000 National Gallery of Art in 1937 to house his $50,000,000 art collection. Now his son, Paul Mellon, is planning another public gallery in Washington for his 500-plus works of art.[25]

The late C. D. Jackson [SR, NY] was a leading official of Time, Inc., an adviser to President Eisenhower, and a member of the board of directors of the Boston Symphony.

E. Roland Harriman, Averell's brother, heads the American Red Cross.

THE GATEWAYS TO THE UPPER CLASS

Acceptance into the American upper class of today is not an impossible task, although a passport to its innermost citadels may be issued primarily

---

* In 1937 Dixon Wecter characterized now-statesman Averell Harriman as an "industrialist and polo player." [21] We mention Harriman because he is one of the "red threads" that runs throughout our narrative. Industrialist, financier, ambassador, Secretary of Commerce, State Department official, and special emissary for Presidents, he is an ideal prototype of the member of the power elite who moves from command post to command post in different institutional hierarchies.

† *Social Register,* San Francisco. We have adopted this shorthand method of identifying listees in the *Social Register* because of the lack of elegance in such phrases as "socially registered" and "social registerite."

to succeeding generations. For the newly arrived rich, the first step as a family is participation in charitable and cultural projects. Working on the organization of such ventures, and giving a considerable sum of money to them, will often lead to private dinner invitations in addition to invitations to other upper-class activities. Another important avenue for the aspiring family is to hire a social secretary, who, interestingly enough, we have usually found to be a member of the upper class herself. The social secretary will have many suggestions to make; she will arrange guest lists, caterers, and music for parties to which she will invite her upper-class friends and clients. The social secretary is especially important for planning debutante parties, for she has guest lists from other clients and from private school enrollment rosters. To be accepted as a client by one of these important persons is almost a guarantee that one is on the status elevator to the social upper class. The importance of this seemingly trivial person cannot be overemphasized, for she functions to screen and mold applicants for membership in the social upper class.

For the man of the family, the most important gateway into the upper class is election into one of the exclusive gentlemen's clubs. Baltzell notes that there is a status order among these clubs, and quotes Allen's *Lords of Creation* to show how each generation is brought a step closer to the inner sanctum:

The following progress is characteristic: John D. Rockefeller, Union League Club; John D. Rockefeller, Jr., University Club; John D. Rockefeller III, Knickerbocker Club.[26]

Election into a club, as Osborn Elliott (SR, NY) of *Newsweek* points out in his *Men at the Top,* is often one of the first signs that the bright young executive is in line for a significant promotion. For the woman of the family, the most typical gateway to the upper class is the Junior League. Founded in 1901 by Mary Harriman Rumsey (Averell's sister) and other New York socialites, the League, as of the early 1960's, had about 78,000 members in chapters in over 180 American cities. It is not as exclusive as many upper-class organizations, and has been one of the most important in co-opting the wives of the small-city aristocrats and of the successful corporation executives. One of the League's best features is its national structure, for its transferable membership is an important social entree into the new community for the wife of the oft-transferred organization man. In many cities hospital boards serve a similar function.[27]

The attainment of upper-class status is perhaps slightly less painful and self-conscious for the children of the newly arrived rich. Most important, the child is sent to a private school. To be able to afford this is "proof," so to speak, to the hereditary members of the upper class that the upstart has arrived financially, for private schooling is a very expensive proposition. Tuition is often only the beginning; travel expense, room and board, and, occasionally, sheltering a horse can raise the cost as high as $3000 to $5000 per year. Then too, being admitted to a private school often "proves" that one is "well connected," for it sometimes takes recommendations from alumni and friends of the school to be admitted. Attendance at one of the exclusive private schools automatically guarantees that the child will mingle with upper-class children. For one thing, his name is on the school's enrollment list, which will be circumspectly revealed to the nearby private schools for the opposite sex, as well as to social secretaries and dancing classes. This results in invitations to the schools' social functions, to dancing classes, and to debutante parties. At the school itself the child learns upper-class values, upper-class manners, and most of all upper-class speech, one of the most telltale signs of class and regional origin. From private school attendance it is but a short hop to the debutante parties and social gatherings of school acquaintances; the result is usually intermarriage into the hereditary upper class.[28]

Sweezy, in discussing social classes, states that they have an identifiable core but very vague boundaries. At the fringes, says Sweezy, social classes seem to flow into each other.[29] While this is true at the lower levels of society, leading some social scientists to abandon the rigid-sounding concept of "class" for more permeable-sounding terms such as "social groups," "status groups," or "social strata," it can be seen that social secretaries, clubs, leagues, private schools, and similar institutions give a surprising definiteness to the upper class.[30] It takes a considerable amount of money even to knock on the door of the co-opting institutions, the right contacts to gain entrance, and a certain amount of training to gain certification. Once inside the castle there are many rooms, but that should not overshadow the formidable nature of its moated entrance.

THE COHESIVENESS OF THE AMERICAN UPPER CLASS

Every major city in the country has upper-class social institutions with similar structures and functions, but that is not sufficient evidence for the existence of a cohesive national upper class. It may be that these institutions merely have parallel structures, and that the members from one city or region seldom interact with like-minded souls from other parts of the country. How can it be determined that the interactions are national in scope? The first and most important way is through intermarriage. The *Social Register* has a special section entitled "Married Maidens" which enables one, among other things, to find old acquaintances who have moved to other cities. A perusal of "Married Maidens" suggests that the intermarriages are national in scope. The intercity character of upper-class intermarriage can be demonstrated in another way, by studying the society pages of major newspapers. Our cursory study of *The New York Times,* the *San Francisco Chronicle,* the *Los Angeles Times,* the *Houston Post,* and the *New Orleans Times-Picayune* revealed a number of intercity marriages. Perhaps an example from the *San Francisco Chronicle,* August 2, 1965, will give the flavor. Everyone mentioned in the following marriage announcement, except for Winston Churchill's nephew, is listed in the *Social Register.* This includes Texan Gillian Spreckels Fuller, the daughter of a Texas oilman and a San Francisco sugar heiress. She is listed in the New York edition:

SYIDA HAAS TO WED
CLAXTON ALLEN LONG

Mr. and Mrs. Edward Thompson Haas announced the engagement of their daughter Syida to Claxton Allen Long at a cocktail party yesterday evening at the family home in Hillsborough.

Syida has been living in New York for the past year, and she met her fiancé there six months ago. The bride-elect has been working in an art gallery, and the young man is associated with the Morgan Guaranty Trust Company in New York.

The bride-elect, a fourth-generation Californian, is a graduate of Finch College. She spent her senior year studying in Europe, where she majored in art.

Syida was a Cotillion deb in 1957, and was presented that same year at a ball given by her parents at their Hillsborough home.

She has a brother, Edward Thompson Haas, Jr., and is the cousin of Ed Conner, president of the Bachelors.

She is the granddaughter of the late Mr. and Mrs. Edward Francis Haas and the late Mr. and Mrs. Seward Arthur Griggs, all of San Francisco.

Her cousin, the former Gillian Spreckels Fuller, married Lord Charles Spencer-Churchill, second son of the Duke of Marlborough, on July 23 in London.

The young man is the son of Mr. and Mrs. Isaac Addelbert Long of St. Louis. He has two sisters, Ada Long, who attends Stanford, and Mrs. Roland Baer, Jr., of St. Louis.

He graduated from the St. Louis Country Day School, and the University of Virginia, where he was a member of St. Anthony Hall.

He is a member of the St. Louis Country Club, the University Club in New York, and the Brookville Polo Club in Long Island.

A fall wedding on the Peninsula is planned.

Further documentation on the national scope of intermarriages can be found in the works of Amory, Baltzell, Lundberg, and Wecter. Baltzell's examples are important because they also show considerable intermarriage among Catholic, Jewish, and Protestant members of the upper class, at least among the better-known families.

A second way to demonstrate the cohesiveness of the national upper class is to study attendance at private schools, Ivy League colleges, and summer resorts, as well as the multiple memberships in gentlemen's clubs. The writings of Baltzell provide impressive evidence for the overlap in all four institutions, while Cleveland Amory's *The Last Resorts* is well-nigh definitive in its anecdotal way on interactions at summer resorts. Baltzell's examples are again of considerable interest because they show the interaction of Protestant, Catholic, and Jewish youth at the private school and the Ivy League college. On the other hand, they show the exclusion of Jews from the gentleman's club and the summer resort. Rather than repeating information from these sources, we will present some new data:

The Parents Committee of St. Paul's School met on Saturday, February 6, 1965. Nineteen of the 27 members were present. Among the cities represented were San Francisco; Concord, N. H.; Oyster Bay, N. Y.; Winnetka, Ill.; Groton, Mass.; Arlington, Vt.; New York City (2); New Orleans, La.; Boston, Mass.; and Haverford, Pa.[31]

Regional alumni chairmen for St. Paul's can be found for every *Social Register* city except Cleveland and Baltimore, as well as for, among others, Denver, Detroit, Houston, Indianapolis, Los Angeles, Louisville, Memphis, Minneapolis, Phoenix, Portland, and Salt Lake. The regional chairman from Greenwich, Conn., is a Rockefeller; the chairman from Wilmington, Del., is a du Pont.[32]

Pomfret School, Pomfret, Conn. "This well-known prep school attracts students from as far away as Wyoming and Texas." [33]

Shattuck School, Faribault, Minn. "Shattuck is both a military and a church school (Episcopal). It has good academic standing. Students between the ages of 13 and 19 come from all over the United States. Tuition, room, and board come to $2000. Uniforms cost about $235." [34]

"Tourists drop by from almost everywhere, but it [Jackson Hole, Wyo.] is a summer retreat for well-to-do families from California, Illinois, Colorado, and Utah. . . ." [35]

The Harbor Point Association, Harbor Point, Mich., is an exclusive summer retreat for 82 families from Cincinnati, St. Louis, Detroit, and Chicago.[36]

"[Sea Island, Ga., is] mostly favored by reasonably well-to-do and well-bred Southern families and honeymooners who like Southern ways, though a fair number of Midwesterners and Yankees show up each year also." (Most of the relatively few members of the Southern branch of the upper class are at best "reasonably" well-to-do by Northern upper-class standards.)[37]

"Today, Nathan Pusey, Walter Lippmann, Thomas Gates, and Nelson Rockefeller go there [Mount Desert, Me.] to enjoy some of the world's best sailing, with the major derivation of the visitors remaining Boston and Philadelphia." [38]

"Yet if society is prominent American families, this town [Miami, Fla.] has it. Firestone, du Pont, Deering, McCormick, Bell, Palmer, Vanderbilt, Astor—their children are here [visiting]." [39]

According to Baltzell: "The fashionable summer neighborhood fosters the development of upper-class solidarity on a national scale in America, and summer romances on the enchanting island of Mount Desert have not infrequently resulted in intercity family alliances. Among such alliances, the grandson of Joseph Pulitzer (St. Louis) is now married to the granddaughter of Samuel M. Vauclain, a former president of the Baldwin Locomotive Works . . . ; the former wife of Nelson Rockefeller (NY) is the granddaughter of George Roberts of the Pennsylvania Railroad; and the former Louise De Koven Bowen, descendant of an old Bar Harborite from Chicago who lent her social prestige to the service of Jane Addams' Hull House, now lives in Chestnut Hill as the wife of young John Wanamaker, vice-president of his great-grandfather's department stores." [40]

Club memberships provide further evidence for the national scope of the American upper class. The point can be made from a study by Ann Bicknell on the club memberships of directors of the 20 largest industrial corporations.[41] There are only a handful of interlocking directorates in this group, since it is against the law for companies that compete to have directors in common. However, at least one director from 12 of the 20 companies was a member of the Links Club, which Baltzell calls "the New York rendezvous of the national corporate establishment." [42] Best represented at the Links were General Electric with seven, Chrysler with four, Westinghouse with four, IBM with three, and U. S. Steel with two. The figures for other famous clubs are as follows: Century (New York), eight companies represented; Duquesne (Pittsburgh), seven; Chicago (Chicago), seven; Philadelphia (Philadelphia), five; Bohemian (San Francisco), five; and Pacific Union (San Francisco), four. When Barry Goldwater rested at the Bohemian Club's Bohemian Grove north of San Francisco, *Time* Magazine described it as a "walled-in Walden for the well-to-do," and added that "among its 1950 members are, besides a collection of little-known but influential people, such diversified types as Henry Ford II, former President Hoover [himself quite a successful businessman], Bing Crosby,

Edgar Bergen, Earl Warren, Ernie Ford, Lucius Clay, retired General Albert Wedemeyer (Barry's host), former defense secretary Neil McElroy [SR, Cincinnati], and old aviator Jimmy Doolittle." * [43]

A third method for demonstrating the national scope of the upper class is to ask members whether they in fact know each other. This is in effect what Floyd Hunter did as part of his study, *Top Leadership, U. S. A.;* there is a considerable overlap between his top 100 leaders for the late 1950's as determined by polling knowledgeable people (the "reputational" method), and the men isolated in this study by our quite different methods. By the criteria to be presented at the end of this chapter, 45 of Hunter's top 100 leaders are members of the upper class, while another 30 qualify as members of the power elite. The rest are non-upper-class senators (12), congressional representatives (4), union leaders (3), cabinet members (2), former President (1), Chief Justice (1), Presidential adviser (1), and religious leader (1). Hunter interviewed most of these top leaders and, among other things, asked them how well they knew each other. The results were quite impressive, particularly within the top one-third of the group. As another example of this method of determining upper-class interactions, we cite questionnaire studies by David Guggenhime and Tony Mohr.[44] They chose 25 prominent names from the San Francisco *Social Register* and 20 California Club members from the Los Angeles *Blue Book,* then mailed a questionnaire to each of these people asking them to judge how well they knew the other persons on the list: (1) "very well," (2) "casually," (3) "by reputation," and (4) "not at all." Based upon a 76 per cent return by the San Franciscans and a 70 per cent return by the Angelenos, they established that both groups were quite tightly knit and that there was a considerable amount of acquaintance between the San Francisco and Los Angeles branches of the upper class.

The findings from the final method used to demonstrate the nationwide character of the upper class, interlocking corporation and foundation directorates, will be detailed in subsequent chapters. However, it would appear on the basis of the findings already presented that the burden of argument now lies with those who would deny the national character of the American upper class. The fact that Thursday is the maid's night out throughout the United States is no mere coincidence.

* The following are the club memberships of Herbert Hoover, Jr. (SR, SF), who is a director of Hanna Mining, Monsanto Chemical, Southern California Edison, American Mutual Fund, Investment Company of America, and Pacific Mutual Life Insurance as well as a special adviser to the State Department on worldwide petroleum matters: Century (NY), University (NY), Bohemian (SF), California (LA), Metropolitan (Washington), and Chevy Chase (Maryland).

THE ANTAGONISMS WITHIN THE UPPER CLASS

It should be clear by now that the group which concerns us truly deserves the designation "social class." However, this by no means implies that every member knows every other member personally, or that every member loves and admires every other member. Sheer size assures that members of the American upper class will know "of" each other as much as they will know each other. This makes the proper credentials, such as schools and clubs, all the more important. The relative lack of intimacy also makes various "go-betweens" important. The men who know everybody perform an essential information-transmitting and opinion-organizing function. They include such well-known people as John J. McCloy, Averell Harriman, and Robert Lovett, and, more generally, men such as those identified in Hunter's study of top national leadership.

The most important antagonisms within the upper class are due to the fact that business interests often clash. This has been ameliorated somewhat by diversified stock portfolios, oligopolistic corporations, and the use of hired managers, but the fact remains that American business is a very competitive system. One of the most fundamental business splits is between the heavy industrialists, on the one hand, and the big retailers and light manufacturers on the other. Then too, differences of opinion can arise between bankers and industrialists; according to James W. Gerard (SR, NY), some manufacturers were angry about the machinations of certain Wall Street firms during the late 1920's.[45] Stressing these particular splits does not imply that differences between other business enterprises never occur. For example, when the suppliers of natural gas tried to induce the government to allow them to raise their prices, they were defeated by the industries which use natural gas in their manufacturing.[46] Most important of all, there is a split between what Mills called the "business liberals" and the "old guard." The business liberals, who usually come from the biggest, most internationally minded companies, speak through such organizations as the Council on Foreign Relations, the Business Advisory Council, the Committee for Economic Development, the Democratic Party, and the moderate wing of the Republican Party, while the "old guard" of practical conservatives, who tend to be nationally oriented businessmen, speaks through the National Association of Manufacturers and the conservative wing of the Republican Party. Mills elaborated as follows:

In the higher circles of business and its associations, there has long been a tension, for example, between the "old guard" of practical conservatives and the "business liberals," or sophisticated conservatives. What the "old guard" represents is the outlook, if not always the intelligent interests, of the more narrow economic concerns. What the business liberals represent is the outlook and the interests of the newer propertied class as a whole. They are "sophisticated" because they are more flexible in adjusting to such political facts of life as the New Deal and big labor, because they have taken over and used the dominant liberal rhetoric for their own purposes, and because they have, in general, attempted to get on top of, or even slightly ahead of, the trend of these developments, rather than to fight it as practical conservatives are wont to do.[47]

Overlapping and reinforcing the business antagonisms within the upper class are the religious antagonisms. Protestants, who usually became Episcopalians or Presbyterians, very much controlled the industrial revolution, while the immigrants of the late nineteenth and early twentieth centuries, some of whom became the ethnic rich, arrived in time to share in the consumer revolution. Indeed, as will be shown in a later chapter, these ethnic rich have joined with a significant number of very old upper-class families to control the Democratic Party, while the Republican Party has been the instrument of the Protestant industrialists and bankers who came to power in the last part of the nineteenth century.

The seriousness of these religious differences cannot be denied. As Baltzell shows, they make for bitter controversy, and for in-group hatreds that are not easily forgiven. The behavior of the upper-class Protestants in the first half of this century was little short of incredible, the least cruel of their actions being the exclusion of rich Jews and Catholics from social clubs and summer resorts.[48] This led the upper-class Jews to organize their own clubs and resorts. (The most important of these, the Harmonie of New York, is one of our indexes of upper-class membership.) However, such ethnocentrism was not always the case to the extent that it was manifested in the first four decades of this century, and perhaps this gives reason to believe that its importance will once again decline. As Baltzell notes, class interests tend to push aside other factors at the highest levels of society,[49] and it must be added that many of the rejected were not merely "Jewish" or "Catholic," but "new rich" and "immigrants" as well.[50]

In recent years there have been several indications of a breakdown in religious discrimination within the upper class. First of all, there seems to have been a decline in the importance of the puritanical Protestant ethic which played such an important role in the upper class of a generation ago. Then too, many members of the upper class are resigning from gentlemen's clubs that practice anti-Semitism, and the very fact that such upper-class authors as Amory and Baltzell are openly and vigorously condemning this ethnocentrism is a symptom of change in itself. Catholicism in particular has become respectable. The grandchildren of Henry Cabot Lodge, for instance, are being raised as Catholics, Henry Ford II is a Catholic, Marshall Field III is a Catholic, John McCone is a Catholic convert, and even

Texan Luci Baines Johnson is now a Catholic, having forsaken the Episcopalianism that was shared by Mrs. Lyndon Johnson and Mrs. Harry Truman. Perhaps the most interesting case is that of Henry Ford II. His grandfather was one of the leading Protestant anti-Semites of his time, but "young" Ford is a Catholic and a close friend of Sidney Weinberg of Goldman, Sachs. Weinberg sits on the board of the Ford Motor Company. Another Jewish member of the upper class, Charles Wyzanski, Jr., is a trustee of the Ford Foundation. Further evidence of the breakdown of the religious antagonisms within the upper class will be presented in subsequent chapters by identifying Jews and Catholics, a practice that otherwise would be distasteful.

There are other antagonisms within the upper class. For example, the tensions between new and old money are proverbial, and can be understood at least in part in terms of the different upbringings of the old rich and the newly arrived. Inability to spend money gracefully, coupled with feelings of rejection, can lead the new rich to the ostentation and the search for "celebrity" and "publicity" which Amory found to be prevalent in first and second generations of new families.[51] However, ostentation is not necessarily the case, as has been shown by a study of the new rich of the second half of the twentieth century.[52] We believe that the tensions between new and old rich are due largely to the barriers thrown up by the old rich. These barriers, whether or not anyone is aware of it, have important functions, and they are utilized as if they had been designed by drawing on the latest findings in the social psychology of small groups. They make the new rich strive desperately to meet the requirements for admission into the mysterious world of clubs and *Social Registers;* in the process of striving, the seekers assimilate the values and manners of those they wish to emulate. This serves to preserve the standards long since built into the upper class.

A major antagonism of the past that is fast losing its importance concerns regional differences within the upper class. We believe that most of these differences are actually based on the more important types of antagonisms already discussed. For example, in the case of business antagonism, there is the competition between Wall Street financiers and non-Eastern businessmen, and between Eastern-owned and Texas-owned oil companies. Then too, these seemingly regional differences sometimes reflect new-rich–old-rich antagonisms, as is the case with the behavior of some Texans.[53] What remains of regional differences after these other factors are eliminated from consideration are minor differences in style of living and in folklore which reflect the geography, climate, and history of a particular region. Southerners will continue to talk about "Yankees" and enjoy warm-weather sports, Texans will continue to wear cowboy hats and enjoy riding and ranching, and San Franciscans will continue to brag about their city and go snow skiing at Lake Tahoe, but these colorful superficialities should not be confused with the core of interests, values, and institutions that unite the American upper class. The presence of Southerners, Texans, and San Franciscans at Eastern private schools and Ivy League colleges, as well as the pattern of intermarriage, demonstrates the insignificance of these regional differences.

Finally, in our discussion of antagonisms, there are, as both Baltzell and Sweezy point out in discussing divisions within the upper class, differences between liberals and conservatives.[54] Indeed, whatever the social class, and whatever the causative factors may be, there are syndromes—constellations of interests and attitudes—that describe liberal and conservative personalities. Of all the evidence that could be marshalled to support this claim, perhaps the best study is one conducted at the University of Minnesota, where students tested during their college years were retested many years later as middle-aged adults. It was found, among other things, that those who had called themselves "liberal Democrats," as opposed to "conservative Republicans," were more interested in the arts, less interested in business and practical matters, more likely to have obtained advanced degrees, and more likely to have finished their undergraduate work despite the fact that there were no differences in ability between the two groups.[55] The findings of this and other studies are very reminiscent of the distinction made by Baltzell between the "aristocratic" and "caste" tendencies within the upper class. Perhaps it is such psychological differences that would lead one branch of some prominent families to be Democrats and the other to be Republicans, or one brother to be a New Deal Democrat (Averell Harriman) and the other to be a Republican (E. Roland Harriman).

By concentrating on diversity within the upper class, we hope to go a long way toward dispelling the notion that the two political parties, just because they are both controlled by members of the upper class, are merely a sham.

THE PREOCCUPATIONS OF THE UPPER CLASS

Contrary to the stereotypes, most members of the American upper class are and always have been hard-working people, even at the richest levels. The American upper class is a business aristocracy, and business is its primary concern. Mills found in a study of the 90 richest men of 1950 that only 26 per cent were men of leisure.[56] Taking a larger compass, only 13,500 of the 450,000 families with incomes of $25,000 or more in 1959 lived entirely on dividends and other "unearned" (that is what the

Census Bureau calls it) income.[57] These figures suggest that few members of the upper class are full-time participants in the games known as "café society" and "jet-set society." These games, which are necessary for the continued box office success of the entertainers, producers, and movie–TV moguls who make up a considerable part of the contingent, are the bane of many of the old guard of the upper class, leading them to assert that "Society" is dead. This means that members of the upper class are no longer in the limelight. The debutante, for example, has been replaced by the starlet in the public eye. Unfortunately, business comes first, and the tremendously large and profitable entertainment industry has usurped one of the diversions of the upper class of yesteryear. It is the impression of both Mills and Kavaler that the presence of upper-class participants in café society has decreased considerably since 1937, when a *Fortune* Magazine study showed that two-thirds of the members were listed in the *Social Register*.[58]

If most members of the upper class are not "functionless genteels," what do they do? The first answer is that they are actively involved in business, law, and finance. As Mills summarizes, members of the upper class are the bulwarks of the financial and legal aristocracies of America's major cities.[59] This involvement in business, finance, and law will be explored in detail in the next chapter. The second answer is that they are busy achieving eminence in a great many fields. As Baltzell shows, using the 1940 *Who's Who in America* as an index of eminence in one's chosen field, 23 per cent of the *Who's Who* listings from the *Social Register* cities were also listed in the *Social Register*.[60] Nor is there a shortage of Ph.D.'s and M.D.'s within the upper class. A representative sample from the 1965 *Social Register Locater* revealed that 8 per cent of the 182 adult men sampled had the title "doctor" before their names. While there is no way of telling from the *Social Register* alone, it is likely that most of these doctors are physicians. Whatever the case—M.D.'s or Ph.D.'s—we can add that members of the upper class are represented in the academic world. According to one observer, "one has but to skim the marriage columns in *The New York Times* to realize that a very large proportion of the well-educated sons and daughters of businessmen and industrialists do not enter business and industry. A surprising number are pursuing academic careers or preparing for such." * [61] Baltzell's study of Philadelphia is consistent with

* In addition to Baltzell, the most prominent examples would be philosopher Corliss Lamont, sociologists David Riesman (SR, Boston), Barrington Moore (SR, NY), and George Homans (SR, Boston), and psychologists Henry Murray (SR, Boston), Edward Chace Tolman, and Robert W. White. Riesman, originally trained as a lawyer, is from a prominent Philadelphia family and was originally listed in that city's *Social Register*.

these observations of the medical and academic worlds at the national level. He concludes that medicine, along with architecture, has been traditionally an upper-class profession in the United States.[62] He supports his statement with the fact that 39 per cent of the Philadelphia architects and physicians listed in the 1940 *Who's Who* were also in the *Social Register*.

As another indicator of what members of the upper class do, we classified the occupations listed by St. Paul alumni of the past 20 years in the Spring, 1965, issue of that private school's alumni journal. There were seven physicians, seven academic scholars, and four authors, in addition to the 20 financiers and 16 businessmen who made up the bulk of the sample. The rest of the sample was divided among small numbers of ministers (five), government officials (four), private school teachers (four), military officers (two), architects (two), playwrights (one), and lawyers (one). This St. Paul's sample, which should be considered no more than a set of examples, is consistent with the findings of Baltzell on the activities of members of the Philadelphia branch of the upper class. In short, while the American upper class is overwhelmingly a business and financial aristocracy, it nonetheless harbors a considerable amount of expertise in a wide variety of fields. To quote Baltzell:

In fact, America is probably now producing more leaders who have had inherited advantages than at any other time in the twentieth century. For we live in an age of radically conflicting social forces, and, along with the alienated genteel and deracinated marginal man, the 1950's also produced such old-stock leaders as Robert Fiske Bradford, a Mayflower descendant, as Governor of Massachusetts; Sinclair Weeks, Secretary of Commerce; Robert Cutler, Assistant to President Eisenhower; Christian Herter and Dean Acheson as Secretaries of State; Henry Cabot Lodge, Ambassador to the United Nations, and his brother, Governor of Connecticut and Ambassador to Spain; John Cabot, Ambassador to Brazil (11 Cabots are listed in the 1958-59 edition of *Who's Who in America*); one Taft in the Senate and another a leader in civic and church affairs; one Saltonstall in the Senate and another head of Phillips Exeter Academy; a Lowell, a Pulitzer Prize-winner in Poetry, and Charles Francis Adams, the head of Raytheon.[63]

THE CRITERIA FOR UPPER-CLASS MEMBERSHIP

If this chapter has been successful, it should have demonstrated that there is in the United States an intermarrying social upper class, based upon business wealth, that has a rather definite set of boundaries which are guarded by social secretaries, private schools, social clubs, and similar exclusive institutions. Thus, it should have laid the groundwork for our criteria of upper-class membership, which are basic to the following chapters. To paraphrase Dahl, these criteria isolate a particular socioeconomic category which will be studied in later chapters in terms of the nature and extent of participation in national affairs by persons in this category. Just as Dahl used the invitation lists to the annual debutante assemblies held in the New Haven Lawn Club as his criterion of upper-class standing in New Haven, we have used the following criteria as evidence for membership in the national upper class:

1. A person is considered to be a member of the national upper class if he is in any *Social Register* other than the Washington edition. (For the reason the Washington edition was not used, see page 15.) While the 11 city editions we will use as criteria will include a few persons who are not long-standing members of the upper class, this merely reflects the relatively rapid mobility and assimilation that is characteristic of this country's business-oriented aristocracy. At the same time, it is also undoubtedly true that these volumes list a few families that have "lost their money," although it is difficult to assess what this statement means in terms of the net worth of the "impecunious families." However, we would estimate that the families worth tens of millions of dollars are the exceptions within the American upper class.

2. A person is considered to be a member of the upper class if he has attended any one of the private preparatory schools listed below:*

Asheville (Asheville, N. C.)
Buckley (New York, N. Y.)
Choate (Wallingford, Conn.)
Cranbrook (Bloomfield Hills, Mich.)
Deerfield (Deerfield, Mass.)
Episcopal High (Alexandria, Va.)
Groton (Groton, Mass.)
Hill (Pottstown, Pa.)
Hotchkiss (Lakeville, Conn.)
Kent (Kent, Conn.)
Lake Forest (Lake Forest, Ill.)
Lawrenceville (Lawrenceville, N. J.)
Loomis (Windsor, Conn.)
Middlesex (Concord, Mass.)
Milton (Milton, Mass.)
Pomfret (Pomfret, Conn.)
Portsmouth Priory (Portsmouth, R. I.)
St. Andrew's (Middletown, Del.)

* This list was compiled from the works of Baltzell and Kavaler. Exeter and Andover have been excluded from the list because of their large minority of scholarship students. However, attendance at Exeter and Andover will be noted when we discuss specific individuals in later chapters.

St. George's (Newport, R. I.)
St. Mark's (Southborough, Mass.)
St. Paul's (Concord, N. H.)
Shattuck (Faribault, Minn.)
Webb (Bell Buckle, Tenn.)
Woodberry Forest (Woodberry Forest, Va.)

According to Baltzell, exclusive private schools are an even better index to upper-class status than the *Social Register,* but as he also shows by comparing the British and American *Who's Who* listings of Adlai Stevenson, Averell Harriman, and Dean Acheson, some members of the American upper class do not mention their private school backgrounds in American publications.[64]

3. A person is considered to be a member of the national upper class if he is a member of any one of the following "very exclusive" gentlemen's clubs:[65]

Boston (New Orleans)
Brook (New York)
California (Los Angeles)
Casino (Chicago)
Chagrin Valley Hunt (Cleveland)
Detroit (Detroit)
Eagle Lake (Houston)
Everglades (Palm Beach)
Harmonie (New York)
Idlewild (Dallas)
Knickerbocker (New York)
Maryland (Baltimore)
Pacific Union (San Francisco)
Philadelphia (Philadelphia)
Pickwick (New Orleans)
Piedmont Driving (Atlanta)
Rainier (Seattle)
St. Cecilia (Charleston, S. C.)
St. Louis Country Club (St. Louis)
Somerset (Boston)

This list of clubs is considerably smaller than the actual number of clubs with a large proportion of upper-class members; therefore, any errors will be on the side of exclusion rather than inclusion. Recalling the statement Baltzell quoted from Allen's *The Lords of Creation,* we do not want to be guilty of inflating our figures by including a great many persons who are still on the fringes of the upper class. The list is also shorter because there are no Washington, D. C., clubs on the list. As is the case with the Washington *Social Register,* many Washington clubs take a somewhat liberal view toward the extension of membership to politicians. While there is a Washington branch of the national upper class, we would have to use more subtle criteria than the *Social Register* and gentlemen's clubs to distinguish it from the non-upper-class politicians that mingle with its members at the whirl of Washington parties. A third reason that the list of clubs is shorter than it could be is that we have excluded upper-class clubs which try to include in their membership men of artistic, literary, and intellectual achievement regardless of their social standing. Examples of such clubs would be the Tavern in Boston, the Century in New York, and the Bohemian in San Francisco. Excluding such "liberal" clubs, which according to Baltzell are more likely to be joined by Democratic Party members of the upper class, does not deny that most of their members are from the upper class.[66] It only ensures that men of talent—the "elites" of various fields—are not confused by definition with the upper class. Despite the relatively small number of clubs deemed exclusive enough to be near-perfect indicators of upper-class status, the underreporting of private school attendance in standard biographical sources makes club memberships the most valuable criterion we have for persons from cities where there is no *Social Register.*

4. A person is considered to be a member of the upper class if his or her father was a millionaire entrepreneur or a $100,000-a-year corporation executive or corporation lawyer, *and* (a) he or she attended one of the 130 private schools listed in Kavaler's *The Private World of High Society, or* (b) he or she belongs to any one of the exclusive clubs mentioned by Baltzell or Kavaler. The list of private schools and exclusive clubs can be larger here than for the second and third criteria above because it is known that the person is a member of the second generation of a wealthy family. Women's schools and clubs are included here because of the next criterion.

5. A person is considered to be a member of the upper class if he or she marries a person defined as a member of the upper class by criteria 1-4 above. Co-optation by marriage is one of the ways by which the upper class, whether its members are aware of it or not, infuses new brains and talent into its ranks. As one of Kavaler's informants reminded her, "But you haven't mentioned the biggest crack in the wall around the inner circle. I mean marriage, of course." [67] Thus, for example, President Kennedy's ambassador to Germany, George McGhee, married into an old Houston family based on oil money, while Thomas Schippers, conductor of New York's Metropolitan Opera Company, married Elaine Lane Phipps, who was from an old-line New York family. In the case of marriage into the

upper class, we are assuming that the person's interests and values will tend to become similar to those of the people with whom he mingles. This must be emphasized because there may be some social scientists who think of social class only in terms of social origins, and who would thus question the assumption that those who marry into the upper class become a part of it.

6. A person is considered to be a member of the upper class if his father, mother, sister, or brother is listed in the *Social Register,* or attended one of the exclusive private schools listed in criterion 2, or belongs to one of the exclusive gentlemen's clubs listed in criterion 3. This criterion allows us sometimes to obviate the reticence of some individual members of the upper class, especially those who refuse to list in the *Social Register.*

7. A person is considered to be a member of the upper class if he is a member of one of the old and still-wealthy families chronicled by Amory in *Who Killed Society?* or *The Proper Bostonians.* This criterion is based upon the assumption that Amory is an accurate ethnographer of the American upper class.

There may be other criteria, such as membership in exclusive clubs at Harvard, Yale, and Princeton, that would be useful in future studies of the upper class. However, we have found the seven given here to be the best possible when relying on autobiographies, biographies, and reference sources such as *Who's Who* for information. We would stress, with Baltzell, that no sociological index is likely to be perfect.[68] High-level corporation, foundation, and university employees who are merely on the fringes of the upper class may on occasion find their way into the *Social Register* or an exclusive gentlemen's club, and even the most exclusive of private schools give a few scholarships to the bright-but-needy. On the other hand, there are many people who do not bother to list in the *Social Register,* to list their private schools in *Who's Who,* or to list all the clubs to which they belong. Then too, there are a great many reticent members of the upper class on whom there is no published information. In short, we think that when both the "false positives" (those who should not be included but who are) and the "false negatives" (those who should be included but who are not) are considered, these seven criteria will give an accurate picture of the extent of participation by members of the national upper class in the institutions and decisions which are of concern to us in this study.

Convinced of the existence of an American upper class of intermarrying families that is national in scope, and armed with criteria for identifying its members, we can now turn to a consideration of their participation in the dominant institutions and important decision-making groups in American society.

Chapter Two . . . . . .
The Control of the .
Corporate Economy

It would seem that an American business aristocracy would control the American business system by definition. Unfortunately, matters are not as simple as they were in the past, when it could be determined readily that a family or a group of families owned and managed each business enterprise. However, the principal changes since the "breakup of family capitalism"—the dispersal of stock ownership and the increased number of hired executives—do not have all the implications that are sometimes attached to them. Members of the American upper class continue to be intimately involved in the business world, but the relationship is now more complex and confusing. We will have to proceed with some caution and at some length through this tangled jungle, because the information necessary to resolve all the problems is hard to locate; the ownership and control of major businesses is the most secret aspect of American society.

If it is not immediately obvious that members of the American upper class control the nation's economy, it does seem to be a generally accepted hypothesis that the economy is controlled by a relatively small number of very large corporations, banks, and insurance companies. There is no need to present in great detail the awesome statistics that buttress this statement —the relevant studies are summarized in the works of David Lynch, A. A. Berle, Jr., and the Hart Committee.[1] Although we will concentrate in our discussion on these giant businesses, we do not wish to give the impression that members of the American upper class are involved with only the biggest of the big businesses. We know from our studies of the alumni bulletins of St. Paul's and Lawrenceville and from the writings of Amory and Baltzell that many "smaller" companies are controlled by members of the American upper class. We also know from financial writers that there are "more than 25,000 family-owned or closely held corporations with assets of more than $1 million which have grown and prospered. . . ."[2] As important as these smaller companies are in understanding all aspects of upper-class life in America, we would emphasize that this chapter is concerned with demonstrating control of the economy rather than with determining the number of companies owned and controlled by members of the American upper class.

What is the nature of control in the large businesses that dominate the economy? According to most authorities, control is in the hands of the board of directors, a group of men usually numbering between ten and 25 who meet once or twice a month to decide upon the major policies of the company. In addition to the "outside" directors who are not regular company employees, the board always includes at least the top two or three officers in charge of day-to-day operations. In some cases, such as the large retail companies we studied, the board may include a great many regional or divisional vice-presidents; this has led at least one observer to assume that such managers are dominant within the board.[3] We consider the boards decisive because, despite the necessity of delegating minor decisions and technical research, they make major decisions, such as those of investment, and select the men who will carry out daily operations.[4] In fact, their power to change management if the performance of the company does not satisfy them is what we will mean by "control." There is no better authority on the importance of the directors than A. A. Berle, Jr. (SR, NY),* a corporation lawyer who is a director himself in addition to a writer, and who has written extensively on the modern corporate economy:

The control system in today's corporations, when it does not lie solely in the directors as in the American Telephone and Telegraph Company, lies in a combination of the directors of a so-called control block (a misnomer, incidentally) plus the directors themselves. For practical purposes, therefore, the control or power element in most large corporations rests in its group of directors and it is autonomous—or autonomous if taken together with a control block. And inheritance tax distribution of stock being what it is, the trend is increasingly to management autonomy. This is a self-perpetuating oligarchy.[5]

Berle is a constructive starting point, not only for his insights but for his shortcomings. He believes the directors to be autonomous in the sense that they are not beholden to stockholders, and he emphasizes that most of the directors do not have a significant percentage of the company's stockholdings. This leads to a situation of power without property.[6] In short, Berle is pointing to the problems we noted at the beginning of this chapter

---

* Berle is one of the most scholarly and liberal upper-class members of the power elite. He went to Versailles with Woodrow Wilson after World War I and was sent on a mission to Latin America shortly thereafter. Later he became one of the leaders of Franklin D. Roosevelt's Brain Trust and he has served as an adviser to Democratic Presidents ever since, usually as an expert on Latin American affairs. He had a coordinating role in the 1962 invasion of Cuba.

—the distribution of stock ownership and the rise of autonomous managers who are without significant property holdings. The first of these points has been called "people's capitalism" by the National Advertising Council and the United States Information Agency.[7] The second point is usually termed the "managerial revolution," a thesis which holds that the wide dispersal of stock and the need for expertise in running modern corporations have combined to allow a nonstockholding group of professional managers from the middle levels of society to take control of the corporations. Talcott Parsons, one of the country's leading sociologists, emphasizes the managerial revolution in criticizing Mills.[8] He continually points to confiscatory taxes and the need for expertise in claiming that there is no one ruling group within this country. Daniel Bell, another eminent sociologist, uses the managerial revolution thesis to argue that the American upper class no longer has a community of interest because it has lost responsibility for its corporations.[9]

However, these changes must be looked at more closely. First of all, the decline of family capitalism does not mean widespread stock ownership within the general population; it means *dispersal within the upper class.* Family A does not own Company X while Family B owns Company Y, as it may have been in the past; instead, Family A and Family B both have large stockholdings in companies X and Y, as does Family C, which used to be the sole owner of Company Z. Furthermore, it is not necessary to control a company in order to be socially responsible. That is, members of the American upper class now have an interest in the success of the business system as a whole. Contrary to Bell, this may give members of the upper class an even greater community of interest than they had in the past when they were bitterly involved in protecting their standing by maintaining their individual companies. Then too, the fact that many members of the upper class are not tied to a given corporation frees them to be involved in other aspects of the socioeconomic system, such as governmental service. This may well lend to the stability of the system. Nor, as we shall see, does the fact that members of the upper class do not own their own individual companies mean they do not involve themselves in the management of large corporations in which they own only a small share. To support our arguments, we will present systematic information on stock ownership and on the participation by members of the upper class in the management of major corporations.

STOCK OWNERSHIP

Ascertaining the distribution of corporate stock ownership is fraught with difficulties, for such figures are seldom a matter of public record. The meager disclosure laws that exist are circumvented in a variety of ways, such as by putting the stock in the name of one's wife or some other relative. In 1966, when the Securities Exchange Commission demanded that a wife's holdings be disclosed, it was found that some propertyless directors were major stockholders after all.[10] Despite these difficulties, a technique has been developed which leads to fairly accurate estimates. However, before presenting the findings based on this method it is necessary to distinguish the problem of stock distribution from four easily confused issues: standard of living, income distribution, wealth distribution, and number of stockholders.

Standard of living—living level—has to do with consumption, with how well people live. In terms of standard of living, most Americans do very well indeed. As many as 75-80 per cent have consumer goods in sufficient quantities—cars, TV's, food, and houses. As a matter of fact, the "job-rich," as Floyd Hunter calls the high-salaried professionals of the upper-middle class, often live just as well as their upper-class counterparts.[11] Harold Hodges, in another detailed study of the Bay Area, also found that living level did not distinguish the upper-middle class from the upper class.[12] However, living level is not related to the relative distribution of income or wealth within a population. A person may have the same share of yearly income or national wealth he has always had and still have more "things," a higher living level, if the size of the national economy has grown.

Income distribution has to do with the percentage of the wages and profits paid out each year to families at various income levels. In 1959, for example, 45 million families had incomes totaling $300 billion. The top 0.1 per cent of families received 1.5 per cent of the income, the top 1 per cent received 8 per cent, the top 5 per cent received 18 per cent, and the top 20 per cent received 44 per cent.[13] The top 0.1 per cent were 45,000 families who received an average of $110,000 per year, or 15 times as much as their numbers would warrant if income were equally distributed. The top 1 per cent were 450,000 families who received an average of $53,000 per year, which is eight times as much as would be received under conditions of complete equality. The comparison of this income distribution with earlier decades of the twentieth century is a matter of dispute. Gabriel Kolko argues in *Wealth and Power* that the income distribution has not changed since 1910 if all factors are considered. According to Kolko, the factors that must be considered include increased withholding of dividends by corporations, underreporting of dividend income, and the rewarding of the corporate rich by expense accounts, company-paid insurances, company-owned cars and yachts, and other nontaxable compensation.

On the other hand, Herman Miller claims in *Rich Man Poor Man* that there was a tendency toward more equality in income distribution from 1929 to 1944, with the share of the top 5 per cent of the families dropping from 30 per cent to 20 per cent of the income, but that since that time the distribution has remained about what it is today. Miller denies Kolko's claim that greater withholdings by corporations, underreporting, and non-taxable compensations are large enough to explain the reported changes. Miller bases his argument on the accuracy of census reports, which he shows to compare favorably with estimates by the Office of Business Estimates. However, it is also true that the census estimates are much lower than those of the OBE in the category that contains dividends.[14] Then too, income from tax-exempt securities does not have to be reported.[15] Nevertheless, from the broad perspective of this study the differences between Kolko and Miller as to the earlier decades of this century are not important, for they agree about the last 20 years. They also agree that taxes do not affect this picture. In Miller's language: "When all tax payments are taken into account, there is a real question as to whether taxes have a significant effect on the equalization of income." [16]

Miller's statement is borne out by economist Leon Keyserling, who notes that a study of 1960 income figures showed that those who made under $2000 per year paid 38 per cent of their income in all types of taxes, those who made $2000 to $5000 paid from 38 per cent to more than 41 per cent, those who made $7500 to $10,000 paid only 22.3 per cent, and those who made above $10,000 paid only 31.6 per cent.[17] Nor do the figures presented by Keyserling tell the whole story, for the job-rich pay higher taxes than the property-rich. We have a tax system that "soaks the high salaried" rather than the really rich. (Mills lists most of the ways in which this minimization of taxes by the property-rich is accomplished.)[18] The success of the system can be seen in studies which show that those who make over $750,000 a year pay a percentage of their income to income taxes which is not much greater than that of the typical wage earner.[19] We can conclude our survey of income distribution by saying that the unequal distribution of income is not affected by the tax structure. If Marxist William A. Williams and *Washington Post* reporter Bernard Nossiter are right in pinpointing the tax structure as a sensitive indicator of the power structure of a society, perhaps the "outcome" of tax legislation can be considered as an example of what Polsby advocates when he urges social scientists to study outcomes in specific issue-areas. In terms of Polsby's question, "Who benefits?" the outcome of tax legislation points to the existence of a power structure dominated by the very rich.[20]

Wealth distribution is a still different question from standard of living and income distribution. It has to do with ownership of various marketable assets, which "may include such tangible things as land, buildings, machinery, raw materials, goods in process, and animals, and such intangible things as franchises, patent rights, copyrights, and good will." [21] (Wealth, it should be noted, is a broader concept than "stock ownership," which is one form of wealth.) Little was known about wealth distribution in an accurate way in the United States until a study by economist Robert Lampman, who later became President Johnson's major economic adviser on the anti-poverty program. Lampman applied a method that has been used with considerable success in other countries, the "estate multiplier method." He developed an accurate picture of wealth distribution by studying the estates of deceased individuals worth $60,000 or more, aided by the comments of such experts on wealth distribution as Raymond W. Goldsmith, Simon Kuznets, and J. Keith Butters. Lampman's studies showed a slight drop in the amount of wealth held by the top 1 per cent of adults between 1922 and 1956, a drop from 31.6 per cent to 26.0 per cent (see Table 1). How-

TABLE 1. SHARE OF PERSONAL SECTOR WEALTH (EQUITY) HELD BY TOP WEALTH-HOLDERS, SELECTED YEARS, 1922-1956*

Year	Top 1 Per Cent of Adults	Top 0.5 Per Cent of All Persons	Top 2 Per Cent of Families†
1922	31.6	29.8	33.0
1929	36.3	32.4	
1933	28.3	25.2	
1939	30.6	28.0	
1945	23.3	20.9	
1949	20.8	19.3	
1953	24.2	22.7	28.5
1956	26.0	25.0	

* Lampman, The Share of Top Wealth-Holders in National Wealth, 1962, p. 24. Reprinted by permission of Princeton University Press. Copyright © 1962 by Princeton University Press.
† Families are defined here as all adults less married females.

ever, he quickly points out that half of the drop disappears if families rather than individuals are considered, for tax laws have now made it expedient to distribute legal ownership among all members of the family. Lampman provides a refinement of these findings in two other tables, which we have condensed into one table using only the figures for 1953, the last year for which these figures are available (see Table 2).

TABLE 2. SHARE OF PERSONAL SECTOR WEALTH HELD WITHIN THE TOP
1 PER CENT OF ADULTS AND THE TOP 1 PER CENT OF THE
TOTAL POPULATION IN 1953*

Per Cent of Adults	Per Cent of Wealth	Per Cent of Population	Per Cent of Wealth
top 0.44	18.3	top 0.27	18.0
0.79	22.3	0.37	20.0
0.89	23.3	0.47	22.0
0.98	24.1	0.50	22.7
1.00	24.3	0.58	23.8
		0.65	24.8
		0.80	26.6
		1.04	28.5

*The figures for adults are from Table 94 on page 204 and the figures for the population as a whole are from Table 93 on page 202 of Lampman, *The Share of Top Wealth-Holders in National Wealth*, 1962. Reprinted by permission of Princeton University Press.

Several points should be stressed in examining Lampman's findings. First, wealth is much more unequally distributed than income. Whereas the income of the top 0.1 per cent of the population is disproportionate by a factor of 15, the wealth of the top 0.5 per cent of the population for 1956 is disproportionate by a factor of 50. Second, the figures for the 1950's suggest that the top wealth-holders' share may be increasing from a low point in the 1940's. British wealth expert Richard Titmus, who has done exhaustive studies on wealth distribution in Great Britain, interprets this finding to mean that the rate of increase from 1949 to 1956 was twice as rapid as the rate of decline between 1929 and 1949.[22] A third point which must be stressed in examining Lampman's results is that a percentage considerably less than 1 holds the greatest proportion of the wealth held by the top 1 per cent. This is consistent with our belief that members of the American upper class comprise about 0.5 per cent of the population. Finally, in commenting on Lampman's findings, it seems certain that there has been very little change in wealth distribution in the past several decades. Nor is there any reason to believe that there is any tendency whatsoever toward increasing equality. This would seem to refute Berle and Parsons' belief in the devastating nature of the tax system.

With Lampman's findings clearly in mind, the problem of the number of people who own stock—one form of wealth—can be considered in its proper perspective. If there are many millions of stockholders in the United States, as the New York Stock Exchange claims, it is also the case that most of them own very little stock. Lampman gives the exact picture when he dissects the types of property held by the top wealth-holders (see Table 3). Lampman's findings on the concentration of stock ownership are con-

TABLE 3. SHARE OF PERSONAL SECTOR ASSETS AND LIABILITIES HELD BY TOP 1 PER CENT OF ADULTS, 1922, 1929, 1939, 1945, 1949, AND 1953 (PER CENT)*

Type of Property	1922	1929	1939	1945	1949	1953
Real estate	18.0	17.3	13.7	11.1	10.5	12.5
U.S. gov't. bonds	45.0	100.0	91.0	32.5	35.8	31.8
State and local bonds	88.0	†	†	†	77.0	†
Other bonds	69.2	82.0	75.5	78.5	78.0	77.5
Corporate stock	61.5	65.6	69.0	61.7	64.9	76.0
Cash	—	—	—	17.0	18.9	24.5
Mortgages and notes	—	—	—	34.7	32.0	30.5
Cash, mortgages, and notes	31.0	34.0	31.5	19.3	20.5	25.8
Pension and retirement funds	8.0	8.0	6.0	5.9	5.5	5.5
Insurance	35.3	27.0	17.4	17.3	15.0	11.5
Miscellaneous property	23.2	29.0	19.0	21.4	15.0	15.5
Gross estate	32.3	37.7	32.7	25.8	22.4	25.3
Liabilities‡	23.8	29.0	26.5	27.0	19.0	20.0
Economic estate	33.9	38.8	33.8	25.7	22.8	27.4

* Lampman, The Share of Top Wealth-Holders in National Wealth, 1962, p. 209. Reprinted by permission of Princeton University Press. The data come from Table 90 and Appendix Tables A-17 through A-21, col. 13. National balance sheet data used for 1922, 1929, and 1939 are from Goldsmith, Saving in U.S., III; for 1945, 1949, and 1953, from preliminary unpublished tables prepared by the National Bureau of Economic Research.

† In excess of 100 per cent.

‡ Total wealth variant.

sistent with other results. Robert Heilbroner quotes a Senate committee estimate that less than 1 per cent of the families own over 80 per cent of all publicly held industrial stock, while a trio of Harvard economists, by their "residual method," estimated that 0.2 per cent of the "spending units" own 65 per cent to 71 per cent of the publicly held stock.[23] Using the 65 per cent figure, the top 0.2 per cent hold a proportion of stock that is disproportionate by a factor of 325. Whatever the exact figures may be—they may never be known because of the secrecy surrounding stock ownership —our conclusion is very similar to that drawn by Mills: ". . . at the very most, 0.2 or 0.3 per cent of the adult population own the bulk, the pay-off shares, of the corporate world."[24]

It is probable that corporate stock ownership would be even more concentrated if certain factors, economic and political, did not work against it. First, municipal and state bonds are tax free. As can be seen in Table 3, the very rich own all of these, for obvious tax reasons.* Second, there are sound economic reasons for encouraging people with small savings to become stockholders. Most of these reasons are included in the following statement by Perry Hall (SR, NY), a partner in the investment banking firm of Morgan, Stanley and Company:

What are the advantages of the common-stock way to the corporation? First, it's ownership money, and doesn't ever have to be paid back to anybody. Second, not all the stockholders exercise their rights. Some of them sell, instead, and that means new stockholders, which, in turn, means new customers—a fellow wants to buy his own company's product. That was certainly a factor, General Motors being a sales-minded company. Third, that low debt ratio keeps the borrowing power in reserve for future needs, acting as a sort of anchor to windward.[25]

Finally, in considering why members of the upper class do not own all of the corporate stock, a possible political reason must be mentioned. Efforts by the New York Stock Exchange to increase the number of stockholders may well serve to counteract hostile propaganda to the effect that only a handful of people own the American corporate economy.

Unfortunately, demonstrating overwhelming stock ownership by less than 1 per cent of the population does not completely answer all the questions with which we are concerned. There remain three problems—the relationship of top income and top wealth, the relationship of top stockholders to the American upper class, and the relationship of stock ownership to corporate control.

According to Lampman, rankings by income and wealth are not interchangeable. When talking in terms of the top 1 per cent or 2 per cent of both groups this is true, for the top 1 per cent of the income group in 1960 included those earning as low as $25,000 per year, while the top 1.04 per cent of wealth-holders in Lampman's study includes those with estates worth as little as $60,000 to $70,000. However, when Lampman's findings on the concentration of wealth within the top few tenths of a per cent of the distribution are combined with the fact that most of the income of the top few tenths of a per cent of income earners comes from property, the statement must be amended to say that the relationship between wealth and income breaks down very rapidly as one moves from the highest summits. Mills's figures for 1949 can be considered representative. He determined that 94 per cent of the income of the 120 people reporting $1 million or more in earnings came from property, while 67 per cent of the earnings

---

* Tax advantages also partly explain the growth in the number of personal trust funds. Each fund is taxed separately.

of the 13,702 who reported $100,000 to $999,000 in income came from that source.[26]

As to the second problem: Are the less than 1 per cent who stand at the top of the income and wealth distributions also the same less than 1 per cent who make up the American upper class? The answer may seem obvious, but it is hard to document in a systematic way. The Internal Revenue Service, for example, released names for the last time in the early 1920's. Fortunately, the names released in 1924 furnished the basis for Lundberg's *America's Sixty Families,* which has been shown by Baltzell to have a large overlap with one index of upper-class membership, the *Social Register.* We can also recall Mills's finding that one-half of the 90 richest men of 1900 had descendants in the *Social Register,* as well as the statements by Amory and Baltzell, respectively, that the Boston and Philadelphia branches of the upper class are based on corporate stock ownership.[27] As further evidence, we studied a list compiled by Don Villarejo of the 99 corporate directors with $10 million or more in stock in leading corporations.[28] Sixty-seven (74 per cent) of the 90 men on whom information could be found were members of the upper class by our criteria. Of the 23 who could not be so classified, 12 were people who were local in their affiliations, 9 were new-rich who had not been assimilated, and 2 were unassimilated Jews.

If it is not yet clear that members of the American upper class control the corporate economy, at least it is fairly certain who reaps most of its benefits. We must now turn to the third question, the relationship between ownership and control.

OWNERSHIP AND CONTROL

The relationship between ownership and control in major corporations, which used to be taken for granted because of the legal rights of stock ownership, has been in dispute since the early 1930's, when Berle and Gardner Means (Exeter, Harvard) reported in *The Modern Corporation and Private Property* that salaried managers controlled 44 per cent of the 200 then-largest nonfinancial corporations. However, as Sweezy notes, their data were not as detailed as those later compiled as part of the TNEC investigations, which showed that large stockholders controlled about 140 of the top 200 corporations. Sweezy himself, writing in the late 1930's, carried the argument one step further with a methodologically sophisticated study of corporate histories, interlocking directorships, and corporate financing; it showed that there were eight major "interest groups" centered around large banks and finance houses which controlled a great many of the major corporations through minority ownership and legal device.[29] According to another Marxist, Victor Perlo, who has done work which updates Sweezy's study, Sweezy's groupings accounted for control of 11 of the companies deemed to be under management control by Berle and Means, while the TNEC reports accounted for another 15.[30] A more experience-based study by Lundberg agrees with those of Sweezy and Perlo, pointing out that six companies listed by Berle and Means as under management control were "authoritatively regarded in Wall Street as actually under the rule of J. P. Morgan and Company: United States Steel Corporation, General Electric Company, Electric Bond and Share Company, Consolidated Gas Company (now Consolidated Edison Company), AT & T, and New York Central Railroad." [31] Lundberg, for many years a Wall Street financial reporter, explains further:

. . . control of corporations by legal device, while excluding small stockholders from a voice in affairs, does not exclude the big interests. What has happened is this: the big proprietors, unable to exercise as wide control over as many companies as they would like by means of simple ownership, have in certain instances abandoned simple ownership of a corporation as a means of control and have substituted for it control by legal device. The liquid capital they have by this means been able to repossess has then been used to obtain an ownership stake in other additional enterprises. . . . The fact is, however, that the managers under the legal device have in virtually all cases been installed by the big proprietors." [32]

The nature of these "interest groups" can be seen from an angry outburst in the mid-1960's over the existence of the Cleveland group whose hub is the Cleveland Trust Bank. Through a holding company, A. A. Welsh and Company, Cleveland Trust controlled the Cleveland *Plain Dealer,* Sherwin Williams, Cleveland Cliffs Iron, Island Creek Coal, and many other prominent Cleveland corporations. In addition, it also held large blocks of stock in the National City Bank and the Union Commerce Bank in Cleveland, the Firestone Bank in Akron, and banks in other Ohio cities.[33] Its chairman and its president, George Gund and George Karch, both of whom are listed in the Cleveland *Social Register,* are directors of 43 corporations between them.

Robert Gordon questions the cohesiveness and vigor of interest groups as well as the amount of active control by corporate directors and large stockholders.[34] If they are looked at as so many separate economic units, it is perhaps plausible to argue that such stockholding groups are not closely knit. However, when looked at as intermarried families and social cliques who operate through holding companies, family trusts, and family foundations, it is unlikely that such criticisms as Gordon offers are relevant. The Rockefellers, who hold minority control in several Standard Oil companies, are an excellent example. Their companies provide several of the examples of "inside" or "management" boards. Still another example would be the Morgan interest group, which is based upon several extended families who put their voting rights in the hands of Morgan financial institutions. An even better example would be the huge du Pont clan, which is the center of still another interest group. However, the best example of all would be the Mellon interest group, which controls, among others, Mellon National Bank, Gulf Oil, Westinghouse Electric, Aluminum Corporation of America, and Koppers. As *Forbes* Magazine explains:

When Gulf executives speak reverently of "the board," they are normally referring to a single man, diffident Richard King Mellon, senior member of one of the world's richest families. The only Mellon on Gulf's board, Dick Mellon looks after his family's $2 billion, 32 per cent interest in Gulf—though he rarely concerns himself with its day-to-day operations.[35]

As a final example of a tight-knit interest group, we would point to the intermarriage which cemented the interest group built around the First National City Bank of New York. The two largest stockholders in that bank were William Rockefeller and James Stillman. Two of William Rockefeller's sons married two of Stillman's daughters; today the head of the bank is James Stillman Rockefeller, whose son by Nancy Carnegie is Andrew Carnegie Rockefeller.*

While a concern with interest groups has subsided within the academic community, research continues on the problem of ownership and control. Information developed during the 1960's has been summarized by Earl F. Cheit, who concludes that "it is far from clear that attenuation of ownership control is as complete as is generally assumed." [36] He points in particular to a study by Villarejo which found usable data on 232 of the 250 largest corporations for 1960. It showed that in at least 141 of the 232, the directors as a group held enough stock to control the company. Cheit emphasizes that these are probably minimal conclusions because the stock of relatives does not have to be reported to the Securities Exchange Commission. Nor do the trust holdings of a bank, "even if a director of the bank is a director of the corporation in question." [37] Cheit's comments are also supported by the fascinating findings of Kolko, which Cheit summarizes as follows: "For example, when TNEC and current stock ownership figures for the same corporations are compared, in board after board the same family names appear but with very much less stock ownership visible in the current figures." [38]

In summarizing our discussion of ownership and control, we believe that the circumstantial evidence developed by TNEC, Sweezy, Perlo, Lund-

* Mrs. Rockefeller is a niece of Andrew Carnegie.

berg, Kolko, and Villarejo points to only one conclusion—the biggest share-holders in large corporations are actively involved in determining the general policies and selecting the managers of these companies. If, like Richard Mellon, they do not bother with day-to-day operations, they still have the power to change management when they are not satisfied with the company's performance. This fact has been demonstrated time and time again throughout the past 30 years. Villarejo uses the examples of Chrysler Motors and Commercial Solvents during the late 1950's. The following quote from Villarejo concerns the latter:

To the investor interested in Commercial Solvents it was apparent by late 1958 that the company was not flourishing under Woods's leadership. Whereupon, the Milbank family, the dominant interest, took steps to replace Woods with another man. These steps merely involved informing Woods, through H. H. Helm, a director of Commercial Solvents and Chairman of Chemical Bank New York Trust Company, that his term was up. Woods, underestimating the shares the Milbanks represented, was reluctant to surrender without a fight. Upon learning that the Milbanks spoke for 30 per cent of the stock, representing personal holdings as well as some holdings of friends and business associates, Woods expressed some surprise and quickly resigned.[39]

However, as Cheit admits, quoting Villarejo, "the issue of management control can only be settled finally if lists of, say, the largest 150 shareholdings in each corporation of interest became available to the public." [40] The lack of such lists is hardly an argument in favor of those who would claim that control is somehow separate from the members of the American upper class who own most of the stock.*

CORPORATE DIRECTORS

As convincing as the indirect evidence on ownership control may be, and as fascinating as the study of interest groups may be, we have tried to supplement such findings by the more direct method of ascertaining the social class of corporate directors. Such a study will tell us about control in general, although not about the nature of control in specific companies. In order to understand control in specific companies, each company would have to be studied in great detail, including its history and present ownership. For example, to find that most of the directors of a company are non-upper-class vice-presidents may be understandable only when it is also

---

* We want to emphasize once again that the question of management control concerns only the very largest of corporations. We do not know of any social scientists who would claim that the "smaller" big businesses that are still independent have been taken over by managers. These companies are an important source of income and power for many members of the upper class, but they are not the key to the question which concerns us here, the control of the economy.

known that the company's chairman, a *Social Register* listee, owns most of the stock and took over control from his father. Or it may be understandable only when it is known that Morgan Guaranty Trust has the voting rights to 25 per cent of the stock. That is, not all members of a board are equally important. A company may well be run by one person or by a handful of persons on the board. At any rate, well aware of the differences among boards, we studied the corporate directors of the top 15 banks, the top 15 insurance companies, and the top 20 industrials for 1963 on the assumption that these companies are the dominant elements in the American economy. A long story can be made very short by saying that 53 per cent of the 884 men from the banks, insurance companies, and industrials were members of the American upper class. However, we will also tell the story in more detail.

Before turning to a detailed consideration of each area of the economy, it might be well to deal with the question which will immediately occur to many readers: Who are the 47 per cent of directors who are not members of the American upper class? The answer is as follows:

1. The largest number of non-upper-class directors are hired executives who have risen to positions of prominence. This phenomenon has been documented in a great many studies. We would add that these people are in the process of being assimilated into the upper class and that their goal is similar to that of long-standing members of the upper class—an adequate profit by the corporation. We will return to this point later in the chapter.

2. Another important group on the corporate boards, particularly in insurance, are the "experts" who have risen to positions of prominence. This group includes engineers, agriculturists, economists, and statisticians. For example, an engineer with a Ph.D. from the University of Chicago sits on the board of Prudential Life after many years with Bell Telephone Laboratories. However, the experts come from other fields as well. A prominent example would be former FBI agent John Bugas, a vice-president of Ford Motors, who sits on the boards of Standard Oil of Indiana, Ford, and the One William Street Fund.

3. A third important group consists of college presidents. We would emphasize that these men are mostly employees of the major universities controlled by members of the upper class (see pp. 77-79) and thus are members of the power elite. The one best example would be James R. Killian, Jr., chairman of the Massachusetts Institute of Technology, who sits on the boards of General Motors, Polaroid, and the Cabot Corporation.

4. A fourth group, whose numbers are usually greatly overestimated, are former military men. As with college presidents, we believe that they can be considered members of the power elite, if it is assumed that the

Defense Department in which they were formerly employed is controlled by members of the American upper class (see Chapter 5).

5. A fifth group consists of corporate lawyers, often from big Wall Street law firms controlled by members of the upper class, or from trusts and estates of members of the upper class. In short, many are members of the power elite.

6. Another small group of corporate directors who can be counted as part of the power elite are the foundation executives. The two most prominent examples in our sample are Henry T. Heald, president of the Ford Foundation in the early 1960's, and John Gardner, who was president of the Carnegie Corporation until he became President Johnson's Secretary of Health, Education, and Welfare. Heald sat on the boards of Lever Brothers, U. S. Steel, Equitable Life, and AT & T, while Gardner was on the board of Shell Oil.

7. Another minor group of directors can be classified as local small businessmen, usually owners of their own companies.

8. We also found a handful of very wealthy Jews on major boards who could not be considered by our criteria as assimilated members of the upper class. The best example would be Lester Crown, son of the founder of General Dynamics. He married Renee Schine, the daughter of a wealthy Jewish real estate owner, but neither gives any evidence of schools or clubs that would qualify them as members of the social upper class. They are members of a small, parallel Jewish upper class which may or may not be more fully assimilated into the national upper class in the next several decades.

9. Finally, there were a small number of Canadians and Europeans on corporate boards. The companies with one or more foreign directors included Travelers, Gulf Oil, Shell Oil, and General Motors.

In summarizing these nine types of non-upper-class directors, we do not see any reason to doubt that members of the upper class continue to control the corporate economy. Executives and experts who have risen are trusted employees. College presidents, foundation presidents, and most lawyers are employees of other upper-class-dominated institutions, while the number of unassimilated rich Jews, local businessmen, and foreigners is too small to matter.[41]

The Banks

Returning to a consideration of corporate boards in specific areas of the economy, we decided to study the banks in great detail because, among other reasons, they are reputed to be the centers of "interest groups." Even if this is not always the case, it is true that the top ten banks have 25 per cent of the assets of all banks, and it is also true that the major banks are the trust representatives for a very large amount of corporate stock.[42] Further, we believe that the major banks are the glue of the economic system: as can be seen by studies of corporate interlocks, they have ties with every important business in the country.[43] Bankers are the most important carriers of information and opinion from one sector of the business establishment to another. Among the top 15 banks as a group, one-third of the 350 directors are listed in the *Social Register*. Applying all criteria for upper-class standing, 62 per cent are in that small social group. This increase from 33 per cent to 62 per cent is due primarily to the inclusion of men from cities that do not have *Social Registers*. This is a very important point because we will see that studies done by other authors on lawyers and university trustees, which used only the *Social Register* as a criterion for upper-class membership, showed that about one-third of those groups were also in that index. In addition to our thorough study of the boards of the top 15 banks, using data gathered by Fred Nuss,[44] we quickly checked the directors of banks 17, 18, and 19 against the *Social Register* because they were the biggest banks in Boston, Cleveland, and Philadelphia, respectively. The *Social Register* figures were 46 per cent, 41 per cent, and 52 per cent. We have no hesitation in saying that this overrepresentation by a factor of 125 in the top 15 banks is impressive evidence for control of the banking system by members of the American upper class.

The Insurance Companies

Second only to the banks in their importance to the financial life of modern America are the insurance companies. While most of them are not profit-making institutions, they are important as a source of investment funds for the large corporations. They supplement the banks with which they are so tightly interlocked. However rich the banks and industrial corporations may be, they are not rich enough for the large financing needs of giant enterprise in the second half of the twentieth century. In the words of Peter Drucker: "Our economy has made the small man the major supplier of capital. . . ." [45] This need for financing, along with the fear of losing control to rival stockholding groups, was an important factor in the mutualization of insurance companies around the turn of the century. Not having to pay dividends, the insurance companies were able to accumulate a large amount of money very rapidly. And not being a profit-making venture, they have enjoyed very liberal tax rates, further intensifying the buildup of funds.*

The insurance companies, according to data compiled by Ronald Schaffer,[47] are not very different from the banks in terms of participation

* There are other sources of investment funds which are controlled but not "owned" by members of the upper class. For example, Berle points out that Bankers

in directorships by members of the upper class. Again, one-third of the directors were listed in the *Social Register,* with the figure jumping to 44 per cent upper-class participation when all criteria are applied. The difference from the figure for banks is due to a greater number of experts and college presidents on the insurance boards, as well as to many persons from the state of Connecticut who could not be classified as members of the upper class by our criteria. Like the banks, the insurance companies interlock with the entire corporate economy. The 311 men we studied sat on 1844 other corporate boards. However, the most significant finding on the insurance companies is their great overlap with the major banks. It is simply not true, as Berle claims, that the insurance companies are "independent fiduciaries." [48] On this point our findings are consistent with previous research. For example, the Cellar Committee reported that the Big Four of life insurance, which sell almost half of all the life insurance written in this country, had 24 New York bankers on their boards in 1948. Parkinson found that Chase Manhattan, the Rockefeller bank, had four interlocks with Metropolitan Life, two with Travelers, one with Equitable Life, and one with New York Life. First National City Bank interlocked with Metropolitan, Prudential, New York Life, and Travelers, while Manufacturers Hanover Bank interlocked with Prudential, Northwestern Mutual, Travelers, and Mutual Benefit Life.[49] To choose examples not presented in other reports, Schaffer's study showed that 12 major insurance company directors interlocked with Connecticut Bank and Trust, ten with Chemical Bank of New York, seven with Hartford National Bank, and three with the Federal Reserve Bank of New York.

The Top Twenty Industrials

The 20 largest industrial corporations for 1963 include such well-known companies as General Motors, Ford, General Electric, International

---

Trust controls AT & T's $2.2 billion employee pension fund. Drucker calls the managers of such monies, including the insurance executives, the "new tycoons" who serve the people in general: "When General Motors set up its pension fund seven years ago, it hired Clarence Stanley—then a partner of Morgan, Stanley and Company, the country's most powerful investment bankers—to manage the fund. There could be no more perfect example of the 'capitalist revolution' than this move of J. P. Morgan's direct successor from heading the very symbol of Wall Street to managing the savings of 'proletarians.' . . ." [46] Drucker also mentions Wallace Dunkel of the pension fund department of Bankers Trust and Merrill Griswold of Massachusetts Investors Trust, the biggest mutual fund, as examples of these new tycoons. He neglects to mention, however, that two of the three, Stanley and Griswold, are old-line members of the upper class, that Bankers Trust is controlled by members of the upper class, and that General Motors is tightly interlocked with Morgan financial institutions. General Motors did not "hire" Clarence Stanley. Rather, Stanley and his company gained control of a vast amount of investment funds, the savings of Drucker's "proletarians."

Harvester, Lockheed Aircraft, and four Standard Oil companies. In this study by Ann Bicknell, only the outside directors and the chairmen of the board were included.[50] However, the *Social Register* figure remained at one-third. The overall percentage of upper-class participants was 54 per cent. Once again, the interlocks with the rest of the corporate economy were extensive. Each man sat on an average of six to seven other boards, a figure almost identical with that for bank directors. In the case of U. S. Steel, for example, the 16 men studied were also directors or trustees for 20 major industrials, 18 banks, 11 insurance companies, 9 railroads, 8 utilities, 5 universities, and 3 charitable foundations. The directors of Lockheed, one of the largest of the defense corporations, also served 27 industrials, 14 banks, and 5 universities.

Other Large Businesses

Assuming that banks, insurance companies, and industrials control the American economy, we believe our findings on the 50 companies that dominate these sectors of the economy are evidence for control of the corporate economy by members of the national upper class. However, there are other major sectors within the business community—transportation, utilities, and merchandising—which we will look at briefly. Little need be said about the 15 largest transportation companies, for their percentage of upper-class directors—53 per cent of 230 inside and outside directors—is not different from that for the 20 largest industrials. On the other hand, the top 15 utilities, where only 30 per cent of 218 directors are members of the upper class, and the 15 leading merchandising firms, where only 26 per cent of 227 directors meet our criteria, require further comment.[51]

The utilities are interesting for the light they throw on the problem of determining ownership in big businesses. Because the Federal Power Commission requires that the ten largest stockholders of all operating electric utilities be reported, it might seem that adequate information would be available for at least this sector of the economy. However, the actual situation can be seen from a list of the top ten stockholders of Pacific Gas & Electric, the fifth largest utility in the country:

1. Merrill Lynch
2. Equitable Life
3. New York Life
4. Savings Fund and Plan
5. Prudential Life
6. King & Co.
7. Raymond & Co.
8. Sigler & Co.
9. Mac & Co.
10. Cudd & Co.

The companies in the first column are identifiable, but it comes as a surprise to many people to learn that the names in the second column are the "street names," the aliases, of leading banks, which in turn hold the stock in trust funds for unnamed individuals.[52] Mac & Co., for example, translates to Mellon National Bank, the center of the Mellon family interest group. According to Perlo, many banks use at least a half-dozen different street names, and he lists 12 that are used by Morgan Guaranty Trust. While outsiders can eventually piece together their own code book, this system plays havoc with reporting rules:

Let us suppose that Lynn & Co., representing the Guaranty Trust, is listed as one of the ten largest stockholders in a power company. There is no information as to how many additional shares Guaranty Trust may hold in the names of its other 11 nominees (providing they are not among the top ten holders), or even through brokerage houses.[53]

This system may be important at times in the secretive struggles among financial interests:

When a particular group seeks to buy up a controlling interest in a corporation, it does so over a period of time and through a myriad of channels, so as to cover its tracks. At the same time, the incumbents use their excellent sources of information to uncover any attempts to unseat them. The American Telephone and Telegraph Company keeps a dossier on every stockholder of 500 shares or over.* [54]

The ubiquity of this system can be seen from the fact that 16 of the 22 leading owners of utilities are street names. These 16 aliases are among the top ten owners in 275 utility companies. To take an extreme geographical example of this control of the utility business by financiers, the Montana Power Company's ten leading stockholders are street names from New York (6), Delaware (2), Boston (1), and Kansas City (1).[55] Fitting nicely with this financial information is our finding that bank, insurance, and industrial corporation employees make up the bulk of the outside directors on utility boards.

Turning to merchandising, we see that it has a smaller percentage of members of the upper class than other sectors of the business community. This reflects the relative newness of many of the companies, particularly the food store and dime store chains. It also reflects the presence of more Jewish persons in this area of the economy than in any other which we examined. However, this second point can easily be overstated, for we found only 24 identifiable Jewish persons in our sample (eight of whom could be classified as members of the upper class), and they were concen-

---

* It is a relief to know that such steal-the-company games are played, deadly serious though they may be, for it answers the criticism that corporate life is becoming dull and routinized.

trated primarily in Food Fair, Federated Department Stores, Sears, and the financial houses of Lehman Brothers and Goldman, Sachs. The latter finding is interesting because Perlo notes that the closely allied Jewish firms of Lehman Brothers and Goldman, Sachs were the investment bankers for seven of the eight largest department store chains in 1952, which are in turn Jewish-owned to a large extent.[56]

Summary

Our findings on all corporate boards studied can be summarized as follows. Interlocking directorates show beyond question that there is a national corporate economy that is run by the same group of several thousand men. *Social Register* listings, private school attendance, and club memberships suggest that this group is very much a part of the American upper class described in Chapter 1. Furthermore, our findings on the representation of the American upper class in corporate life are in agreement with other studies. Mills studied the business elite born between the years 1570 and 1879. For the generation born between 1850 and 1879, *i.e.,* those who were prominent during the first three or four decades of this century, the percentage with upper-class origins was 41.3 per cent.[57] A figure between 40 per cent and 50 per cent also seems to be implied by this remark in W. Lloyd Warner and James Abegglin's study of the corporate elite: "A check on the *Social Register* shows that less than half were members, indicating that it takes time for those who come from the lower ranks to achieve social recognition for their economic and occupational accomplishments." [58] In short, we believe that overrepresentation by a factor that varies from 52 to 125, and the existence of a majority of directors in three areas of the economy, are indicative of control of the corporate economy by members of the American upper class. To us, the vastness of the corporate economy and the smallness of the upper class make it understandable that this social group does not have more *men* (which cuts the pool of potential candidates in half) *willing* (they also go into the arts, medicine, and politics) or *able* (not all members of the upper class are born bright) to be corporate directors. We believe that hired managers are a necessity and that they serve the interests of members of the American upper class.[59]

THE MANAGERIAL REVOLUTION

There yet remains of the "managerial revolution" thesis the fact that there are a great many director–managers who are not of the upper class. The importance of stock ownership is relevant to a consideration of this problem. The first point is that the success of a top manager is ultimately rated in terms of the company's earnings. The aims of the manager are necessarily those of the stockholder—an adequate profit. *Claims by some observers that the managers are more interested in stability and public image than are the owners implies that the aims of members of the upper class are less farsighted. This is simply not the case, for those working hardest to change the image of the corporation—the "business liberals"— are usually hereditary members of the upper class.* This very important fact will become apparent in the next chapter. Perhaps more important from a sociological point of view than the economic fact of corporate profit-seeking is that the personal goal of the manager is to be a stockowner himself. As he rises in the corporate hierarchy, this reward becomes more and more accessible. Indeed, contrary to the thesis of the split between managers and stockholders, survey studies show that corporate managers hold more stock than any other occupation in American society.[60] Gordon argues that the small percentage of stock held by these manager–directors is relatively insignificant, but at the same time he shows how large the holdings are in absolute terms. To take an extreme case, a 0.63 per cent interest in AT & T was worth $17 million in the 1930's.[61] In short, from a psychological and sociological point of view, the holdings of the successful manager are not small. The manager becomes a millionaire. For example, Charles Wilson of General Motors had accumulated $2.5 million in stock in that company before he became Secretary of Defense, while Robert McNamara had accumulated $1.5 million worth of stock in the Ford Motor Company before he became Secretary of Defense. The latter sum, assuming a 6 per cent rate of return, insures the McNamara family of an income of about $90,000 a year. Stock options and stock "tips"—inside information—have become the major economic means by which the successful manager is assimilated into the American upper class.* Stock ownership certifies the permanence of the manager's status and ensures the future of his children and grandchildren at a high socioeconomic level, another point which cannot be overemphasized. The American upper class, whether its members are aware of it or not, has developed means for assimilating the successful corporate executive.[63]

THE CORPORATION LAWYER

There are a handful of large law firms, located chiefly in New York City, that are closely linked with the business community. "They serve the banks and larger corporations, and not infrequently sit on the boards of

---

* A minor example of this can be seen in the case of astronaut John Glenn, who is now a director of Royal Crown Cola Company. Glenn was given an option to buy 60,000 shares of the company's stock at $19.81 per share. The price of the stock at the time was $24.00, so his paper profits were $250,000 from the outset.[62]

the latter. They are particularly active in mergers and reorganizations; they do the legal work involved in the issuance of new securities; they represent various of the large firms in their dealings with the government agencies. Their influence goes far beyond the giving of advice on legal matters." [64] The above sentences, which completely summarize this section, were taken from Robert A. Gordon's *Business Leadership in the Large Corporation*, as was the following partial list of companies that have been managed at one time or another by presidents or board chairmen who began their careers in the law: U. S. Steel, General Foods, American Sugar Refining, Anaconda Copper, American Car and Foundry, Commonwealth and Southern, and the Atchison, Topeka, and Santa Fe.

Who are these major law firms, and who controls them? The answer is not hard to find, thanks to an excellent study by sociologist Erwin O. Smigel, *The Wall Street Lawyer*. Smigel studied the 20 largest Wall Street firms, those with 50 or more lawyers, in considerable detail. He also studied 20 smaller Wall Street firms, as well as the 17 firms outside of New York with 50 or more lawyers. Smigel found that 30 per cent of the 468 partners in the 20 largest Wall Street firms were in the *Social Register*, a figure not very different from those previously noted for corporate directors. Slightly over half of these 468 men had received their undergraduate training at one of seven Ivy League colleges—Harvard, Yale, Princeton, Columbia, Cornell, Dartmouth, and Williams—and 72 per cent had received their law training at the unquestionably upper-class-controlled law schools of Harvard, Yale, and Columbia. (See Chapter 3 for evidence on this matter.) Says Smigel: "Only 17 per cent of all partners in the large law firms do not have some combination which includes either a socially acceptable college or one of the preferred law schools." [65] Smigel did not calculate the percentage of *Social Register* affiliates from the 17 largest firms outside of New York, but it is undoubtedly lower due to the location of the firms and their very rapid growth in the past 10 to 20 years. However, he did determine their reliance upon the Ivy League law schools for partners. The analysis showed that these firms depend, first of all, on the best local law school, followed by Harvard and Yale. For example, 39 per cent of the partners in the large California law firms had graduated from Harvard or Yale law schools.

The large law firms of New York also serve as postgraduate training centers for corporation lawyers who eventually join other law firms, corporations, or law school faculties. Of the 20 small Wall Street firms studied by Smigel, all had at least one partner who had worked for one of the big firms. In fact, many of the smaller Wall Street firms are "spin-offs" or "satellites" of the larger firms. Although figures are not presented, it is apparent from some of Smigel's interviews that a few of the members of large firms outside of New York also had their first experience with the large Wall Street firms. However, the most important functions of the large Wall Street firms, aside from their legal service to the large corporations, are the training of men who later go to work (1) for corporations, (2) for the government, or (3) for the major law schools. As far as government service is concerned:

Firms like Donovan, Leisure, Newton & Irvine and Simpson, Thacher & Bartlett encourage their lawyers to participate in politics, in government, and in professional activities. Few, however, are active in grass-roots politics; Senator Case is one, Justice J. Edward Lumbard, Jr. (Donovan's firm), of the United States Court of Appeals is another. Former Justice Simon J. Rifkind (Paul, Weiss, Rifkind, Wharton & Garrison) helped manage Mayor Wagner's New York City campaign for that office. R. Burdel Bixby (Dewey's firm) was very active in Governor Rockefeller's bid for the 1960 Presidential nomination. The late General Donovan, noted for his management of the OSS and his World War I record, ran for Governor of New York. Others, like Dewey, Willkie, Davis, and Stevenson, who had been very important in government, all have or had important posts in large law firms. . . . Some like John T. Cahill, senior partner in the firm of Cahill, Gordon, Reindel & Ohl, seem to commute between government public service and the law firm. They are constantly shuttling between Washington and Wall Street.* [66]

Not all prestigious law firms are large. This is evident, for example, from Baltzell's studies of the seven leading law firms in Philadelphia, none of which is big enough to be found in Smigel's study. Baltzell found that over 80 per cent of the partners and 100 per cent of the senior partners in Philadelphia's most eminent gentile firms were listed in the *Social Register*.[68] The importance of "smaller" firms is also evident on Wall Street, where there are smaller upper-class firms, termed "social" firms by Smigel, with important clients. Thus, the conclusions to be drawn on corporation lawyers are those of Mills and Berle. We will quote first from Mills, then from Berle. Says Mills:

The inner core of the power elite also includes men of the higher legal and financial type from the great law factories and investment firms, who are almost professional go-betweens of economic, political, and military affairs, and who thus act to unify the power elite. The corporation lawyer and the investment

* When Donald Matthews called lawyers "the high priests of American politics" in *The Social Background of Political Decision Makers,* he was not referring to corporation lawyers alone, but it is nonetheless worth noting that 40 per cent of American diplomats, 50 per cent of federal politicians, and 100 per cent of the Supreme Court Justices have been lawyers.[67]

banker perform the functions of the "go-between" effectively and powerfully. By the nature of their work, they transcend the narrower milieu of any one industry, and accordingly are in a position to speak and act for the corporate world or at least sizable sectors of it. The corporation lawyer is a key link between the economic and military and political areas; the investment banker is a key organizer and unifier of the corporate world and a person well versed in spending the huge amounts of money the American military establishment now ponders. When you get a lawyer who handles the legal work of investment bankers you get a key member of the power elite.[69]

Says Berle:

The law firms become virtually an annex to some group of financial promoters, manipulators, or industrialists; and such firms have dominated the organized profession . . . what they have contributed . . . is the creation of a legal framework for the new economic system, built largely around the modern corporation.[70]

Richard Kronish has provided documentation for Berle's claim that corporate law firms dominate the organized law profession.[71] He studied the 258 men who made up the House of Delegates of the American Bar Association in 1961. His findings can be summarized as follows:

1. Thirty-two were members of the upper class (12 per cent).

2. Another 16 were from large corporate law firms such as those described by Smigel (5 per cent).

3. Another 42 were graduates of the Harvard, Yale, Columbia, and University of Virginia law schools (16 per cent).

4. Among the others, those who listed representative clients invariably served major corporations. For example, Ross Malone of Roswell, New Mexico, had as clients Gulf Oil, Ohio Oil, and the New Mexico Transportation Company among others, while Frank Holman of Seattle, Washington, served Boeing Aircraft, Crown-Zellerbach, General Foods, United Airlines, and Armstrong Cork Company. We believe that the systematic findings of Smigel and Kronish, in conjunction with the experience-based conclusions of Berle, allow us to consider leading corporate lawyers as members of the power elite. As Smigel says, "the large law firms are indisputably the spokesmen for big business." [72] This is in keeping with D. C. Blaisdell's claim in 1941, at a time when only 16 per cent of the country's lawyers were members of the American Bar Association, that the association was the "special pleader" for American business before the government and the people.[73]

We conclude that the large businesses and law firms which dominate the American economy are the keystone of the power elite. We agree with

Mills that the American upper class has not been displaced by managers, but has been fortified and reorganized by their presence:

What has happened, I believe, is the reorganization of the propertied class, along with those of higher salary, into a new corporate world of privilege and prerogative. What is significant about this managerial reorganization of the propertied class is that by means of it the narrow industrial and profit interests of specific firms and industries and families have been translated into the broader economic and political interests of a more genuinely class type. . . . As men of status they have secured their privileges and prerogatives in the most stable private institutions of American society. They are a corporate rich because they depend directly, as well as indirectly, for their money, their privileges, their securities, their advantages, their powers on the world of the big corporations.[74]

From this point on, then, we will assume that any high-ranking official in a large corporation, or any member of one of the large corporate law firms studied by Smigel, is a member of a power elite which serves the interests of members of the American upper class. This power elite serves these interests by maintaining a profitable business system whose dividends, salaries, and expense accounts are the basis of the style of life and political power of the American business aristocracy. We can now turn our attention to other aspects of the power elite, beginning with the nongovernmental institutions which are so important in shaping American society and American opinion.

Chapter Three . . . .
The Shaping of the
American Polity . .

"Control" is too strong a word to use when it comes to the problem of understanding the relationship of the power elite to the framework within which American opinion reaches its decisions. Nevertheless, the institutions to be discussed in this chapter have a strong and never-ending influence on the shape of that framework. By showing that these institutions are closely related to the corporate economy we will be adding support to Richard Rovere's claim that the establishment "has very nearly unchallenged power in deciding what is and what is not respectable opinion in this country." [1] We will also be taking his advice as to how best to understand the decision-making process in this country: "If I were a C. Wright Mills and were seeking to show the influence of the interlocking directorate of corporate, political, and military leaders, I think I would look not to the large decisions but to small ones and to the whole tone and temper of our society at the present time." [2] We will study first tax-exempt charity foundations, such as the Ford Foundation and Rockefeller Foundation. These foundations provide funds for a great variety of cultural, intellectual, and educational activities. The second type of institution is the association which has been formed to influence government and public opinion on significant issues. Examples of these associations would be the Council on Foreign Relations (CFR) and the Foreign Policy Association (FPA), which engage in a wide variety of activities related to foreign affairs. In addition to the CFR and FPA, we will look at the Business Advisory Council (BAC), the Committee for Economic Development (CED), the National Advertising Council (NAC), and the National Association of Manufacturers (NAM). A third institution to be studied in this chapter is the university, namely, the elite universities which train most of the country's leading lawyers, academicians, and physicians. These universities are important as a source of expertise. Finally, we will look at the mass media, which are important in the dissemination of information and opinion, and secondarily in the formation of opinion.

Our study of these four types of institution—foundation, association, university, and mass media—will show that the biggest and most prestigious are closely intertwined with each other and the corporate economy. However, as was the case within the corporate community, we will see that there are differences of opinion within the group.

THE FOUNDATIONS

The growth of this twentieth-century phenomenon, the foundation, has been amazing. From 1960 to 1964 alone, the resources owned by foundations climbed $3 billion to a total of at least $14.5 billion.[3] Although no one knows for sure just how many foundations there are, it is known that most of their assets are controlled by the top several hundred: Congressman Wright Patman found that 546 foundations have a total of $10.3 billion in assets.[4] And it is not only family foundations which are growing. Corporate foundations, which are also tax free, now give 20 per cent of the funds handed out by foundations. Family or corporate, the foundation's influence is felt everywhere—the arts, science, medicine, educational television, and most especially, the university. In considering the foundations, their independence from their rich donors cannot be underemphasized, as the following quote from the *Virginia Law Review* suggests:

It is this peculiar circumstance—retention of control—which largely explains the emergence of family foundations as the dominant feature of the foundation scene today. Men who have built successful enterprises and seen the value of their equity swell have sought, naturally, to keep control within the family. They have accordingly established charitable family foundations, minimized their tax, enjoyed the satisfaction of promoting good works, and retained practically all but the dividend benefits of ownership. Such persons, it has been said, actually do not give their property away at all, but only the income thereon—though this is perhaps an overstatement.[5]

In fact, the summary in this quote is an understatement, not an overstatement. As Patman has revealed, income can be retained by paying very high salaries to officers and trustees of the foundation. The foundation can also serve as a holding company—a great amount of Rockefeller stock in several Standard Oil companies is held by foundations which are controlled by the Rockefellers.

For the purposes of this study we will concentrate on the biggest and most influential of these philanthropies, the 13 foundations with $100 million or more in assets in the early 1960's. They are the Ford Foundation, the Rockefeller Foundation, the Duke Endowment, the Hartford Foundation, the Kellogg Foundation, the Carnegie Corporation, the Sloan Foundation, the Moody Foundation, the Rockefeller Brothers Fund, the Lilly

Endowment, the Pew Memorial Trust, the Danforth Foundation, and the Commonwealth Fund. However, there are many lesser-known, but quite powerful foundations. They do not become prominent because the backers choose to spread their gifts among several foundations rather than concentrating them in one enterprise. Thus, the Mellons control at least six foundations, the du Ponts at least nine, and the Rockefellers at least ten others besides their two in the top 13. In addition to a detailed study of the 13 largest foundations, certain lesser Carnegie foundations will be touched upon because of their tie-in with the Council on Foreign Relations and major universities. If combined, the assets of these three additional Carnegie foundations, the Carnegie Endowment for International Peace, the Carnegie Foundation for the Advancement of Teaching, and the Carnegie Institute of Washington, would total $137 million.

Our data should be presented on a foundation-by-foundation basis, but to avoid tediousness we will restrict ourselves to several examples after making the following generalizations.[6] Twelve of the top 13 foundations are controlled by members of the power elite, with two-thirds of their trustees coming from the upper class (51 per cent) or major corporations (16 per cent). The only exception is the Kellogg Foundation, which is controlled by local interests in central Michigan. The one-third of the trustees who are neither members of the upper class nor corporate executives are professional persons, most of them college presidents or college professors. Just over half of all trustees attended Harvard, Yale, or Princeton; 22 earned Phi Beta Kappa keys; 20 are in the Links Club of New York; and eight are on the board of the RAND Corporation, the Air Force "think factory" supported primarily by government contracts. There is a considerable interlock among the Ford, Rockefeller, Carnegie, Sloan, and Commonwealth foundations, and this group has weaker ties to the Duke Endowment and the Danforth Foundation. No generalizations can be made about the ideological commitments of the foundations. Some support liberal and educational projects, others are quite conservative. These differences reflect the factional interests and ideological struggles which we have seen to be present within the upper class. In the following paragraphs we will go into more detail on six of the foundations: Ford, Rockefeller, Carnegie, Lilly, Pew, and Danforth.

The Ford Foundation

By far the biggest individual foundation, the Ford Foundation came into prominence during the 1950's through its financing of universities, the arts, and educational television. It has spent more than $80 million on Educational Television (ETV), a figure that grows by $6 million a year. The president of ETV in the mid-1960's was Jack White, a former college dean:

White is theoretically responsible to a board of directors composed of school superintendents, corporation presidents, and college presidents, but the board plays mostly a public relations function. White's chief responsibility is to the Ford Foundation, which subsidized and created NET (National Educational Television), chose White as its executive, and reserves the right to inspect every NET program produced with Ford Foundation money.[7]

National Educational Television, a network of 90 independent stations, provides late afternoon and evening viewing of children's programs, cultural events, and informational programs. Audience surveys suggest that it is viewed by those of above-average income and a college education. We believe that NET may be described as one of the many lines of communication between liberal members of the upper class and the intelligentsia of the upper-middle class.

Ford has sponsored other projects which are an important part of American intellectual life. It gave a $15 million grant to the Fund for the Republic, which in turn set up the liberal-minded Center for the Study of Democratic Institutions in Santa Barbara, California. The grant was made during the presidency of millionaire Paul G. Hoffman. Hoffman is best known as the former president and chairman of the Studebaker Company. He is one of the leading "business liberals" in the American upper class and, as shall be seen, the founder of the influential Committee for Economic Development.* Turning to another Ford benefaction in the educational realm, the foundation has taken over the financing of Harvard's Russian Research Center from the Carnegie Foundation. It gave $131,000 of the center's budget for 1965, with the remaining $9000 coming from Carnegie funds. With a staff of 57 scholars drawn from the many colleges and universities in the Boston area, this center provides consultants to the State Department and the CIA, as well as lecturers to the Army War College, the Foreign Service Institute, and the Council on Foreign Relations.[8] The board of the Ford Foundation is presented in Table 4. It consists, by and

TABLE 4. TRUSTEES OF THE FORD FOUNDATION

UPPER-CLASS TRUSTEES

Stephen Bechtel is head of the little-known, but very large, Bechtel Construction Corporation of Oakland, California. Mr. Bechtel is also a

---

* Less controversial than the Santa Barbara center is another Ford-sponsored center in California, the Center for Advanced Study in the Behavioral Sciences, invitingly ensconced in the wooded hills of Palo Alto, where successful scholars repair for a year at a time to think and write books at Ford's expense.

director of Morgan Guaranty Trust, Southern Pacific, Continental Can, Bechtel-McCone Corporation, and Stanford University, among others.

Eugene Black is a Southern-born aristocrat who is a long-time employee of the Rockefeller interests. He is a director of Chase Manhattan, IT & T, *The New York Times,* Cummins Engine, the Brookings Institution, and Johns Hopkins University, among others.

John Cowles (Exeter, Harvard) of Minneapolis is co-owner of the family publishing empire, which includes *Look* Magazine and newspapers in Minneapolis and Des Moines. He is also a trustee for the Carnegie Endowment for International Peace, and a director of the First National Bank of Minneapolis and the Equitable Life Insurance Company of Iowa.

Donald K. David is a Harvard Business School professor and dean who sits on several corporate boards.

Benson Ford (Hotchkiss, Princeton) is a director of the National Safety Council and chairman of the board of the Traffic Safety Committee. He is a vice-president at Ford Motor Company.

Henry Ford II (Hotchkiss, Yale) is a director for General Electric, General Foods, and Philco. He runs the Ford Motor Company.

Roy E. Larsen (SR, NY) is chairman of the executive committee of Time, Inc.

John J. McCloy (SR, NY) is a director of many corporations. As a former chairman of the board at Chase Manhattan he is a key interlock between the Ford Foundation and the Rockefeller empire. Mr. McCloy is chairman of the Ford Foundation trustees.

Joseph Irwin Miller, the head of Cummins Engine Company, is a director of AT & T and many other corporations.

Bethuel Webster (SR, NY) is a corporation lawyer who was a consultant for John J. McCloy when McCloy was High Commissioner of Germany.

Charles E. Wyzanski, Jr. (Exeter, Harvard), is a Jewish member of the upper class. Judge Wyzanski is married to another member of the Jewish aristocracy, Gisela Warburg, who came to this country to escape the Nazi persecution.

OTHERS

Mark F. Ethridge is the editor of the *Louisville Courier-Journal,* which is owned by Barry Bingham, who sits on the board of the Rockefeller Foundation (see Table 5).

Laurence Gould is president of Carleton College.

Julius Stratton is president of MIT.

Henry T. Heald was president of Ford Foundation at the time of this study. He was the president of Illinois Institute of Technology (1940-1952) and NYU (1952-1956) before joining the Ford Foundation. His training was as an engineer. He is a director of AT & T, U. S. Steel, Equitable Life, and Lever Brothers.

large, of the same men studied in the previous chapter, with an added dash of journalism and scholarship.

The Rockefeller Foundation

If the Ford Foundation is now the largest, the Rockefeller Foundation is still the most famous of the foundations. Its activities have ranged over a larger field and for a longer period of time. They include studies of tropical diseases, a Population Research Center at Harvard, a Russian Research Center at Columbia, and support for universities. The Rockefeller Foundation is also a guiding light behind the famous Lincoln Center for the Performing Arts in New York City. Details on the foundation's trustees can be found in Table 5.

TABLE 5. TRUSTEES OF THE ROCKEFELLER FOUNDATION

UPPER-CLASS MEMBERS

Barry Bingham (Middlesex School, Harvard) is the publisher of the *Louisville Courier-Journal* and the *Louisville Times,* and an heir to a Standard Oil fortune. He is an Episcopalian, a Democrat, and like many upper-class Southerners, a listee in the Washington *Social Register.*

Lloyd D. Brace (SR, Boston) is a Boston banker who sits on many corporate boards.

Arthur Amory Houghton, Jr. (SR, NY), is president of Corning Glass and a director of New York Life Insurance and U. S. Steel, among others.

John R. Kimberly (Phillips Andover, MIT) inherited the Kimberly-Clark Company of Wisconsin, which was originally a paper-making firm. He sits on the boards of Northwestern Mutual Life, First National City Bank of New York, Corning Glass, Lawrence College, and the Episcopalian Church Foundation, as well as being president and chairman of the family firm.

Lord Franks of Headington, chairman of Lloyd's Bank, Ltd., London.

John D. Rockefeller III (SR, NY) is the Rockefeller brother who specializes in cultural matters. As chairman of the foundation he has a firm grip on its activities. Other trustees come and go—he does not.

He is president of the Japanese Society, the Asia Society, and the Council on Economic and Cultural Affairs. He is chairman of the National Council of the United Negro College Fund.

Thomas J. Watson, Jr. (SR, NY), is head of IBM and a director of Bankers Trust, Time, Inc., Cal Tech, and Brown University.

William B. Wood, Jr. (SR, Baltimore), is vice-president of Johns Hopkins.

REPRESENTATIVES FROM UPPER-CLASS BUSINESSES

Frank Stanton is president of CBS, a director of New York Life Insurance Company, and chairman of the Center for Advanced Study in Behavioral Sciences.

George D. Woods is chairman of the board at First Boston **Corporation,** which is the biggest underwriter of utilities in the world.

OTHERS

Ralph Bunche (AB, UCLA; Ph.D., Harvard) is one of the nation's most prominent Negro citizens. A professor before he became a United Nations official, he won the Nobel Peace Prize in 1950.

Lowell T. Coggeshall, formerly a research physician with the foundation, is a dean at the Rockefeller-founded University of Chicago, and a director of Commonwealth Edison of Chicago.

John S. Dickey is president of Dartmouth.

Lee A. DuBridge is president of Cal Tech.

Robert F. Goheen is president of Princeton.

Clifford M. Hardin is president of the University of Nebraska.

J. George Harrar, a former professor, is an expert on plant pathology who is the foundation's director for agriculture as well as its president.

Theodore Hesburgh is president of Notre Dame.

Clark Kerr was president of the University of California.

The Carnegie Corporation

The Carnegie Corporation, and the other Carnegie funds, are among the most important in the philanthropic world. They are also among the oldest, all four having been incorporated between 1902 and 1911. Twelve of the 14 trustees of the Carnegie Corporation are members of the American upper class. They include Frederick Eaton, who sits on the Commonwealth Fund as well as on several corporate boards; C. D. Jackson of Time, Inc.; Devereux Josephs, who sits on the Sloan Foundation board as well as on a multitude of corporate boards; Margaret Carnegie Miller;

and Charles A. Thomas, president of Monsanto Chemical Company. One of the two trustees not of the American business aristocracy was the corporation's president, psychologist John W. Gardner. Gardner was also the president of the Carnegie Foundation for the Advancement of Teaching. As already noted, in the mid-1960's he left the Carnegie Foundation to become President Johnson's Secretary of Health, Education, and Welfare.

The situation is very similar for the other Carnegie boards, except that there are a greater number of educators. There is also a considerable amount of overlap among the four Carnegie institutions. Of the 72 persons who sit on the boards of the three minor Carnegie foundations, 46 (64 per cent) were corporate executives or members of the upper class. The others, with two exceptions, were college presidents (15) or college professors (9).

The Lilly Endowment

Five of the seven trustees of this foundation are members of the Lilly family. The remaining two are directors of Lilly companies. The Lillys are well known as right-wing aristocrats. Their foundation helped found the National Foundation for Education in American Citizenship (NFEAC), which also receives funds from Texas H. L. Hunt's Life Line Foundation and Roger Milliken's (SR, NY) Deering-Milliken Foundation. Most of NFEAC's money goes into the financing of *Human Events,* an ultra-right weekly.[9]

The Pew Memorial Trust

Very little is known about this foundation. It lists its purposes and activities as "broad purposes; general giving" and its trustees as Glenmede Trust Company. Congressman Wright Patman has complained about this foundation's defiance of his investigations of such philanthropies. He finally issued a subpoena when it refused to divulge any information. However, it is known that the Pews own Sun Oil Company, the sixtieth-largest industrial in the nation, and that there are 21 of them in the Philadelphia *Social Register.* It is also known that they have given multimillions to the Republican Party, were staunch Goldwater supporters in 1964, and own *Pathfinder* and the *Farm Journal,* two major agricultural publications, as well as trade magazines in other industries.

The Danforth Foundation

The major efforts of the liberal-minded Danforth Foundation are directed toward higher education. For example, it supports the training of college professors and seminar workshops for college personnel. Four of the foundation's nine trustees are Danforth descendants, two of whom are in the St. Louis *Social Register*. One of them, William H. Danforth, is a Harvard-trained physician who heads the St. Louis Psychoanalytic Foundation. The Danforth Foundation would seem to be at the other end of the pole from the Lilly Foundation and the Pew Memorial Trust.

In summarizing our study of leading foundations, we would emphasize that the "seed money" they provide for important intellectual and cultural projects helps to shape the framework of American society to a great extent. Sponsorship of a project by one of these foundations implies that it meets with the approval of at least some members of the upper class. By encouraging some projects and discouraging others, the foundations create implicit values and set the limits within which cultural and intellectual quests are undertaken.

We will now turn to five associations or committees which are equally important in shaping this cultural–intellectual framework and equally closely associated with members of the American upper class. Further, several of these associations work closely with the large foundations.

THE ASSOCIATIONS

The importance of the associations we are about to consider—the Council on Foreign Relations, the Foreign Policy Association, the Business Advisory Council, the Committee for Economic Development, and the National Advertising Council—has been hinted at by Washington newspaper reporters. However, a detailed study of these important links of the power elite to politics and public opinion has been left by and large to an ultraconservative, Dan Smoot.[10] Smoot's thesis, aside from the notion that these rich businessmen are part of or dupes of a one-world socialist conspiracy, is that these five organizations have a great deal of overlap in membership and intent. If he is wrong about the motives of these men, he is nonetheless accurate in showing the interlocks of these groups and their tie with the corporate elite.

The Council on Foreign Relations

The story begins with the oldest and perhaps most influential of the groups, the Council on Foreign Relations, which was founded in 1921 but was of little consequence until the late 1920's, when it began to receive considerable financial support from various Rockefeller and Carnegie foundations. Members of the council were deeply involved in State Department affairs during World War II, and such upper-class members of the CFR as Secretary of State Edward R. Stettinius, John Foster Dulles, John J. McCloy, Nelson A. Rockefeller, Adlai Stevenson, and Thomas Finletter were members of the United States delegation to the organizational meeting of the United Nations. For our purposes, the important points concerning the CFR are its membership, its financing, and its activities. The membership is restricted to 700 resident members—citizens whose residences or places of business are within 50 miles of the New York city hall—and 700 nonresident members. As Smoot points out, most members occupy important positions in business, finance, communications, and education. Our study of a sample of 210 resident members of the CFR shows that 82 were listed in the *Social Register,* which is 39 per cent upper-class membership by this one criterion alone. However, even more significant is our study of the 51 men who have been directors since the council's inception. Ten of the 51 are currently trustees of one of the foundations studied in the previous section. Of the 22 recently or currently directors, 14 are in the *Social Register.* Among the better-known upper-class directors, past and present, are Paul Cravath, Norman Davis, Arthur H. Dean, Allen Dulles, Lewis Douglas, Averell Harriman, Devereux Josephs, Walter Lippmann, Adlai Stevenson, Myron Taylor, Paul Warburg, and Owen D. Young. Perhaps it is enough to say that John J. McCloy and David Rockefeller have been high officers in the association in recent years.

If the membership and leadership of the council do not belie its upper-class base, perhaps its financing does. Of its $925,000 income in a recent year, $231,700 came from foundation grants and $112,000 from its "corporation service," which entails a minimum fee of $1000.[11] The contributing corporations are among the biggest in the country, including several of those studied in Chapter 2. The CFR also receives a considerable sum, $210,300, from the publication of one of its major activities, the very influential magazine *Foreign Affairs.* Other important activities of the council include the presentation of speakers and seminars to subscribers to the corporation service and to the Committees on Foreign Relations which the council has created in 30 cities. The committees are composed of 40 to 80 men who are leaders in their city. The groups usually include professors, public relations executives, lawyers, and corporate vice-presidents as well as several of the leading members of the American business aristocracy in the given city:

About once a month, from October through May, members come together for dinner and an evening of discussion with a guest speaker of special competence. . . . Since the beginning in 1938, the Carnegie Corporation of New York has continued to make annual grants in support of the committee program.[12]

In the light of the upper-class status of 12 of the 14 trustees of the Carnegie Corporation, there can be little doubt that these committees are a key link between the more liberal members of the Eastern branch of the upper class and people of high status and a similar viewpoint in other areas of the country.

The relationship between the major foundations and the CFR has been documented by Smoot. For example, 10 of the 14 trustees of the Carnegie Corporation were members of the CFR in 1961. The overlap of the CFR with other major foundations is as follows: 10 of the Ford Foundation's 15 trustees are also members of the CFR; 12 of the 20 from the Rockefeller Foundation; 18 of the 26 from the Carnegie Endowment for International Peace; 15 of the 26 from the Carnegie Foundation for the Advancement of Teaching; 12 of the 16 from the Sloan Foundation; 6 of the 10 from the Commonwealth Fund; 13 of the 20 from the Twentieth Century Fund; and 7 of the 18 from the Fund for the Republic.[13]

The Foreign Policy Association

Similar in purpose to the CFR is the Foreign Policy Association. While the CFR is concerned with communication and opinion-formation within the highest levels of American society, the FPA includes judges, schoolteachers, mayors, and other lesser community leaders among its members; its role is to educate a broader audience on problems of foreign policy. The leading educational efforts of the FPA are its Councils on World Affairs, which bring speakers to many communities, and its Great Decisions Programs, which are "an annual nationwide review, by local groups under local sponsorship, of problems affecting United States foreign policy." Groups are formed for Great Decisions Programs by five to 15 interested persons who meet once a week for eight weeks to discuss the topics chosen for the year. "You need no 'teacher' or 'trained discussion leader,'" explains an FPA pamphlet. "The only material required is the nonpartisan Fact Sheet Kit. . . ." In the mid-1960's the discussions could be supplemented by eight weekly half-hour television shows on National Educational Television.[14] However, even though the function and membership of the FPA differ from those of the CFR, its leadership is equally upper class (see Table 6).

TABLE 6. OFFICERS OF THE FOREIGN POLICY ASSOCIATION

Eustace Seligman (SR, NY), the chairman, is a partner in Sullivan & Cromwell, the same firm that contributed John Foster Dulles.

John W. Nason, FPA president, is a member of the CFR, a *Social Register* listee, and a trustee of the Danforth Foundation.

Walter H. Wheeler, Jr., vice-chairman, is a member of the CFR and an affiliate of the J. Henry Schroeder Banking Corporation of New York.

Mrs. Andrew G. Carey (SR, NY), is secretary. Her husband is a member of the CFR.

Emile E. Soubry, chairman of the executive committee, is a director of Standard Oil of New Jersey and a member of the CFR.

Benjamin Buttenweiser, member of the executive committee, is a Jewish member of the upper class, married to Helen Lehman, and a partner in Kuhn, Loeb. A CFR member.

Harold F. Linder, member of the executive committee and one of the biggest donors to the Democratic Party, is a former associate of Carl M. Loeb, Rhoades, & Co. (1933-1938) and American Investors (1948-1955), and is now chairman of the Export-Import Bank in Washington. Also a CFR member.

Henry Siegbert, member of the executive committee, is a member of the CFR and a partner in the investment banking firm of Adolph Lewisohn & Sons.

Joseph E. Johnson, member of the executive committee, succeeded Alger Hiss as president of the Carnegie Endowment for International Peace, a position he still holds. He is a member of the CFR.

A. William Loos, member of the executive committee, is executive director of the Church Peace Union. Not a member of the upper class or power elite.

The Committee for Economic Development

Concerned primarily with issues of an economic nature, the Committee for Economic Development, which was founded in 1942 by Paul G. Hoffman of Studebaker and the Ford Foundation, is made up of representatives of the nation's leading corporations. As of 1957, 47 of its trustees were also members of the CFR. Among its chairmen have been Marion B. Folsom of Eastman Kodak; Meyer Kestnbaum of Hart, Schaffner & Marx; J. D. Zellerbach of the Crown-Zellerbach Corporation; and Donald K. David of the Harvard Business School, Ford Foundation, and Atlantic & Pacific Company (A & P). The CED has two major functions, suggesting new economic policies and promoting and improving economic education. For example, a 27-member CED commission made a study which was one of the bases for the Kennedy Administration's tax cut. Among that commission's members were 13 members of the CFR. As of 1957, CED's training program in economics for prospective teachers was being used in 20 colleges, and 20 school systems around the country were trying out a program to introduce economics into the curriculum as early as the first grade. Over 19,000 teachers have participated in the CED's summer workshops on the teaching of economics. In 1961 the committee's information division distributed 3,716,676 books and pamphlets.[15]

The Business Advisory Council

Whatever the importance of the CED as an educational and research organization, the Business Advisory Council is "the" organization of the internationally minded wing of the American business aristocracy. According to Smoot, 41 of 120 past and present BAC members are also members of the CFR. From its formation in 1933 by financier Sidney Weinberg until its withdrawal in 1961, the BAC functioned in a semi-official advisory capacity to the Department of Commerce. The phrase "semi-official" must be used because very little is known about its status or its functions. There is available no administrative order or ruling formally establishing it or delineating its functions. In 1955-1956, a House committee was denied access to its files. No minutes are taken at its meetings and reporters are barred. The group holds six meetings a year, four one-day meetings in Washington and two longer meetings at such resorts as White Sulphur Springs, Virginia, and Sea Island, Georgia. After a tiff with the Kennedy Administration, which Kennedy later did everything possible to patch up, the BAC changed its name to Business Council (BC) and offered its consultative services to any governmental agency that wished them.* Its influence was at its height during the Eisenhower Administration when several of its members were tapped for government service. According to Rowen, the BC may have triggered the squelch of McCarthy that had been smoldering in many upper-class minds. The incident which triggered McCarthy's censure, according to this version, was his high-handed treatment of yet another member of the power elite, corporate leader Robert T. Stevens of Andover, Yale, J. P. Stevens & Company, General Electric, and Morgan Guaranty Trust. He was serving as Secretary of the Army when embarrassed by McCarthy on nationwide television:

During the May 1954 meeting at Homestead, Stevens flew down from Washington for a weekend reprieve from his televised torture. A special delegation of BAC officials made it a point to journey from the hotel to the mountaintop airport to greet Stevens. He was escorted into the lobby like a conquering hero.

---

* See Hobart Rowen's *The Free Enterprisers* for the story of Kennedy's relationship to the BC. Rowen is perhaps the country's most knowledgeable reporter on the BC. He feels that the following was significant evidence for the BC's importance: "The BC has indeed become the very symbol of the larger business establishment in the United States. And in those sad first moments after President Kennedy's death, when President Johnson needed to establish contact with the business world, he called not the head of the Chamber of Commerce, nor the President of the NAM, but Frederick R. Kappel, Chairman of the BC in 1963." [16]

Then, publicly, one member of the BAC after another roasted the Eisenhower Administration for its McCarthy-appeasement policy. The BAC's attitude gave the Administration some courage and shortly thereafter former Senator Ralph Flanders (a Republican and BAC member) introduced a Senate resolution calling for censure.[17]

The National Advertising Council

The final major association of the American business aristocracy is very different from the other four. It is the National Advertising Council. The NAC was formed during World War II as the War Advertising Council and was designed to promote such government programs as rationing and war bonds. After the war it continued as a public service paid for by the large corporations. "It's a voluntary gift to America by U. S. business," explained a two-page advertisement in a 1965 issue of *Time* Magazine.[18] The council's best-known figure is Smokey the Bear, but it also supports the Red Cross, the Peace Corps, the United Nations, Traffic Safety, Youth Fitness, and Radio Free Europe. As of 1958, eight of the 19 members of its Public Policy Committee were members of the CFR. Four of the eight who are in the CFR, along with four others, are corporate executives or members of the upper class. The others are college presidents (three), labor leaders (two), and a variety of professional persons. Among the upper-class members of this council are John J. McCloy, a leading figure in the CFR, Benjamin Buttenweiser, a leading figure in the FPA, and Paul G. Hoffman, a leading figure in the CED. However, the most obvious basis of control in this case is corporate financing.

Radio Free Europe, one of the NAC's benefactions, is the largest of the nongovernmental radio stations beamed at the Communist world. It is aimed exclusively toward the five Communist countries of Eastern Europe. RFE is an operation of the Free Europe Committee, Inc., founded in 1949 and backed by funds raised by the Committee's Crusade for Freedom. General Dwight Eisenhower, later president of Columbia University and of the United States, and General Lucius D. Clay led the first fund-raising campaign, and its first directors included Clay, Allen Dulles (SR, NY), C. D. Jackson (SR, NY), and A. A. Berle, Jr. (SR, NY). Other upper-class Americans who have been officials of the Free Europe Committee or one of its subcommittees include William Clayton, Henry Ford II, Herbert H. Lehman, Henry R. Luce, and Charles M. Spofford (SR, NY).[19]

National Association of Manufacturers

There is one association conspicuous by its absence from our list which should be mentioned at this point—the National Association of Manufacturers (NAM). This organization was at one time a leading spokesman for the dominant interests within the American upper class. Its early successes in lobbying were notorious. However, it now represents interests within the upper class which have failed to come to terms with the New Deal and the governmental needs of internationally oriented corporations. The battles over foreign policy between the NAM and the CFR–CED–BAC coalition, which the NAM usually loses, according to a decision-making study by David McLellan and Charles Woodhouse, are another piece of evidence for the division within the upper class between Mills's "business liberals" and "practical conservatives." [20] However, a detailed study of the NAM by Richard Gable showed that it continues to be dominated by very large corporations, and that it was notably successful in its campaign to amend the National Labor Relations Act: "There is a startling similarity between the numerous NAM labor proposals since 1937 and the final version of the Taft-Hartley Act." [21] Indeed, Gerald D. Morgan (SR, NY), the lawyer hired by Fred A. Hartley to serve as special counsel to the majority members of the House committee, sought advice at one point from the NAM's general counsel.*

It is difficult to determine how successful these groups are in attaining their objectives. However, it is incontrovertible that they attempt to be influential within the government and in shaping public opinion on a wide variety of issues. It is also incontrovertible, we believe, that these organizations are arms of the power elite which have the function of attempting to influence the framework of the American polity.

THE UNIVERSITIES

Control of America's leading universities by members of the American business aristocracy is more direct than with any other institution which they control. Nevertheless, this control over the university machinery and its long-term goals does not give members of the upper class day-to-day control over the opinions that emanate from it. Tenure, which essentially means that the time-tested professor can be dismissed only for extreme misconduct, makes it difficult for members of the upper class to quash any but the most extreme of opinions with which they disagree. Upper-class control of major universities is achieved through such financial support as family endowments (*e.g.,* Duke, Stanford, Vanderbilt), personal gifts, foundation gifts, and corporate gifts, and through service on the boards of trustees. These mechanisms give the upper class control of the broad framework, the long-run goals, and the general atmosphere of the university. This point is made with considerable emphasis and a great deal of

* If the NAM and CED clash over foreign policy, they are not very far apart on labor policy: the CED, as of the early 1960's, favored right-to-work laws.

evidence by Merle Curti and Roderick Nash in *Philanthropy in the Shaping of American Higher Education*. They stress that the gifts of the corporate rich created model universities, which publicly supported universities later followed, and set standards of quality that other universities tried to emulate. As might be expected, members of the American business aristocracy stressed technical and practical training in the universities they influenced, as opposed to traditional classical education. Thus, Joseph Wharton gave the University of Pennsylvania $600,000 to found the Wharton School of Business and Finance, and George Eastman gave $20 million to MIT between 1912 and 1920. According to Curti and Nash, the role of the Carnegie foundations and Rockefeller's General Education Board cannot be overestimated in understanding the structure of American higher education. The relationship between the corporate rich and academia is best exemplified by a school such as the University of Rochester. Most of the university's board is made up of officers of such Rochester-based corporations as Eastman Kodak, Xerox, and Taylor Instrument. The chairman of the board, who is also the president of Xerox, explained the relationship as follows:

To put it as crassly as possible, it's a matter of sheer self-interest—dollars and cents. Xerox will live or die by technology.[22]

A detailed study by Hubert Beck, entitled *Men Who Control Our Universities,* provides the systematic information necessary to determine whether or not members of the power elite control the nation's leading universities. Beck studied 727 trustees from 30 major universities, 14 private and 16 public. Among the universities were such prestigious Eastern schools as Harvard, Yale, Princeton, Columbia, Johns Hopkins, and Cornell, as well as such highly regarded public institutions of the Midwest and West as Ohio State, Illinois, and the University of California. At the time of the study, 1934-1935, the 30 schools, which comprised the United States universities in the elite Association of American Universities, made up only 2.2 per cent of the total number of institutions of higher education. However, they had 20 per cent of the undergraduate students, 24 per cent of the faculty, 47 per cent of the graduate students in professional schools, 50 per cent of the graduate students in the arts and sciences, and 77 per cent of the awarded doctoral degrees. Needless to add, they also possessed a corner on talent. Nearly one-half of the college graduates in the *Who's Who* for 1929 had attended one of these institutions. In 1936, 50 graduates of Yale alone were college or university presidents.

As was the case for corporate directors and Wall Street lawyers, just about one-third of the trustees were in the *Social Register*. This percentage is especially impressive when it is added that the Southern-based University of North Carolina had 104 (!) trustees, and that most of the others not listed in the *Social Register* came from state universities which have no *Social Register* cities nearby. As might be expected, the trustees listed in the *Social Register* were much more likely to be at private institutions, and it goes without saying that Harvard, Yale, Princeton, and Columbia are controlled by members of the upper class. Beck developed other interesting information on the trustees of the elite universities which shows that they are members of the power elite. Nearly half of the top 200 industrial corporations and the top 200 financial corporations were represented on the 30 boards. One hundred seventy-five men from 194 of these top 400 companies held 1321 positions as corporate directors, an average of seven to eight per trustee. This average is very similar to those found in our studies of corporate directors. Other findings by Beck include the fact that lawyers and judges made up 25 per cent of the total group of trustees, while bankers and manufacturers each contributed 15 per cent of the total. Some 45 per cent of the trustees were listed in Poor's *Register of Corporations, Directors, and Executives*. The trustees held 54 directorships in 29 major foundations; 24 trustees were on J. P. Morgan's 1929 "preferred list" to receive "new issue securities at less than their market value"; and 12 were on mining magnate James W. Gerard's (SR, NY) list of "52 men who run America." [23] Seven of the trustees were on two boards in the top 30.

There is only one possible objection to Beck's little-known but definitive study: It is based upon the years 1934-1935. While these years are within the time span with which we are concerned, it might be claimed that changes have taken place over the past 30 years. There is no reason to believe that the dominance of the elite universities by members of the power elite has diminished, however. A study of 100 men from the 12 foundations we found to be part of the power elite in a previous section of this chapter showed that one-third of them also served as university trustees or university presidents. There were six interlocks with Duke University, three with Yale, two with Princeton, two with Amherst, two with Dartmouth, two with Cornell, and one each with such elite schools as Harvard, Smith, Stanford, Cal Tech, and Vanderbilt. As another example of this continuing interlock, there were 60 interlocks with universities among the top 20 industrials studied in chapter 2.

MASS MEDIA

Between outside reality and inner consciousness, to paraphrase Mills, stand the mass media—newspapers, magazines, television, and radio. Few would doubt the importance of these disseminators of information and opinion, but it is often difficult to demonstrate when and how much they are influencing opinion on a specific issue. We agree with sociologist Morris Janowitz' concise summary of a great deal of research on the influence of the mass media, which appears in his discussion of the public relations efforts of the military:

It remains outside the capacity of social research—even with the most elaborate field techniques available—to give a clear answer to the question: What are the consequences of these public information programs on public attitudes and political decisions? Available research knowledge suggests that mass communications can be decisive in moments of crisis and tension, but that, in general, their influence is limited and has effect gradually, over a long period of time. The influence of mass media, supported by networks of interpersonal contacts among opinion leaders, is not in dramatic conversion of public opinion, but rather in setting the limits within which public debate on controversial issues takes place.[24]

Once again, in Janowitz' summary, we see an emphasis on the point made by Rovere at the start of this chapter—the importance of certain institutions, not in controlling opinion but in setting limits within which discussion can take place. The mass media, in short, play an important role in shaping the American polity, in determining the framework within which decisions are made.

Except in the area of foreign affairs, where most people have no personal observations to rely upon, the primary role of the mass media is the dissemination of information and opinion. There is even reason to believe that much of the communication between disparate parts of the federal government takes place through such trusted mass media as *The New York Times* and *The Reporter*. Douglass Cater (Exeter and Harvard), formerly a writer for *The Reporter,* summarizes the situation as follows:

The press, bearing a loosely drawn mandate to probe and pry, exercises first of all an intelligence function within the government. No ordinary member of Congress has the same opportunity to pose a pertinent question to a President or a bureau chief with expectation of an answer. . . . It is indispensable as the independent conveyor of news to the various possessors of power, none of whom is willing to trust the other's propaganda.[25]

Not only do certain newspapers and magazines have an important role as information and opinion disseminators, but certain of their leading columnists have an equally important role as interpreters of information and leaders in opinion formation. The most influential of these opinion leaders by far during the period which concerns us was Walter Lippmann, a Jewish member of the upper class who attended Harvard and who belongs to such clubs as the Century, Harvard, Coffee House, and River in New York, the Metropolitan and Cosmos in Washington, and the Tavern in Boston.[26]

The most pervasive influence of members of the upper class on the mass media is an indirect one—corporate advertising. Newspapers and magazines, for example, are highly mechanized business operations which are run on a profit-making basis, and only a small part of their income is from reader support. When advertising is important, the threat of its discontinuance can often have effects upon editorial policy. However, what is even more important is that the dependency on advertising keeps the subscription price of the magazine or newspaper very low and thus makes it impossible for publications to exist which must depend in their infancy on reader support. The problem, in short, is getting a newspaper or magazine started in the first place.[27] The role of advertising in keeping subscription prices low has precluded the entrance of new periodicals into the field. Thus, when a new magazine begins, it is dependent upon large financial backers, as was the case when sociologist Daniel Bell and publishing executive Irving Kristol founded *The Public Interest* in 1965. According to *Time* Magazine, they relied "on backing from Wall Street, and other friends. . . ." [28]

Members of the upper class secondarily control many of the mass media through ownership. As the number of newspapers and magazines becomes fewer and fewer, the importance of these large, upper-class-owned publications will increase. There is at least one newspaper owned by a *Social Register* listee in every city with a *Social Register* except for Pittsburgh. Outside of *Social Register* cities there are such aristocratically owned newspapers as those of the Chandlers of Los Angeles, the Hobbys of Houston, and the Binghams of Louisville, but no systematic research was undertaken for other than the *Social Register* cities. Perhaps the most important newspaper of the American upper class is *The New York Times,* owned by an aristocratic Jewish family which also operates its original newspaper venture, the *Chattanooga Times.*[29]

Equally important in understanding the newspaper business are the newspaper chains, the most famous of which is the Hearst chain, originally based upon a mining fortune. The Hearst empire includes 12 newspapers, 14 magazines, three television stations, six radio stations, a news service, a photo service, a feature syndicate, and Avon paperbacks. Another important chain is that of John S. Knight (SR, Chicago), who owns newspapers in Akron, Ohio, and Charlotte, North Carolina, as well as the better-known *Miami Herald* and *Detroit Free Press.* The Ridder clan, with ten of its members listed in the *Social Register,* controls 14 newspapers, including those in St. Paul, Minnesota, and San Jose, Long Beach, and Pasadena, California. The Scripps-Howard chain, which is run by three members of the upper class—Jack R. Howard, Charles E. Scripps, and E. W. Scripps II—includes 20 daily newspapers, four television stations, four radio stations, a press association, a photo service, and a feature syndicate.

It is likely that most newspapers are not owned by members of the upper class, but a majority of the major magazines—left, right, and center —are so owned. Perhaps the most famous are *Time, Life, Fortune,* and *Sports Illustrated* of Time, Inc., which is the nation's 158th largest industrial corporation. In addition to magazines, Time, Inc., also owns radio and television stations, a book club, paper mills, timberland, oil wells, and real estate. Co-founder Henry Luce attended Hotchkiss and Yale, but was merely "well connected" to begin with; he borrowed the money to start his enterprise in conjunction with a more wealthy member of the upper class, Briton Hadden, who was a friend from private school and college. Their backers included many well-known members of the Eastern branch of the upper class, including representatives of the Morgan and Rockefeller interest groups.[30] Two other important magazines owned by members of the upper class are part of newspaper empires. The Cowles, who own newspapers in Minneapolis and Des Moines, publish *Look.* In the mid-1960's they also purchased a half interest in *Harper's Magazine* from Harper & Row. John Cowles, a graduate of Exeter and Harvard, is married to the stepdaughter of Harper & Row chairman Cass Canfield (SR, NY). *Newsweek,* once saved from financial disaster by Harriman and Astor funds, is now the property of the *Washington Post,* the successful newspaper of the late banker Eugene Meyer.

The most famous of ultraconservative magazines, the *National Review,* is partially financed by editor William Buckley's (SR, NY) oil inheritance, while its arch-nemesis, the *New Republic,* is subsidized by other elements of the upper class. To the left of the *New Republic* stands *The Nation,* which has enjoyed the backing of upper-class persons for most of its 100-year history. Until the mid-1960's it was published by George Kirstein (Berkshire School, Harvard), the son of a wealthy department store owner. In early 1966 the publication of *The Nation* was taken over by another liberal, old-line member of the upper class, James Storrow, Jr. (SR, Boston). Equally liberal is the newspaper–magazine controlled by New York members of the upper class, *The New York Review of Books,* a fortnightly with *Social Register* listees performing the roles of publisher, advisory editor, associate editor, and editorial assistants. Perhaps the most important source of political information within the power elite is *The Reporter.*[31]

It is published and edited by Max Ascoli, who married a descendant of the founders of Sears. The Ascolis gave $15,000 to the 1960 Democratic campaign.

All three of the major radio-TV networks, NBC, CBS, and ABC, were managed by Jewish members of the power elite during the mid-1960's. Robert W. Sarnoff, son of NBC founder David Sarnoff, attended Andover and Harvard, and married Felicia Warburg of the aristocratic Warburg banking family. William S. Paley, whose father was a millionaire cigar manufacturer, bought CBS in 1928 for $400,000. He is now married to Barbara Cushing Mortimer of an old-line family. The president of ABC was Leonard H. Goldenson, who received his A.B. and LL.B. at Harvard and is a member of the Harvard Club of New York.

In the final analysis, we do not believe that the majority of the mass media are owned or directly controlled by members of the national upper class. There are thousands of locally owned newspapers, hundreds of locally owned radio and TV stations, and dozens of little magazines for every race, creed, and color. However, by controlling every major opinion-molding institution in the country, members of the upper class play a predominant role in determining the framework within which decisions on important issues are reached.[32] Such factors as diversity within the upper class, the American libertarian tradition, the non-upper-class backgrounds of most reporters and scholars, and the myriad of locally or religiously controlled colleges, newspapers, and magazines keep this upper-class domination of major opinion-molding institutions from being translated into complete and monolithic control of American opinion.

We can now turn our attention to the federal government, which is the most decisive institution in deciding whether or not the upper class is a governing class. The following quote from Cater will prepare us for the findings in the next chapter:

Likewise, it can be observed that a recognizable group of skilled operatives shuttles back and forth between private enterprise and the key posts of foreign policy, defense, and finance. For evidence, a diligent scholar would do well to delve into the role of the purely unofficial Council on Foreign Relations in the care and breeding of an incipient American Establishment.[33]

Chapter Four . . . . . .
The Control of the . .
Federal Government

Members of the American upper class and their employees control the Executive branch of the federal government. That much we will be able to demonstrate with considerable ease, and from it we will argue that they also control the Judicial branch and the regulatory agencies. But does the Executive branch dominate the Congress? That is a question political scientists have by no means resolved. It is important to us because few legislators are members of the power elite. While most observers would probably agree that the Executive branch has gained ascendancy, few would go as far as Senator Joseph S. Clark (SR, Philadelphia), who called Congress "the sapless branch." However, perhaps all would agree with Sir Denis Brogan that the American Congress is the only important legislative body left in the world. In short, twentieth-century governments have been dominated by the Executive branch; the question is how far this process has gone in the United States.[1]

What are the powers of the Congress in an age when the congressman must resort to theatrical ballyhoo to compete with the national political figures and movie celebrities who dominate the mass media?[2] If Congress seldom initiates legislation, it still has the power to block legislation and force compromise. If it does not debate issues of war and peace, or enter into high-level decisions, it still has the power to investigate the decisions which are made—it can hold the Executive branch accountable for its actions. If Congress does not suggest the men who will be appointed to important positions in the regulatory agencies and federal judiciary, it does have the power to veto appointments that do not meet with its approval. However, in spite of these legislative powers, we find ourselves in agreement with Cater, who is by no means unaware of the pockets of real strength in Congress:

Whether guided by the more active or passive concept of the job, the President is now the central figure in the legislative process. The President's program occupies the dominant place on the congressional agenda. Most of the major laws are drafted in the President's office; the budget is put together there and presented to Congress as a packaged entity. A bill initiated by the individual congressman faces giant obstacles unless it has been submitted first to the President's Budget Bureau for "legislative clearance." [3]

To establish that members of the power elite control the Executive branch it is first necessary to show that they control the Presidential nominations that are held every four years. This can be done by studying the financing of political campaigns. By emphasizing that members of the power elite control only the Presidential nominations we are agreeing that American political parties are highly fragmented structures whose different levels —national, state, and local—may be controlled by different interest groups and different social classes. By emphasizing campaign finances we are not claiming that money alone is enough to win elections. The pre-eminent place given to finances in the following pages would not be justified if it were merely a matter of the November election. Although a certain minimum is obviously necessary, especially for new candidates, money alone is not enough to win an election.[4] What makes money the key to understanding party control is the problem of gaining the nomination for a major political office in the first place. Unless a person has large financial reserves or the backing of wealthy men, he cannot hope to develop a national following or compete in party primaries. The cost of winning the privilege to represent one's party gives an important role to the political fund raiser, who is usually a rich man representing a clique of wealth-holders who are in agreement with the goals and values of the potential candidate.[5]

As a second method of demonstrating power elite control of the Executive branch, we will study the social backgrounds of the cabinet members, advisers, and diplomats who played major roles within it between 1932 and 1964. This tack is based on the assumption that finding a great many men with upper-class social backgrounds or previous employment in institutions controlled by members of the upper class would justify the inference that these men have power within the victorious party.

There are few who would deny that the Republican Party is controlled by members of the power elite. It is often stereotyped as the party of "big business," and we will present evidence which supports this belief. However, this stereotype has been unfortunate because it turns attention from the fact that the Democratic Party is controlled by different members of the same elite group. We cannot overemphasize the falsity of the stereotype of the Democratic Party as the party of the "common man," for it is this stereotype which leads many social scientists to deny that the American upper class is a governing class. They agree that the Republican Party

is controlled by big business, but then they point to the success of the
Democratic Party, the party of the common man.[6] The facts are that the
Democratic Party appeals to the common man for its support but is controlled by aristocrats. We will devote much more space to the Democrats
than to the Republicans in order to support this important point. For now,
we can present a summary view of the Democrats by Cater:

From Jefferson's time to Lyndon B. Johnson's, the party of the common man
has been commanded with remarkable regularity by men of wealth and/or cultural heritage. Harry Truman was the most recent exception, but he had not
been intended for first place on the ticket. John F. Kennedy, while belonging to
an ethnic and religious minority, was a member of an emergent Irish upper
class in America. With the exception of Humphrey, the other chief Democratic
possibilities in the 1960 contest—Symington and Stevenson—also were mil-
lionaires.[7]

Because both political parties are controlled by members of the power
elite there is considerable similarity between them. It is for this reason, we
believe with Cater, that the President "enlists his principal advisers not
from the ranks of party zealots, but from an incipient Establishment in
America which more or less disregards the party label." [8] At the same
time, upper-class control of both parties does not preclude party differences
on a great many issues. The first reason for this is that different elements
of the upper class gravitate to one or the other of the two parties for all the
reasons which lead to the diversity within the upper class described in
Chapter 1. The second reason is that the conflicting programs of these
diverse elements appeal to different socioeconomic groups and professional
castes within the rest of the population. This is probably especially the case
with economic programs, which Harvard economist Seymour Harris has
shown to be somewhat different for the two parties in his book, *The Economics of the Political Parties*. The situation can be summarized as follows:
The leaders of the two parties have intra-class differences; the followers
have inter-class and professional differences. The Republican Party is controlled by the largest manufacturers and bankers of the upper class, men
who are primarily White Anglo-Saxon Protestant in background and who
are from families that became prominent between the Civil War and the
Depression. It receives its support from local upper classes of small businessmen, the upper echelon of white-collar workers, and the lawyers, physicians, and engineers within the upper-middle class. The Democratic Party,
on the other hand, is controlled by very new and very old elements within
the upper class, including Southern aristocrats and the ethnic rich, and
draws its support from the blue-collar workers, the lower echelons of white-

collar workers, and the intellectuals, writers, and artists of the upper-middle class.

REPUBLICAN PARTY FINANCES

The Republican Party has been known for a long time as the party of big business, and with good reason, for it is the biggest of the big business-men who are its major financial supporters. In 1952, for example, Dwight Eisenhower received at least $94,000 from the Rockefellers, $74,000 from the du Ponts, $65,000 from the Pews, and $54,000 from the Mellons. The known contributions for 1956 from these families are even higher—$248,-000 from the du Ponts, $216,000 from the Pews, $152,000 from the Rocke-fellers, and $100,000 from the Mellons.[9] More generally, officers and direc-tors of the largest corporations gave $1,900,000 during the 1956 Presi-dential campaign, of which $1,800,000 went to the Republicans.[10] Herbert E. Alexander, director of the Citizens' Research Foundation, has provided similar information on the donations of prominent upper-class Republican families for 1960 and 1964:[11]

	1960	1964
du Ponts	$125,000	$71,000
Mellons	64,000	93,500
Olins	37,000	44,900
Pews	74,000	94,000
Rockefellers	114,800	65,500
Whitneys	35,500	43,000

Republican financing is easily studied because it is relatively well organized, at least compared to that of the Democratic Party. Leading busi-nessmen are appointed heads of state finance committees, which then contact local businessmen. As Key puts it, ". . . people with money to give may hesitate not to give to such committees." [12] For examples, he points out that Winthrop Aldrich, New York chairman in 1952, and John Hay Whitney, New York chairman in 1956, would be hard men to refuse if one were a businessman. On the national level, Republican finance chairmen during the first five years of the 1960's were Courtney Burton (SR, Cleveland), Ralph Cordiner, formerly president of General Electric, and Lucius D. Clay, a Southern aristocrat who has been a prominent figure in a half-dozen major companies since his retirement from a lifelong career of military service.* In the 1964 campaign there was a slight, but highly exaggerated

* Clay's brother, Ryburn Glover Clay, was a leading Southern businessman who belonged to the Piedmont Driving Club in Atlanta. He was president of Clay Moore, Inc., and a director of the Federal Reserve Bank (Atlanta), Colonial Stores, and Southeastern Greyhound Lines. At one time he was president of the Southeastern Pipe Line Company. Unlike his brother, he was a Democrat.

change in the financing of the Republican Party. An important party leader, supposedly close to its inner workings, summed it up this way for *U. S. News & World Report:*

The Eastern group no longer have the power they once had because they no longer have a monopoly on money. Businessmen from the Midwest and West now do not need to go to New York for a loan. And campaign contributions are not confined to the big cities in the East. . . . the truth is that Goldwater, without help from the East, left the Wall Street group at the post." [13]

If the big money is not confined to the big cities of the East Coast, it is nonetheless wrong to think that Goldwater did not have the financial support of many old-line *Social Register* families from all over the country. We believe it would be more accurate to summarize the Goldwater phenomenon by saying that the right-wing aristocrats of the East and Midwest joined forces with the rich of the South and Southwest to take control of the party from the upper-class Republicans who have made their peace with the New Deal. For example, such prominent *Social Register* families as the Irelands and Humphreys of Cleveland, the Stuarts of Chicago, the Olins of St. Louis, the Mellons and Scaifes of Pittsburgh, the Pews and du Ponts of Philadelphia, and the Milbanks and Middendorfs of New York were among Goldwater's major financial backers.* Roger Milliken, perhaps the biggest Goldwater backer of them all, is usually listed as a Southern textile owner (he once closed down an entire plant in the South rather than allow unionization), but he is also a member of the board of directors of the First National City Bank of New York and a listee in the New York *Social Register*:

At the 1960 Republican Convention, Milliken felt so strongly about his champion that he personally put up all the money for a blitz drive and huge rally to nominate him for Vice-President, despite Nixon's avowed preference for Henry Cabot Lodge as running-mate. . . . This time [1964] it is all Goldwater and, as four years ago, the unknown but all-powerful Milliken is in the inner center of the all-pervasive and irresistible Goldwater organization, quietly but firmly supervising and directing just about everything it does. Milliken has a key voice in every major decision and move, and most others, too. Also, he more than carries his share of footing the bills.[14]

Nor were Goldwater's non-Eastern backers merely "new rich," although there were many of them in the South and Southwest.[15] For example, the Klebergs of the huge King Ranch in Texas are an old and estab-

---

* George Humphrey, former Secretary of the Treasury and a leading figure in the Hanna Mining Company, played a key role in Goldwater's nomination by convincing his friend, former President Eisenhower, to refrain from backing another aristocrat, William Scranton.

lished family, with a ranch that sits atop the largest reserves of natural gas in the world. Most interesting of all, however, is Dennison Kitchel, Goldwater's campaign manager, who is a transplanted New Yorker who still lists in that city's *Social Register.* Kitchel became an Arizonan when he married into the famous Douglas family, which is based upon a mining fortune. He is an important person in questioning the anti-Wall Street theory of Goldwater's candidacy, for he is the main lawyer for Phelps Dodge Mining, a part of the Morgan interest group. Among the Phelps Dodge directors is Percy Douglas, head of Otis Elevator Company in New York, who ushered Goldwater through Wall Street circles during the campaign.* The presence of Kitchel and Douglas, when coupled with the fact that Ralph Cordiner of the Morgan firm of General Electric was campaign finance chairman, shows the presence of at least some members of the Morgan interest group in the Goldwater campaign. While it is not our purpose to even attempt to tie Goldwater to any one interest group or set of interest groups, the presence of these men hardly supports the notion that members of a group other than the power elite have taken over the Republican Party; it instead suggests continuing differences of opinion even within the Eastern branch of the upper class.†

A great deal has been made out of the fact that the Goldwater campaign was financed in part by thousands of small contributions. While this tells us something about the fervency of Goldwater's several million followers, it is more important to understand the very substantial financial backing which helped him win the nomination from such rich and powerful Eastern Republicans as Rockefeller, Scranton, and Lodge. This money was collected within the upper class in typical fashion by well-to-do fund-raisers who called on their friends. The most important of these were Roger Milliken (SR, NY), William Middendorf (SR, NY), Jeremiah Milbank (SR, NY), Stetson Coleman, and Donald Gainey, who raised $3.5 million among them before the nomination.[17] While not in the *Social Register,* Coleman has prototypical upper-class credentials. Southern-born, he graduated from Exeter, Yale, and Harvard, and is a member of such exclusive clubs as The Brook (New York), Chevy Chase (Maryland), and Burning Tree (Washington, D. C.). He is different from most members of the upper class we have encountered thus far in that he is only involved in minor companies—*e.g.,* Fannie May Candy, Universal Oil Products, and Zapata Petroleum. Gainey is another "small" businessman. He is chairman of

---

* Percy Douglas is not of the Arizona Douglas family.

† These differences of opinion also can be seen in a study of corporate ideology by Robert Heilbroner.[18] The most conservative of the five men he studied were Cordiner and Roger Blough, both heads of undisputed Morgan companies, General Electric and U. S. Steel.

Jostens, Inc., whose 2000 employees produce class rings, pins, insignias, yearbooks, diplomas, and greeting cards. His son is a trustee of Shattuck School.

A study of a list of donors of $10,000 or more, compiled by the Citizens' Research Foundation, is even more impressive evidence for Goldwater's support by members of the upper class. Of 52 names, we could find information on 44, and 38 of them were members of the American upper class. And, as Alexander notes from his analysis of these donors, New York remained the best source of Republican funds by this index.[18] It is also interesting that the percentage of upper-class names among big Republican contributors for 1960 is almost identical, with 47 out of 54 on whom we could find information meeting one or more of our criteria. There were 60 such givers in 1960, 52 in 1964, which is hardly a precipitous drop. Most of the difference is accounted for by the absence of six of the seven members of the Rockefeller family who gave $10,000 or more in 1960.

In summary, we believe that the financing of the Republican Party even in 1964 demonstrates its control at the Presidential level by members of the power elite. If finances are not convincing in and of themselves, a quick look at Presidential hopefuls during the 1960's provides further evidence: Goldwater, Scranton, Nelson Rockefeller, and Henry Cabot Lodge are old-line members of the upper class, George Romney is the former president of American Motors, and Richard Nixon is a Wall Street lawyer who was asked to go into politics in the first place by leading Los Angeles businessmen. When Republicans talked of the "future" in the mid-1960's their thoughts often turned to Charles Percy (SR, Chicago), Robert Taft, Jr. (SR, Cincinnati), and John V. Lindsay (SR, NY).

DEMOCRATIC PARTY FINANCES

As previously noted, it is important to go into great detail on the financing of the Democratic Party at the Presidential level in order to refute the notion that it is the party of the common man in anything other than its voting support. Because the question of the control of the Democratic Party is so crucial we will also use this section to present other than purely financial information to support the thesis that it is dominated by members of the power elite. We can begin with a consideration of the supporters of Franklin D. Roosevelt and the New Deal:

From its beginning the "New Deal" was primarily underwritten by those wealthy individuals whose revenues derive primarily from direct exploitation of the retail market—department store owners, textile fabricators, cigarette manufacturers, independent industrialists, processors and distributors, and big real estate operators. Excepting the latter, these comprise the light-industries group[19]

This thesis was first presented by Lundberg in *America's Sixty Families.*
It was based upon lists of campaign donors and on Lundberg's years as a
financial reporter for a leading New York newspaper.* While it would obviously have its exceptions because no one "cause" explains a complex
phenomenon such as party allegiance, it is supported by a more systematic
study which showed that in 1940 and 1944 almost three-fifths of Republican
gifts of $1000 or more came from bankers and heavy industrialists, while
almost one-half of big Democratic gifts came from retailers, light industrialists, and the entertainment industry.[20]

However, the Democratic Party of the New Deal was not merely the
party of the light industrialists and the retailers, who are the "smaller" of
the big businessmen. It was also the party of the old-line aristocrats of
three and four generations as well as the first- and second-generation ethnic
rich who had been excluded by the staunchly Protestant, Anglo-Saxon industrialists and bankers who so clearly dominated the Republican Party.
Again, the correlation is not a perfect one, but in the case of ethnicity it
was enough to earn President Roosevelt the epithet "Rosenfelt" within
some cliques of his upper-class compatriots.[21] Among the Jewish backers
of Roosevelt's nomination campaign were Jesse Straus, Herbert Lehman,
Howard Cullman, and Sidney Weinberg, while the most prominent Catholic was Joseph P. Kennedy. Kennedy, for example, gave $25,000 to Frank-
lin Roosevelt's campaign, lent the party in general $50,000 more, and raised
$100,000 "among his friends and acquaintances, some of them Wall Street
figures worried about the way the wind was blowing." [22]

In addition to Franklin D. Roosevelt himself, who is of course the
most important example, the early New Deal was supported by such rich
and well-bred WASPs as Vincent Astor, Francis Biddle, William Bullitt,
James Gerard, Averell Harriman, and R. Sturgis Ingersoll. Ingersoll, for
example, was chairman of the Pennsylvania Democratic Victory Campaign
in 1932. Bullitt became ambassador to Russia and remained one of President Roosevelt's closest advisors throughout the war period. Biddle eventually took the post of Attorney-General and then played a leading role
in founding Americans for Democratic Action.[23] Most interesting of all,
however, according to Baltzell, was Republican John G. Winant of St.

---

* We were able to locate information on 78 of the 93 names mentioned by Lundberg as big Democratic contributors in 1932 and 1936. Fifty-eight (74 per cent) of
the 78 were members of the upper class. Such aristocratic families as the Astors,
Baruchs, Biddles, Busches, Chryslers, Goelets, Harknesses, Hearsts, McCormicks,
Palmers, Strauses, Vanderbilts, and Whitneys were among the donors. Six other persons could be identified as members of the power elite. Another nine could be considered new rich, such as Jesse H. Jones of Texas, Joseph P. Kennedy of Boston and
New York, Frederick John Fisher of General Motors, and Henry L. Doherty of Cities
Service Company.

Paul's and Princeton, who "gave up all personal ambitions to go to Washington in the service of President Roosevelt, whom he admired to an overwhelming extent":

He took a major part in organizing the Social Security Program. An ardent democrat with a sincere love of, and faith in, the average man, Winant was convinced that Social Security was the very heart of the New Deal. When he thought that the Landon campaign was threatening the program, he resigned from his appointed position and actively campaigned for Roosevelt's re-election. But he never became a formal member of the Democratic Party.[24]

If Franklin D. Roosevelt had ethnic and aristocratic supporters in his quest for the nomination in 1932, he also had ethnic opponents within the party. The most prominent were Jewish financier Bernard Baruch (SR, NY) and Catholic industrialist John J. Raskob. Both supported Roosevelt once he won the nomination, Baruch giving $45,000 and Raskob $23,000.* Raskob, the chairman of the finance committee of General Motors and reputedly worth about $100 million, had switched to the Democratic Party in 1928 to serve as Catholic Al Smith's campaign manager. By 1932 he was chairman of the Democratic National Committee, and he was again backing Al Smith, who had undergone an interesting metamorphosis:

Once the derby-wearing darling of the masses, [Smith] was president of the Empire State Building, a resident of swank Fifth Avenue, and a man seldom seen in his old haunts, unless his chauffeur-driven limousine happened to flash by. Smith, the risen commoner, was the choice of the party's conservative wing.[25]

The chairman of the finance committee during President Roosevelt's first administration was James W. Gerard (SR, NY), a third-generation member of the upper class who had been finance chairman for the Cox–Roosevelt ticket in 1920.[26] Gerard had been involved in Democratic politics since the 1890's. He became somewhat more powerful a few years later when he married a daughter of Marcus Daly, who was a one-fourth owner of Anaconda Copper. Along with his brother-in-law, Marcus Daly II, Gerard was a leader in the mining industry in Montana, South Dakota, Mexico, and Canada during the first three decades of this century. He gave at least $17,500 to Franklin D. Roosevelt's 1932 campaign and at least $51,000 to the 1936 campaign. In 1936 Gerard was kicked upstairs to honorary finance chairman, to be replaced by Forbes Morgan (SR, NY). "I think the reason for this," explained Gerard, "was that the boys feared

---

* Raskob later joined the rest of the du Pont interest group in backing the infamous Liberty League of the mid-1930's. Baruch remained a loyal Democrat and played a significant role in the World War II mobilization.

that if I had been chairman I would have refused the $500,000 contribution given by John L. Lewis on behalf of his labor organization." [27] Gerard was once again honorary chairman in 1940 when his old friend and next-door neighbor, Wendell Willkie, ran for President on the Republican ticket.*

Franklin D. Roosevelt's "New Deal" only took shape after his election, and it alienated many rich Roosevelt backers who had assumed that things would go on as usual. It must be stressed that there was no one "plan" within the upper class as to how to deal with the Depression, so there were many arguments and a considerable turnover of upper-class personnel. For example, Jewish financier James P. Warburg bowed out when President Roosevelt went "too far" in his monetary reforms, while the several du Ponts who had backed Roosevelt were enraged about the Nye Committee investigations into the munitions industry. Even one of President Roosevelt's oldest friends and backers, Vincent Astor, who gave $35,000 in 1932, felt that the President had lost his senses. At the same time, most rich backers remained with him, and several more joined the ranks, the most prominent of these being Walter Chrysler of the Chrysler Motor Company and A. P. Giannini of the Bank of America. One of the most prominent of the old-line aristocrats to remain loyal to President Roosevelt was Ohio Senator Robert Johns Bulkley (SR, Cleveland). Bulkley had sponsored such New Deal reforms as the Home Bank Loan Act and the Securities Exchange Act. Moreover, President Roosevelt continued to enjoy the support of two of the most prominent members of the Morgan Empire, Thomas W. Lamont (SR, NY) and Gerard Swope. As Baltzell notes, Lamont was one of the leading figures in the Morgan complex and a former advisor to Woodrow Wilson and Herbert Hoover. He was an old friend of the President:

As one might expect, Lamont, even though he was often openly critical of Roosevelt's economic policies, was quick to see the essentially conserving nature of the New Deal. Thus, in 1934, he told Harry Hopkins that he considered Roosevelt a "bulwark of sane politics" and that he expected him to remain in office until 1940, or perhaps 1944.[29]

Swope, on the other hand, was an MIT graduate who had worked his way to the presidency of General Electric. According to Baltzell, it was not generally known that he was of Jewish origins.

While the biggest and most established oilmen were important con-

---

* It is not without interest that Gerard's father-in-law gave $300,000 to William Jennings Bryan's campaign in 1896, for, as Gerard remarks, "Bryan's election, of course, would have been a boon to the silver-mining industry." According to Gerard, Daly was Bryan's biggest backer.[28]

tributors to the Republican Party during the 1930's, the Democrats were not without their backers from that industry. Once again, these Democratic backers were "smaller" big businessmen or members of the ethnic rich. Oil contributions are summarized as follows by political scientist Robert Engler, who did a seven-year study on *The Politics of Oil*:

It is now customary to identify oil with the Republican party or the Dixiecrat movement. But oilmen have been active in the Democratic party. During the New Deal they made many cash contributions. In 1936, for example, H. L. Doherty of the Cities Service Company reported giving $55,000. Walter A. Jones, a Pittsburgh oilman, was also an important contributor in that period [$102,000 in 1936, according to Lundberg]. Jacob Blaustein of the American Oil Company (now part of Standard of Indiana) was consistently pro-New Deal. Sid Richardson was friendly with Franklin D. Roosevelt, and his contributions helped maintain a Democratic Congress in the 1942 election. In fact the Democrats received sizable oil sums as late as 1944.[30]

As Engler recounts in some detail, it was oil money that led to one of the early embarrassments of the Truman Administration. In 1946 Senator Charles W. Tobey "challenged President Truman's nomination of oilman Edwin W. Pauley for Undersecretary of the Navy, intended by Roosevelt and then Truman as a steppingstone to his succeeding James Forrestal as Secretary." * Pauley had served as both a leading fund-raiser and the treasurer of the Democratic National Committee between 1941 and 1945. He was succeeded as treasurer by one of his friends, George Killion, who "later became president of the American President Lines, controlled by a syndicate formed by Davies and Samuel B. Mosher, president of Signal." [32] (Ralph Davies was another West Coast oilman who was friendly with Pauley.)

The financial base of the Democratic Party did not change during the 1950's. We were able to find information on 65 of the largest 105 contributors to the Democratic Party for 1952 and 1956.[33] Forty-three of these 65 people—66 per cent—could be categorized as members of the American upper class. Twenty-one of the 65—32 per cent—could be identified as Jewish or as married to Jews. Eight of the 21 were wealthy Jewish businessmen who could not be considered members of the social upper class. They were socially isolated from the larger upper-class community. The Jews who had been assimilated into the social upper class included three of those mentioned as prominent in the 1930's—Straus, Lehman, and Blaustein—and several who had married into such prominent

* "To Tobey and others, the post of Secretary of the Navy seemed an obviously inappropriate reward, especially in view of the industry's recurring interest in the Navy's petroleum reserves." [31]

Jewish families as the Blocks, Rosenwalds, and Lehmans.[34] Needless to say, the Kennedy clan remained the most prominent Catholic contributors to the Democratic Party during this period.

Contributors of $10,000 or more for the 1960 and 1964 elections have been listed by the Citizens' Research Foundation.[35] Of the 35 giving this amount to the Democrats in 1960, 43 per cent of the 28 on whom we could find information were members of the upper class. Half of these upper-class donors were Jewish. In addition, seven other persons on the list could be identified as Jewish, bringing the percentage of Jews in the sample to 50. This compares with three Jews among the 54 big Republican donors for that year on whom we could find information. The figures for 1964 are even more impressive due to some switches in party backing. Thirty-three of 58 large Democratic donors were members of the upper class (57 per cent), with one-third of the 33 being identifiable as Jewish. In addition, there were 13 other Jews among the 58. This proportion of Jews—25 out of 58—once again supports our thesis about ethnic differences in the leadership of the Democrats and the Republicans, for only two out of 44 large Republican donors for 1964 on whom we found information could be identified as Jewish.

If statements about ethnicity and light industry remain true of the Democratic Party in general, it would still be wrong to ignore the continuing presence of old-line aristocrats. Baltzell's *The Protestant Establishment* gives as much evidence for the presence of these aristocrats as it does for the rise of a new, ethnically heterogenous establishment and the decline of the Protestant Establishment of heavy industrialists and Wall Street financiers who ruled until the 1930's:

Like their friends in the arts or in teaching, men of inherited wealth in America are increasingly seeking a sense of personal fulfillment in government service. Their family firms have been sold, and the life of the organization man has little appeal. . . . Thus there were probably more men of inherited wealth— and of the Eastern Seaboard upper class like Angier Biddle Duke—down in Washington at all levels of the New Frontier bureaucracy than at any other time in our history (even including the generation of Franklin Roosevelt).[36]

Then too, such names as William Benton of the *Encyclopaedia Britannica,* Barry Bingham of the *Louisville Courier-Journal,* August Busch of Anhueser-Busch, William Averell Harriman of Brown Brothers, Harriman and Company, Angier Biddle Duke, Marshall Field, Millard Tydings, and William Vanderbilt were among the big contributors of the 1950's and 1960's.

Perhaps a classic example of the WASP presence is multimillionaire

Charles W. Engelhard, Jr., who has multiplied his father's $20 million fortune into an organization worth $120 million. A frequent caller at the White House, he participates in missions for President Johnson, but makes no public pronouncements. His credentials are prototypical—St. Paul's, Princeton, Episcopalian, married to the socially prominent daughter of a Brazilian diplomat, a neighbor of former Secretary of the Treasury Douglas Dillon, a member of the Foreign Policy Association and the Committee for Economic Development, and the owner of 100 horses which he races in the United States, England, and South Africa.[37] However, an even better understanding of the Democratic Party of the 1950's and early 1960's can be gained from this quote concerning Robert F. Kennedy's drive for the party's nomination for Senator from New York:

To cinch it for Bobby, [Stephen] Smith arranged for 12 apostles of liberalism in the New York Democratic Party to declare publicly for Bobby. These are the kind of reliable Democrats who fork over big campaign money, pay $1000 to join the President's Club, and are considered prestigious, liberal, and sound. They were: Averell Harriman; Arthur Krim, President of United Artists; Roswell Gilpatric, former Deputy Secretary of Defense and a prominent lawyer; Mrs. Albert D. Lasker, a philanthropist and a member of the East Side liberal group; Mrs. Edward R. Murrow; Howard Samuels, upstate industrialist and promoter of the Democratic Party; Robert Benjamin, an associate of Krim's; John Snyder, who, as president of U. S. Industries, Inc., is one of the kings of automation; Abraham (Abe) Feinberg, a hosiery baron, who helped make Jack Kennedy palatable to Jews in 1960; Isador Lubin, former State Industrial Commissioner and Mrs. Lubin; and George Backer, businessman and former aide of Harriman's.[38]

Kennedy and his rich brother-in-law, Stephen Smith, are Catholic members of the power elite. Krim, Lasker, Samuels, Benjamin, and Feinberg represent the Jewish element, and Harriman, Gilpatric, Snyder, and Backer are the WASP element.* Mrs. Murrow and the Lubins are what Allan Potter calls "those accepted by them [members of the governing class] on the basis of achievements." [39]

If the financial backing of such upper-class Presidential candidates as Franklin D. Roosevelt, Adlai Stevenson, and John F. Kennedy is not convincing in and of itself for the Democratic Party (Truman and Johnson were Vice-Presidents who were not meant to head the ticket), perhaps a more detailed consideration of the men who have surrounded American Presidents since 1932 will be.

* Mrs. Lasker is not herself Jewish. Although from a well-to-do family, her fabulous wealth comes from her late Jewish husband, Albert D. Lasker.

THE CABINET

The President's Cabinet is made up of the heads of the departments of the Executive branch. A study of the Cabinets for the years 1932-1964 suggests that the power elite dominates the departments that matter most to them—State, Treasury, and Defense.[40] Members of the power elite are also predominant in Commerce and, of all places in a pluralistic society, Labor, while lesser mortals are more likely to be present in the Attorney-General's office, HEW (Health, Education, and Welfare), Interior, and Agriculture. The Postmaster-Generalship has been a frankly political appointment, often going to the chairman of the victorious party.

Of eight Secretaries of State since 1932, five have been listed in the *Social Register*—Edward Stettinius, George C. Marshall, Dean Acheson, John Foster Dulles, and Christian Herter. Three of these five were corporation lawyers—Stettinius, Acheson, and Dulles. Stettinius was a Morgan partner. General Marshall came from a private school background and a moderately well-to-do family with aristocratic Southern origins; he became a listee in the *Social Register* in 1930 when he married Katherine Tupper Brown, the widow of a wealthy Baltimore lawyer who was in the *Social Register* for that city.[41] Christian Herter (SR, Boston) had a distinguished career as State Department adviser, editor, and congressman before replacing Dulles as Secretary of State in the Eisenhower Administration. A sixth Secretary of State, Dean Rusk, is a member of the power elite because he came to the post from the presidency of the upper-class-controlled Rockefeller Foundation. The seventh and eighth secretaries, Cordell Hull (1933-1944) and James F. Byrnes (1945-1947) were respected Southern politicians who do not qualify as members of the power elite.

Since the State Department is so important, it might be worthwhile to look at the people involved in one of its most crucial postwar decisions. As former State Department officer Joseph M. Jones points out in *The Fifteen Weeks,* his account of the origin of the Truman Doctrine and the Marshall Plan, the State Department played a very large role in developing these policies. The key persons during this crucial 15-week period which signaled the switch from isolationism to foreign aid were Acheson, Marshall, James Forrestal, Robert Patterson, Charles Bohlen, and Averell Harriman, all members of the upper class. Two other important upper-class participants were William Clayton, Undersecretary of State for Economic Affairs, and Walter Lippmann, the noted columnist. Clayton, the former head of the Anderson, Clayton Company of Houston, the largest cotton exporting company in the world, was a fervent internationalist with great prestige in the business community. Lippmann was one of the most influential opinion-makers in the country and a strong supporter of foreign aid. Two Republicans figured prominently in turning the tide against isolationist congressmen who wanted to cut $1.75 billion from the military budget and half a billion from aid to Germany and Japan. The first was Henry Cabot Lodge (SR, Boston), who joined Marshall, Acheson, Forrestal, and Harriman very early in the decision-making process. The other was a non-member of the power elite, Arthur Vandenberg. Described as an isolationist, the powerful chairman of the Senate Foreign Relations Committee went along with the policy and carried his colleagues with him. However, Vandenberg may have been more pragmatist than isolationist, for in the early 1930's he campaigned vigorously for the St. Lawrence Seaway, which would allow Michigan to compete in world markets: "Is that not an economic aspiration to which the nation is prayerfully committed?" [42] Whatever Vandenberg's ultimate philosophy may have been, his role was a secondary one, as can be seen in Jones's summary of a program which was consistent with the Free Trade policy that had been advocated by the State Department since at least the Roosevelt Administration:

The State Department therefore took the lead in planning, negotiating, and putting into operation economic and financial institutions on a scale that seemed vast, in the fervent hope and expectation that the leading trading nations of the world could re-establish the liberal world trading system that had existed before 1930.[43]

We have emphasized this crucial period in policy making, which was dominated by members of the power elite, because the Korean War and the Vietnam War must be understood within this context. It was the policy set forth by the Truman Doctrine and the Marshall Plan which provided the framework for the decisions to enter these wars. We have also emphasized this 15 weeks because it shows how minor were the differences within the upper class which led to the charges of "soft on Communism" during the 1950's. The Democratic members of the upper class were following a policy of "containment." While they were not so bold as to pursue the "rollback" policy advocated by some of their Republican opponents, that is hardly enough to justify wild charges against some of the leading financiers and corporation lawyers of the American business aristocracy.

The Treasury Department, like the State Department, is dominated by members of the power elite. Franklin D. Roosevelt's first secretary of this department was William H. Woodin, a Republican big businessman and *Social Register* listee who had backed Roosevelt even before his nomination. He contributed $10,000 to the pre-convention fund, $25,000 after the nomination. He had been a leading figure in American Car and Foundry Motor

Company, and a director of eight other institutions, including the Federal Reserve Bank of New York. Woodin was followed by Acting Secretary Dean Acheson, who left shortly after his appointment because of policy differences with Roosevelt. He was followed by Henry Morgenthau, Jr., a Jewish member of the upper class who was a neighbor of President Roosevelt's in the New York countryside. Morgenthau played a leading role in shaping the New Deal, as well as in selecting the personnel to lead the war effort. His replacement, Fred M. Vinson, was a Kentucky-born lawyer, politician, and judge who was moved to the Supreme Court within a year of his appointment. Following the Vinson interlude, the reins were returned to the bankers and financiers with the appointment of John Snyder, vice-president of the First National Bank of St. Louis, who had served in a variety of ways during the war. George M. Humphrey (SR, Cleveland), head of the Hanna Mining Company, was President Eisenhower's first Secretary of the Treasury, to be followed by Robert B. Anderson, a Texas lawyer and financier who had moved on to New York finance. President Kennedy's choice for the position was Republican Douglas Dillon (SR, NY), the head of the Wall Street finance firm of Dillon, Read Company. Five of the eight—Woodin, Acheson, Morgenthau, Humphrey, and Dillon —were members of the upper class, and two others—Snyder and Anderson —were members of the power elite.

Of the 13 men who have been Secretary of Defense or Secretary of War since 1932, eight have been listed in the *Social Register*. The others are bankers and corporation executives, and clearly members of the power elite. However, different elements of the upper class have occupied the position during different eras. During the 1930's, when economic recovery was the dominant concern and war a lesser one, the department was headed by Western members of the upper class. President Roosevelt's first choice was a Western gold mining magnate, George Dern, a former governor of Utah. His next choice, banker Harry Woodring, was a former governor of Kansas. During the 1940's, the war and postwar years, the Democrats called first on a Wall Street lawyer, Henry L. Stimson (SR, NY), who had been Secretary of State under Hoover. A product of both Yale and Harvard, Stimson was a Republican. His chief aides were also from Wall Street and the *Social Register*: Robert Patterson, John J. McCloy, and Robert Lovett. At war's end Stimson was followed by three more men from Wall Street: Patterson, Kenneth C. Royall, and James V. Forrestal.[44] Following Forrestal's tenure, three men served a year apiece as Secretary of Defense during the final three years of the Truman Administration— lawyer Louis A. Johnson, former Secretary of State George C. Marshall, and investment banker Robert Lovett (SR, NY) of Brown Brothers,

Harriman and Company. Except for one brief interlude, lawyers and financiers from the East did not dominate the Defense Department during the 1950's and early 1960's. President Eisenhower's first two appointees to the position were Midwestern corporation executives, Charles E. Wilson of General Motors and Neil H. McElroy (SR, Cincinnati) of Procter and Gamble. The third person to occupy the position during Eisenhower's Administration was banker Thomas S. Gates, Jr. (SR, Philadelphia), who became president of the Morgan Guaranty Trust Company in 1965. President Kennedy's choice for the position was a Midwestern corporate chief, Robert McNamara of the upper-class-controlled Ford Motor Company.

Four of the 11 Attorneys-General to serve between 1932 and 1964 can be accorded upper-class status: Francis Biddle (1941-1945), Herbert Brownell, Jr. (1953-1957), Robert F. Kennedy (1961-1964), and Nicholas Katzenbach (1964-1966). A fifth, William P. Rogers (1957-1961), came to the government from Kenneth Royall's Wall Street law firm and can be considered a member of the power elite. The remaining six, all Democrats, were local lawyers who had usually worked in city and state politics. Four of the recent Secretaries of Commerce are from the upper class: Averell Harriman, Charles Sawyer (SR, Cincinnati), Sinclair Weeks (SR, Boston), and Lewis Strauss (SR, NY). Four others are big businessmen: Texas banker Jesse Jones; Michigan financier Frederick Mueller; former North Carolina governor Luther Hodges, who was a vice-president of Marshall Field & Co. before receiving the call to run for governor; and John T. Connor, the former president of Merck and Company. As Grant McConnell shows in his book on *Private Power and American Democracy,* big businessmen have developed innumerable ties to the Commerce Department, not the least of which is the Business Advisory Council which had so much prominence during the 1950's.

President Roosevelt's first and only Secretary of Labor, Frances Perkins, was a reform-minded member of the Boston branch of the upper class who had spent many years in social work and in liberal causes. President Truman's choices to head Labor, Lewis Schwellenbach and Maurice Tobin, were a lawyer and a politician, respectively. Tobin had been a white-collar worker for New England Telephone and Telegraph for 15 years before being elected mayor of Boston (1938-1944) and governor of Massachusetts (1945-1946). The Secretary of Labor for all but a few months of the Eisenhower Administration was James P. Mitchell, the vice-president of Bloomingdale's, one of New York's largest department stores. The only man labor has had in the department's leadership since 1932, Martin P. Durkin of the plumbers' union, lasted only a short time before his replacement by Mitchell. Labor had someone who was almost one of its own in the first Kennedy appointee, lawyer Arthur Goldberg, a leading union lawyer and legal counselor. He was followed by W. Willard Wirtz (SR, Chicago), a former law partner of Adlai Stevenson. In summary, three Secretaries of Labor—Perkins, Mitchell, and Wirtz—are members of the power elite; their tenures encompass 23 of the 32 years between 1933 and 1965. This is a very good record in what should be labor's main stronghold in a pluralistic government. It would seem that labor's say-so is filtered through the ear of one or another member or representative of the American business aristocracy.

It is not yet clear what the leadership pattern will be for the Department of Health, Education, and Welfare, which was created in 1953. President Eisenhower's first two appointments were a member of the Houston branch of the upper class, publisher Oveta Culp Hobby, and a corporation executive, Marion Folsom, president of Eastman Kodak and a trustee of Harvard University and the Brookings Institution. However, his third choice was a lawyer–intellectual, Arthur S. Flemming, who was president of Ohio Wesleyan University at the time of his appointment. President Kennedy first appointed Connecticut governor Abraham Ribicoff, a corporation lawyer who was the first major political figure to support Kennedy's Presidential candidacy. He was followed by Anthony Celebrezze, the mayor of Cleveland, Ohio. The Johnson appointment was John Gardner, president of the Carnegie Corporation. At least three of the six—Hobby, Folsom, and Gardner—are members of the power elite. However, it must be remembered that this department is not essential to members of the American upper class, who have excellent health, private schools, and no need for welfare.

The remaining Cabinet posts, Interior, Agriculture, and Postmaster-General, are not outposts of the power elite. Only one person from these three departments, former Postmaster-General J. Edward Day (SR, Chicago), was a member of the upper class or power elite. If the power elite controls the Department of the Interior, it is through special committees such as those which advise the Department of Commerce.[45] If it controls the Department of Agriculture, it does so indirectly. Perhaps this pattern will change, however, for agriculture is fast becoming "agri-business" as large corporations begin to move into what was until recently the least oligopolistic of American industries.

The men who have run the major departments of the Executive branch can also be studied in terms of the administration they served. President Roosevelt drew from the liberal and ethnic elements of the upper class (e.g., Perkins and Morgenthau), and he showed his bipartisanship by choosing renegade rather than orthodox Republicans (e.g., Woodin).

With the coming of the war, President Roosevelt turned to the Wall Street and heavy-industry factions of the upper class (*e.g.*, Stimson and Stettinius). President Truman relied upon the same circles that guided the Democrats during the war years, but he did not replace such New Dealers as Harold Ickes and Henry Wallace with equally liberal men. *Social Register* listees with legal and financial backgrounds such as Forrestal, Acheson, Harriman, Patterson, and Lovett were the key figures of his administration. President Eisenhower's Cabinet was the most obviously tied to the biggest of big businesses, particularly heavy industry, that had been seen in Washington for many years, so much so that some critics claimed Mills was mistaking a momentary aberration for a trend when he used examples from the 1950's to support his thesis that the corporate rich were moving into the federal government. President Eisenhower's Secretary of State, Dulles, was from the largest of Wall Street firms, Sullivan and Cromwell, as well as from one of the largest of foundations, the Rockefeller Foundation. His Secretary of the Treasury, Humphrey, was from one of the largest corporate complexes in the country, the Hanna Mining Company. His Secretary of Defense, Wilson, was the president of the largest industrial firm in the country, General Motors. As was typical of the Republican Party until at least the mid-1960's, there was not a non-WASP in the collection. While the ethnic diversity of the old Democrats returned with Kennedy, the idealistic reformers did not. The Secretary of State, Rusk, was brought in from the same Rockefeller Foundation, although the Secretary of Defense, McNamara, came from a different motor car company —second-ranked Ford. The Secretary of the Treasury, Dillon, was a liberal Republican from Wall Street rather than a conservative one from the Midwest, and the Attorney-General, Robert Kennedy, was a rich Catholic from Boston rather than a rich Protestant from New York. Commerce was guided by a Southern businessman, Hodges, for the first time in several years; Goldberg, the Secretary of Labor, and Ribicoff, the Secretary of Health, Education, and Welfare, were Jewish, and Udall, the Secretary of the Interior, was Mormon.

By departments or by administrations, our analysis reveals that the upper class is very well represented where it really matters within the departments of the Executive branch. The power elite control State, Treasury, and Defense without question, and their influence is very great in Commerce, Labor, and HEW.[46] Ten years of experience since Mills wrote show that he was right when he characterized this epoch as that of the "political outsider"—"a man who has spent the major part of his working life outside strictly political organizations." [47] And, as Mills knew, this political outsider usually comes from the world of corporate business.

We can conclude this section by noting that this policy continued under President Johnson and that it permeates lower levels of the departments as well:

Usually the men Macy [Johnson's private-school-educated "headhunter"] wants for sub-Cabinet positions are men who hold middle-level executive jobs in big corporations or law firms and obviously are headed for the top.[48]

THE PRESIDENT'S INNER CIRCLE

A President's circle does not consist solely of Cabinet members. He also has an entourage of special emissaries, advisers, speechwriters, and secretaries. The first two categories, emissaries and advisers, are of substantive importance, although it is often speechwriters and secretaries who gain notoriety. President Roosevelt relied upon different advisers and emissaries as circumstances dictated. Early in the New Deal the most important members of the Brain Trust, as his advisers were called, included Supreme Court Justice Louis Brandeis, a Jewish member of the upper class who had graduated from Harvard and lived for many years in the inner circles of Proper Boston; A. A. Berle, Jr. (SR, NY), a corporation lawyer; Raymond Moley, a criminologist who was Professor of Public Law at Columbia; and Felix Frankfurter, "scion of a long line of rabbis," who came to this country at the age of 12 and was a law professor at Harvard by the time he was 30.[49] Moley, who had planned a model parole system for Franklin Roosevelt when the latter was governor of New York, brought other Columbia professors to the aid of the President. Frankfurter was also doubly important because he supplied many of the lesser members of the Brain Trust from among his Harvard students. John Carter estimates in *The New Dealers* that there were 75 to 100 Frankfurter-trained lawyers in the early New Deal:

As graduates of Harvard Law School, these New Deal attorneys reflect Brandeis and Frankfurter in their line of thought. Each year for many years a star man from Harvard Law was assigned to Holmes and Brandeis. Eight of them have been prominent in the Roosevelt Administration.[50]

Such conservative Democratic members of the upper class as Colonel Edward House and Bernard Baruch, who were important advisers to Woodrow Wilson, had a lesser role under President Roosevelt. However, two of Baruch's closest associates, Hugh Johnson and Gerard Swope, had important advisory functions. Johnson was the head of the NRA, a plan for the centralized control of big business by big business that very much resembled a plan that had been advocated for some time by Swope, the president of General Electric and first head of the Business Advisory

Council, and the only businessman who really counted in the Brain Trust. Another businessman with some standing was Walter C. Teagle (SR, Cleveland) of Standard Oil of New Jersey, who was head of the NRA's Industrial Advisory Board. Teagle had joined Thomas Watson (SR, NY) of IBM in congratulating James Gerard in 1929 for his acid comments concerning certain Wall Street financial manipulations.[51]

If President Roosevelt turned to friends of the farmer such as Henry Wallace, Rexford Tugwell of Columbia, and George Warren of Cornell for advice on domestic matters, he left foreign problems to members of the upper class. Among the *Social Register* listees who advised him or served as special emissaries were financiers Thomas Lamont and Norman Davis, and lawyer–industrialist Myron Taylor of U. S. Steel.[52] Until his disagreement over a complete abandonment of the gold standard, James P. Warburg, the wealthy Jewish financier whose father helped write the Federal Reserve Act of 1914, was a monetary consultant.[53] This reliance on members of the upper class for foreign policy advice was in keeping with the upper-class composition of the State Department, where William Phillips served as Undersecretary and Sumner Welles and Francis Bowes Sayre were assistant secretaries.

President Eisenhower's advisers did not differ in character from the men who made up his Cabinet.* They included such big businessmen as Lucius Clay, Paul Hoffman, and Robert Cutler, and such nonbusinessmen as lawyer Bernard Shanley (SR, NY), lawyer Gerald Morgan (SR, NY), publisher C. D. Jackson (SR, NY), and former Senator Henry Cabot Lodge (SR, Boston). Democrats Kennedy and Johnson relied upon a quartet of special emissaries—Lodge, Harriman, Ellsworth Bunker (SR, NY), and General Maxwell D. Taylor. Taylor became a *Social Register* listee himself after retiring from the Army to preside over the Rockefeller-sponsored Lincoln Center for the Performing Arts. Another important adviser and emissary for both Democratic Presidents of the 1960's was Republican McGeorge Bundy (SR, Boston).

Lyndon Johnson's personal advisers were mostly corporation lawyers and businessmen. Topping the list in the first category was New Dealer Abe Fortas, a product of Yale Law School and a director of a handful of minor corporations, mostly in retail businesses.[54] Right behind him was another Jewish member of the power elite who rose to prominence, Edwin Weisl, a Wall Street lawyer and New York National Committeeman for the Democratic Party. Weisl was also the millionaire President's personal financial adviser. Another prominent New Deal lawyer who advised President Johnson was Catholic Thomas G. Corcoran, a drug industry attorney

* The most important men around Truman were studied on pp. 97-98.

whose brother is president of three international subsidiaries of Sterling Drugs.[55] A Truman adviser who was also close to President Johnson was lawyer Clark Clifford, revealed in 1965 by Senator Albert Gore of Tennessee to be representing the du Ponts in their efforts for tax relief on the forced sale of their General Motors stock ordered by the courts.[56] The businessmen closest to President Johnson were Democrat Donald C. Cook, president of American Electric Power, a utilities holding company, and Republican Robert B. Anderson, a former Texan and Secretary of the Treasury, who became an investment adviser for wealthy individuals and corporations in New York. Eugene Black, a Southern aristocrat, formerly of Chase Manhattan Bank and the World Bank, was the President's adviser on foreign and domestic economic problems. His first chore was a special aid mission to Southeast Asia. A relatively unknown adviser was George R. Brown, head of the huge, Texas-based construction firm of Brown and Root. Brown had been one of President Johnson's major financial backers since the 1940's. In summarizing the character of Lyndon B. Johnson's circle of influential advisers, Charles Roberts sheds further light on the differences among the cliques within the upper class which control the Executive branch:

Predictably, Lyndon Johnson's friends outside government bear little resemblance to John Kennedy's (mostly wealthy Eastern prep-school and college classmates) or Dwight Eisenhower's (mostly golf-happy millionaire businessmen). Remarkably, nearly all in Lyndon Johnson's outside circle are, like Fortas, lawyers who have dabbled in politics.[57]

THE DIPLOMATIC CORPS

Although not as important as in the past, when transportation and communication were somewhat slower, the diplomat is nonetheless an important part of the President's team. The social backgrounds of diplomats can be summarized with the following formula: Upper-class persons go to important countries; members of the foreign service and political patronage appointments go to lesser countries. The upper-class origins of diplomats to leading countries, almost guaranteed by the low salaries and high entertainment expenses of such diplomats, were shown in an unpublished study by Suzanne Keller, which is summarized in her book *Beyond the Ruling Class*. Keller believes that the "ruling class" has been replaced by "strategic elites" of high intellectual and technical skill. Apparently, wealthy businessmen are not members of the upper class in her classification:

In countries with a feudal past, diplomats are often drawn from the upper classes of society. The United States, lacking such a past, has generally drawn its ambassadors or ministers from circles of wealthy businessmen or from old New

England or Southern plantation families. Keller collected information about the backgrounds of 120 American ambassadors (and ministers, where no embassies existed) sent to the following ten countries between 1900 and 1953: Great Britain, France, the USSR, Germany, Italy, Spain, Turkey, Iran, Japan, and China. (See "Twentieth Century Ambassadors," unpublished manuscript.) One-third of the 120 men could be classified as members of a native aristocracy of old landed wealth; another third, as members of a native plutocracy of financial and commercial wealth. The former was particularly prevalent among career diplomats (one-third of all), whereas the latter prevailed among political appointees (two-thirds of all). The majority of this elite came from families engaged in business or the professions. . . . Four-fifths held college degrees; one-half, graduate degrees, mostly in law. One-third of the group had attended private preparatory schools, and two-fifths had received their degrees from Ivy League colleges. . . .[58]

Keller's findings are in agreement with those reported by Mills. Of 32 top ambassadors and ministers for 1942, almost one-half were graduates of exclusive private schools. Of 118 top officers in the Foreign Service for that year, 51 were from Harvard, Princeton, and Yale.[59] For specific examples Mills mentions President Eisenhower's diplomats to seven leading countries: Great Britain, France, Canada, Australia, Portugal, Italy, and the USSR. Six of the seven—Winthrop Aldrich, Douglas Dillon, R. Douglas Stuart, Amos J. Peaslee, Mrs. Clare Booth Luce, and Charles E. Bohlen— are in the *Social Register*. The seventh, Robert M. Guggenheim, is one of a handful of upper-class Jews who is a Republican. Nor was the situation any different under the Democrats during the New Deal, with five of the seven key appointments going to members of the upper class:

Robert Worth Bingham, a member of the Southern branch of the upper class, was ambassador to England. He contributed $10,000 to Franklin D. Roosevelt's pre-convention fund in 1932.

Jesse Straus of R. H. Macy & Co., a Jewish member of the upper class, was ambassador to France. He too was a pre-convention backer of Franklin D. Roosevelt in 1932.

Breckenridge Long (SR, St. Louis), still another large pre-convention donor, was ambassador to Italy.

Joseph C. Grew (SR, Boston), a cousin of J. P. Morgan, was a career diplomat who was ambassador to Japan.

William C. Bullitt (SR, Philadelphia) was the United States's first ambassador to Soviet Russia after 16 years of nonrecognition.

William E. Dodd, a professor of history at the University of Chicago, was ambassador to Germany. He was not of the upper class.

Nelson Johnson, a career foreign service officer, was ambassador to China.

A cursory look at the 1964 diplomats shows that the picture has not changed since the studies by Keller and Mills. Using the *Social Register* as the only criterion for upper-class membership, unless the person was known to us from other studies, one-fourth of the 103 diplomats for that year were members of the upper class. Most of them were stationed in leading countries. For example:

David K. E. Bruce (SR, NY) was ambassador to England.

Charles E. Bohlen (SR, Philadelphia) was ambassador to France.

George McGhee, a Houston oilman who married a De Golyer of old Texas oil money, was ambassador to Germany. He had previously served as an ambassador to Turkey, a consultant to the National Security Council, and an Undersecretary of State for Political Affairs.

Chester Bowles, one of the more liberal members of the upper class, was ambassador to India.

G. Frederick Reinhardt (SR, SF) was ambassador to Italy.

John M. Cabot (SR, Boston) was ambassador to Poland.

J. Graham Parsons (SR, NY) was ambassador to Sweden.

Outerbridge Horsey (SR, NY) was ambassador to Czechoslovakia.

In summary, we can note that the diplomats to major countries are very likely to be members of the American upper class. While we agree that the diplomatic corps is not the most vital force in the lives of most Americans, it should be emphasized that it is of considerable importance to members of the upper class, who venture far and wide for business and pleasure.

Having shown power elite domination of the Executive branch, we can now turn our attention to the regulatory agencies, the federal judiciary, and the Congress.

THE REGULATORY AGENCIES

The unwieldy bureaucracy of regulatory agencies, which are often styled as a fourth branch of government, is a jungle of self-contained entities, each one beholden to the constituent group it is supposed to regulate. There are 9 such agencies, among the best known of which are the Federal Trade Commission (FTC), the Federal Communications Commission (FCC), the Interstate Commerce Commission (ICC), the Securities and Exchange Commission (SEC), and the Federal Power Commission (FPC). The constituent groups—the industries of the American business aristocracy that the agencies supposedly regulate—control the regulatory agencies in several ways. First, through committees and associations of specific industries, the industries give advice to the agencies. Second, they are able to control key appointments to the agencies by providing as candidates for the positions corporation executives, corporation lawyers, and various other salaried specialists.[60] Most importantly, the industries can appeal to the President to block appointments that are not acceptable to them. Indeed, appointive power is the only power which the Executive branch legally holds over the regulatory agencies, which are not responsible to it. However, the importance of this appointive power can be seen in certain of President Eisenhower's appointments, which were explained by economist Seymour Harris:

Former congressman Albert M. Cole had voted against most public housing measures, so he was made head of the Housing and Home Finance Agency.

John B. Hollister was an outspoken isolationist, so he was the perfect choice to guide the International Cooperation Association.

"The chairman of the Federal Power Commission, Jerome F. Kuykendall, who was supposed to represent the public against the public utilities, had represented gas utilities in cases before the United States Public Service Commission." [61]

Since no government report or academic study yet published contradicts our claim that those who are supposedly being regulated dominate the regulatory agencies, it is not necessary to go into laborious detail on any one agency. The reader is referred to Henry Kariel's *The Decline of American Pluralism,* Bernard Nossiter's *The Mythmakers,* and Grant McConnell's *Private Power and American Democracy* for relevant examples and detailed bibliography. A quote from one of the sources on regulatory agencies will suffice. It is from Judge Lee Loevinger, who was head of the Antitrust Division of the Department of Justice at the time of the drug hearings in the early 1960's:

Unfortunately, the history of every regulatory agency in the government is that it comes to represent the industry or groups it's supposed to control. All of these agencies were fine when they were first set up, but before long they became infiltrated by the regulatees and are now more or less run by and for them. It's not a question of venality, either. More, the agency people consort with this or that representative of some special-interest group, and finally they all come to think alike. Every company that's concerned about government control and is big enough to manage it hires a man—or maybe four or five men —at anywhere from thirty to seventy thousand dollars a year to find out what we're up to. And, by God, they find out! They wine and dine the agency people and get to be great friends with them. Like a lot of people without much money, some bureaucrats are impressed by being around big shots and by the big life. Sooner or later, all of these agencies end up with constituents. And they represent them damned well, too.[62]

THE FEDERAL JUDICIARY

If members of the American upper class control the federal judiciary, it is not through the means which give them control of the Executive branch and the regulatory agencies, for such techniques are not part of the tradition which has given the courts their important place in the American system. Furthermore, members of the Supreme Court and the lower federal judiciary are appointed for life, which gives them considerable independence. However, it is also true that members of the judiciary are selected by the President. Granting that members of the upper class cannot control specific decisions by the courts, we would argue that the President's appointive power gives members of the upper class control of the "character" of the judges in terms of their socioeconomic status, their training, and their beliefs, and that this is, in the long run, control of the federal judiciary by members of the upper class.*

Along with Presidential appointive power, members of the upper class have one other control over the federal judiciary, namely, the Committee of the Federal Judiciary of the American Bar Association:

Working through an 11-member committee of lawyers, the ABA has won for itself the privilege of evaluating at a very early stage in the search for candidates, the merits of each person seriously considered by the Attorney-General for nomination to the federal bench. While the Committee's actual influence has varied with the Administration in power, it has had, at a minimum, considerable success in deterring the nomination of judges it deems unqualified. . . . [During the Eisenhower Administration], Attorney-General Rogers was under instructions not to recommend a nomination over the objections of the Committee except in unusual circumstances. . . . During the first two years of the Kennedy Administration, 158 adverse reports were made, of which eight were disregarded by the Attorney-General.[64]

Members of this committee are selected by the president of the American Bar Association with the advice of the incumbent committee chairman. In the case of Bernard Segal, chairman of the committee from 1956 through 1962, the power to advise the bar president was in effect power to appoint. A graduate of the University of Pennsylvania, Segal is a member of one of Philadelphia's most eminent upper-class law firms, Schnader, Harrison, Segal, and Lewis. He is a Jewish member of the power elite. Who are the other members of the committee? To answer this question Joel Grossman studied a sample of 51 men which included all those who had served from 1946 to 1962.[65] He found that they tended to come from large law firms,

---

* It is true that the Senate has the power to advise and consent on such appointments, but this negative power is seldom exercised.[63]

to have distinguished careers within the ABA, and to live in cities with populations over 100,000. James Moore supplemented Grossman's study by compiling more detailed information on 28 of the men who served between 1953 and 1963.[66] Eight of these 28 men—29 per cent—were members of the upper class. Three more were from large (power elite) law firms, four others had attended Harvard Law School, and five others were corporation directors. The rest came from elite law schools in their region, such as the University of Virginia and the University of Michigan. Except for those who lived in states where we have little information on the upper class, most of the non-upper-class committee members were in socially elite clubs.*

Who are the men finally chosen as judges? In terms of the lower federal judiciary, they are men politically acceptable to local and state politicians, who usually recommended them to Washington friends in the first place, and politically and professionally acceptable to the judiciary committee of the ABA. A study by Moore of 25 judges from six of the 11 circuit courts and the U. S. Court of Customs and Patents revealed that three were members of the upper class and that 20 had attended Ivy League schools. Thirteen of the 25 judges were from Harvard and Yale alone. Twenty had been invited into one or more of the socially elite clubs listed in the 12 city editions of the *Social Register*. Since Moore chose his districts with the hope of maximizing the number of upper-class judges, it was necessary for us to look also at a circuit that would minimize that possibility. The fifth circuit, which encompasses the Deep South and Texas, had two judges who could be considered members of the upper class and four who could not. It can be concluded that most of the judges of the lower federal judiciary are not members of the upper class, but that they have rather substantial professional and political credentials that are carefully checked beforehand by a legal arm of the power elite, the Committee of the Federal Judiciary.

Turning to the Supreme Court, the situation is not different in terms of socioeconomic status, training, and political connections. John Schmidhauser, in *The Supreme Court,* reported on his study of the 92 Supreme Court justices between 1789 and 1959. He found that the justices came

from socially advantaged families. . . . In the earlier history of the Court, he very likely was born in the aristocratic gentry class, although later he tended to come from the professionalized upper-middle class. . . . It seems reasonable to assume that very few sons of families outside the upper, or upper-middle,

* One of the requirements of the committee is that it have at least one member from each federal court circuit, so there are necessarily members from all parts of the country.

social and economic classes have been able to acquire the particular type of education and the subsequent professional, and especially political, associations which appear to be unwritten prerequisites for appointment to the nation's highest tribunal.[67]

In summary, we believe that the findings of Schmidhauser, Grossman, and Moore support our contention that the appointive power of the President, in conjunction with the ABA committee, gives members of the power elite control over the socioeconomic and intellectual character of the federal judiciary. Their studies show that federal judges come from the higher levels of society, have an elite education, and are politically and professionally acceptable to lawyers and politicians who are members of the power elite. This does not deny the obvious fact of diversity of opinion on some issues among federal judges. However, it is unlikely that this diversity of opinion is due to any disagreement with the basic foundations of the American business aristocracy.

THE CONGRESS

Power in Congress lies in the committees, particularly in the committee chairmanships. Like everyone else, members of the power elite try to influence Congress by working through these committees. Although there are few members of the upper class in the Senate, they have a slight advantage over other interest groups because committee appointments are controlled by the Senate Establishment, the leaders of both parties who have gained power through long tenure in office. And, as Senator Joseph S. Clark notes, this establishment has mild overtones of plutocracy.[68] These mild overtones appear more obviously in Donald Matthews' study of the social backgrounds of committee chairmen, reported in his book, *U. S. Senators and Their World*. Matthews found that 7 per cent of the senators who served between 1947 and 1957 were "patricians," men from families of recognized status and wealth.[69] They tended to be elected to the Senate at a younger age than other senators, to stay longer, and to have more than their share of committee chairmanships. In fact, the patricians held 17 per cent of the chairmanships, an overrepresentation of 2.4. Their committee memberships tended to be concentrated in Armed Forces, Appropriations, and Foreign Relations. They tended to be underrepresented on all other committees except for Labor, "on which a small group of patrician reformers served during the postwar years." The situation did not change during the early 1960's. We found that 15 per cent of the senators in the 89th Congress were members of the American upper class. The increase over Matthews' percentage is due to the fact that he used a very strict criterion for "patrician"—senators were assigned to this category "only if the evidence was overwhelmingly in favor of doing so." * The increase is also due to the influx of Kennedys in 1964 and the election of two upper-class senators from Maryland, Joseph Tydings and Daniel B. Brewster. The best known of the upper-class senators in 1964 were J. William Fulbright, Leverett Saltonstall, Stuart Symington, and Thruston B. Morton. One other well-known senator, Clifford Case of New Jersey, was a member of a large Wall Street law firm before being elected to the Senate, so he can be considered a member of the power elite.[71]

However, compared with our findings for corporations, foundations, and the Executive branch, the overrepresentation of the upper class in the Senate is rather small, only 30 times what would be expected if all socio-economic levels contributed their proportionate share of senators. Furthermore, such figures do not take into consideration the House of Representatives, where a cursory check suggested a mere handful of upper-class representatives, concentrated in the states of New York, New Jersey, Ohio, and Pennsylvania. We would therefore conclude that members of the American upper class do not control the Legislative branch but rather have influence. Thus, like other interest groups, members of the power elite have to turn to that well-known activity termed "lobbying," which has been tax deductible since 1962 as part of the Kennedy Administration's tax reforms.†

It is difficult to assess the importance of lobbying, for such an assessment would require a detailed and always difficult study of the decision-making process. Thus, there is no general agreement among scholars as to its efficacy. What the studies show is that most lobbying is done by business associations and that they are most effective when their intent is to block legislation rather than create it.[72] It can also be shown that some lobbyists are more prominent than others. For example, Lyndon Johnson's friend and financial backer, Alfred Dale Miller, lobbyist for Texas Gulf Sulphur, chaired Johnson's inaugural committee, while Irving Davidson, lobbyist for the millionaire Murchinson brothers of Texas, was used by the State Department to contact a person who was a possible candidate to resolve the impasse during the 1965 Dominican Crisis.‡ [73]

There are many historical instances which suggest the power of lobby-

* "Patrician politicians are senators who came from 'old families' and had served ten or more years in public office, or had been in office more than 30 per cent of their adult lives." [70]

† See Bernard Nossiter, *The Mythmakers,* and Hobart Rowen, *The Free Enterprisers,* for two detailed accounts by Washington reporters on the power of big business in the Kennedy Administration.

‡ No one knows how much money lobbyists give to congressional political campaigns, but considerable cash is said to change hands by those who have worked for congressmen.[74]

ing—the exploits of the insurance companies and the National Association of Manufacturers in the early decades of this century are legendary—but there is no better example than that reported by Richard Harris in *The Real Voice,* an account of the drug industry hearings of the early 1960's. Apparently to enhance the value of his investigations, the late Senator Estes Kefauver selected Harris "to be a kind of royal scribe to the proceedings, and he let him in on secrets perhaps more intimate than any politician has ever shared with a journalist." The same reviewer we have just quoted continues, "Harris' subsequent hard work has left a book that tells a great deal, not just about the drug bill, but about the mechanisms and machinations of Congress, and about the uses of power in contemporary America." [75] Suffice it to say here that through its friends in the Congress, on the White House staff, in the regulatory agencies, and in the Department of Health, Education, and Welfare, the drug industry completely eliminated the drug bill's price-cutting provisions, which would have reduced its unbelievable profit rates. Only the sad but timely scandal over thalidomide saved the bill's safety provisions, previously attacked as bureaucratic and unnecessary by the industry. Such examples could be multiplied endlessly, but since they prove nothing as far as most social scientists are concerned, we will not belabor the point. We can conclude that the corporations which are controlled by the American business aristocracy are the most active of lobbyists and are probably as successful as any of their counterparts who make up the multitude of interest groups which are constantly at work in and around the Legislative branch of the federal government.

The American business aristocracy also attempts to influence Congress indirectly through the shaping of public opinion. If the effort is concentrated on one congressman's constituency, hopefully leading to mountains of mail for him to ponder, the technique is called "grass roots publicity." The tactic can also be used on a national scale, as the utilities do in their full-page advertisements decrying public power.[76] On more general issues, opinion is shaped through the President and the prestigious associations and committees detailed in Chapter 3. Sometimes the President works in conjunction with a special committee drawn from the power elite. For example, to counter the attack on foreign aid a new committee was formed, the National Committee for International Development. Its chairman was Sol Linowitz of Xerox Corporation, and its bipartisan membership included Eugene Black, former president of the World Bank, General Alfred M. Gruenther, and John J. McCloy.[77] To counteract agitation against the war in Vietnam, still another committee was formed whose membership read, as *The Nation* noted, like a *Who's Who* of the American Establishment. Its members included Arthur H. Dean of Sullivan and Cromwell, Dean Acheson, Eugene

R. Black, James B. Conant, John Cowles, Thomas S. Gates, Roswell L. Gilpatric, David Rockefeller, and John J. McCloy.[78]

Such less than perfect techniques as lobbying and the manipulation of public opinion must be stressed in the case of Congress because, to repeat, members of the American upper class do not control Congress. The Congressman's business connections tend to be minor and local in nature. For example, one-third of the members of Congress are estimated to have investments in local radio and television stations.[79] The power of these local interests is enhanced by the seniority system which guides the Legislative branch, for the locally oriented representative or senator who is constantly re-elected often has a dominant role on one or more committees. Because of their veto and delaying powers, these local interests have been able in many cases to exact their price for legislation considered essential by an Executive branch which is dominated by representatives of the American upper class. This price is most often limited welfare spending.

In summary, we have argued for the ascendancy of the Executive branch within the federal government, and we agree with Mills when he says:

The growth of the Executive branch of the government, with its agencies that patrol the complex economy, does not mean merely the "enlargement of government" as some sort of autonomous bureaucracy: it has meant the ascendancy of the corporation's man as a political eminence.[80]

This emphasis on the rise of the corporate rich as the key element in the federal government is in agreement with the detailed study, *The Politics of Oil,* by Engler, who concludes by dismissing the theory that big government is somehow a "countervailing power" to big business:

The image of government as a countervailing force fails to meet the empirical test of how legislative policy is made and how government regulation actually works.[81]

Engler's opinion is based upon a decision-making analysis of issues basic to the oil industry. We have reached the same conclusion by studying the sociological composition of the branches and departments of the federal government.[82]

Chapter Five ....
The Military, the CIA, and the FBI ....

The institutions to be considered in this chapter are subservient aspects of the power elite. Nonetheless, they are part of the elite of power because of the enormous resources they are permitted to mobilize once decisions have been made by the members and representatives of the upper class who control them through the Executive branch of the federal government and through other ties which are unique to each one of the three. In relegating the military to a subsidiary role, we are explicitly denying the importance Mills gave to the "military ascendancy." At the same time, the major aim of this chapter, in addition to demonstrating upper-class control of the CIA and FBI, is to show how and why Mills was wrong in his emphasis on the military, thus removing one of the major objections to the idea that the American upper class is a governing class.

THE MILITARY

The military, as historian Bruce Catton documented in 1948 in *The War Lords of Washington,* has become an important part of the American system. About the origin of its new prominence there can be little doubt. The majority of commentaries since Catton's can be summarized by saying that the necessities of World War II and the Cold War inevitably brought the military into its prominent role, while the profitability of a permanent war economy endeared it to those who feared that a depression might result from a drop in defense spending.[1] However, for all its awesome power, which each book on the new military tries to make comprehensible with startling statistics and amazing comparisons, the role of the military remains a subservient one within the American context. It was on this one point that the varied critics of Mills's *The Power Elite* were in unanimous agreement—he attached too much importance to the position of the military.

Much of Mills's argument for the newly acquired status of the admirals and generals was based upon the presence of leading military figures in high posts in business, government, and education. However, a more recent and comprehensive study of retired military officers by sociologist Morris Janowitz shows that the importance of these men continued to decline throughout the 1950's:

The practice of appointing military personnel to politically responsible posts, although it continues, has declined sharply since 1950. Much of the political debate about military personnel in government policy positions centers on a few conspicuous cases where civilian leadership sought to make use of prestigeful military officers to deal with difficult political problems.[2]

Janowitz further buttressed his point by showing that Hunter's list of 475 top leaders for the early 1950's included only three military men in addition to President Eisenhower. They were Carl Spaatz, a contributing editor to *Newsweek*; Lucius D. Clay, the oft-encountered Southern aristocrat; and James H. Doolittle, who has advanced degrees in aeronautical engineering from MIT and who spent the ten years from 1930 to 1940 as the manager of Shell Oil's aviation department before returning to active duty for World War II.[3] These three are hardly typical military men in that one has upper-class origins, a second worked for a large corporation for many years before the war, and the third has journalistic skills. Thus, it is likely that the prominent role given to military men *qua* military men during the late 1940's and early 1950's was a postwar phenomenon that was already beginning to fade when Mills's book appeared in 1956. Mills himself had the means for anticipating this decline in military influence at the highest levels, for he agreed with Janowitz' point that much of the military's apparent power was due to "civilian default." [4] It would seem that civilian default would be a likely occurrence in the first years after a major world war.*

The final reorganization of the Defense Department and the events of the early 1960's are also telling evidence against the thesis that the military has attained an equality of status with its corporate brethren within the

---

* Even though Janowitz is probably right about the decline of military men in *prominent* positions, it is true that they continue to be involved in minor positions within business and the federal government. Thousands of retired military officers are employed by corporations, while a change in the law during the early 1960's which allows retired military officers to draw part of their retirement pay while working for the government has swelled their numbers in the civilian civil service. Angry civilian employees of the government claim that there are 200,000 retired military officers working in the Washington bureaucracy, and that many are hired at very high civil service ranks over civilian employees of long tenure. This would not surprise Janowitz, who warned in 1960 that large numbers of officers would be eligible for retirement in 1962 after 20 years of service.[5]

power elite. In 1959, for example, the Army Chief of Staff noted that there were 19 civilian layers between him and the President, and Robert Mc-Namara subordinated the military even further during the 1960's.[6] Nor were the changes during the late 1950's and early 1960's a sudden reaction to a military upsurge. The whole defense structure had been undergoing change since the postwar period. The heads of the service departments were removed from the Cabinet and made subservient to a Secretary of Defense who by law could not be a military person. To handle military policy, a National Security Council was created which does not include any military officials.

Control of the military by members of the upper class is best demonstrated through a study of the personnel heading the Department of Defense, which is responsible for the selection of top military leaders. There is no automatic succession to the highest ranks of the military, and the Executive branch of the government, through the Secretary of Defense, is free to choose its military chiefs from lesser-ranked personnel. An excellent example would be the selection of George C. Marshall for Army Chief of Staff. A more recent example deserves to be quoted at some length:

Admiral Anderson, like General Lemnitzer, expressed his feelings on the subject of the exercise of authority when he spoke to the Navy League May 3, 1963, at San Juan, Puerto Rico. . . . Three days later the White House announced that Admiral Anderson, who had testified against McNamara in the TFX dispute, had been dropped as Chief of Naval Operations, to be succeeded by Admiral David B. McDonald, a relative unknown.[7]

The secretaries who have headed the Department of Defense have been discussed previously as members of the President's Cabinet, and it is only necessary to point out that of the eight men who have served in the post since it was created in 1947, five were listed in the *Social Register* and the remaining three were a corporation lawyer, a president of General Motors, and a president of the Ford Motor Company. Control by members of the upper class during the 1960's can be seen even more clearly by examining Secretary of Defense McNamara's civilian subordinates:[8]

Roswell L. Gilpatric (SR, NY), a graduate of Hotchkiss and Yale, was Deputy Undersecretary of Defense.

Cyrus R. Vance (SR, NY), a graduate of Kent School and Yale, was Gilpatric's successor.

Eugene M. Zuckert, Salisbury (a minor preparatory school) and Yale, was Secretary of the Air Force.

Paul H. Nitze, Hotchkiss and Yale, was Secretary of the Navy.

Stephen Ailes, Scarborough and Princeton, was Secretary of the Army.

William P. Bundy (SR, Boston), Groton and Harvard, brother of McGeorge Bundy, was Assistant Secretary for International Security Affairs.

Perhaps Mills did not give enough emphasis to the type of information we have just presented because he was influenced in his thinking as to the military's importance by Catton's *The War Lords of Washington*. In addition to borrowing the term "warlords"—he actually uses the phrase "the warlords of Washington" at one point—he gives us reason to suspect this influence by emphasizing Catton's discussion of the similarity of military and corporate views on reconversion to a peacetime economy. This is a particularly important point because Catton is misleading in the prominence he gives to the military in explaining the economic struggles that went on during the war. Mills and Catton are right to emphasize the war years as crucial ones in shaping the postwar power elite, but the conclusion we would draw is the one Catton mentions at the end of his book—the conservative "vested interests" were back in control.[9] This conclusion by Catton is very similar to a conclusion drawn by Mills but not emphasized enough by him:

During the New Deal the corporate chieftains joined the political directorate; as of World War II, they have come to dominate it. Long interlocked with government, now they have moved into quite full direction of the economy of the war effort and of the postwar era. This shift of the corporation executives into the political directorate has accelerated the long-term relegation of the professional politicians in the Congress to the middle levels of power.[10]

We believe that Catton's book, as well as more recent accounts, fully documents this "corporate ascendancy" rather than the "military ascendancy" which Mills stresses. This can be shown by a consideration of the all-important conflict over economic reconversion. Briefly, the dominant elements within the corporate rich were against reconversion to peacetime manufacture while the war was still on. Catton believes that this was due to the fear that gradual reconversion would have given an advantage to small producers, because the industrial giants were still producing for the war effort. In his own words, "devising and executing a reconversion plan would either make big industry more secure than ever or give big industry the scare of its life." [11] The conflict over reconversion began within the War Production Board, which was headed by Donald Nelson, a vice-president from Sears, Roebuck. Nelson had been recommended to Secretary of the Treasury Morgenthau by General Robert E. Wood (SR, Chicago), chairman of Sears. The No. 2 man on the WPB was Charles E. Wilson, the president of General Electric, who was considered indispensable by President Roosevelt and Director of Defense Mobilization James Byrnes. Nelson and Wilson were aided in their task of harnessing American economic power to the war effort by a staff of "500 business executives, the names of whose peacetime affiliations read like American industry's blue book." * [12] Most of these executives were known as "dollar-a-year men" because, although they continued to draw their same salary from their corporate employer, they only accepted a nominal salary from the government.[13] Nelson surprised his corporate brethren by siding with New Dealers and small business advocates who favored a reconversion program which would allow companies to begin peacetime manufacturing when defense spending began to drop, as it did in 1944. But Wilson and a majority of the other dollar-a-year men opposed such a plan, as did the War Department. It is here that Catton (and thus Mills) goes astray, perhaps because he follows an earlier account by his friend Nelson which tried to minimize the conflict within the WPB. Catton and Nelson seem to assume that "War Department" means "military men." In fact, as they well know, the War Department was run by a team of Wall Street lawyers and financiers— Secretary of War Henry L. Stimson and his assistants Robert L. Patterson, John J. McCloy, and Robert M. Lovett.

Equally important in this conflict was Secretary of the Navy James Forrestal, the former president of Dillon, Read, who sided with the War Department and the majority within the WPB. Forrestal had previously defeated Admiral Ernest J. King's attempts to get some autonomy in the procurement of equipment for the Navy.[14] All of this is important because Forrestal, Patterson, and Wilson were the main figures in Catton's story on reconversion.[15] The only military man of any consequence was Lucius D. Clay, the Georgia aristocrat. As the Army's Deputy for Procurement and Production, Clay had a staff which included such corporate executives as S. E. Skinner, later executive vice-president of General Motors; Frank Denton, later chairman of Mellon National Bank; and George Woods, later head of the International Bank.[16]

The disagreement over reconversion was ostensibly a battle between Nelson and Wilson. It ended when Nelson was sent on a special mission (slow boat) to China and Wilson resigned. A New Deal bureaucrat, J. A. Krug, was named head of the WPB. However, the board's real power was switched to former Supreme Court Justice James Byrnes, who was elevated from Director of War Mobilization to Director of War Mobilization and Reconversion.[17] Byrnes, already known to agree with the War Department

---

* For example, Byrnes's special assistant was Fred Searls, president of Newmont Mining Company. Wilson's was Sidney Weinberg of Goldman, Sachs.

position, named Clay as his Deputy Director for War Programs.* The result was that serious reconversion did not really begin until after the war ended.

Catton, and subsequently Mills, overemphasized the role of the military in this decision for two reasons. First, the War Department won out over the WPB, which implies military views dominating over civilian views. However, as Catton shows, the majority of the dollar-a-year men within the WPB were in agreement with the War Department, and, as we have emphasized, the War Department was dominated by members of the upper class. The second reason Catton and Mills overemphasized the military is that the military was in fact against any reconversion whatsoever for psychological reasons—it believed that any return to peacetime manufacture would cause a letdown in the defense effort. However, even though we do not find this psychological fact decisive, it was not merely the military that believed it. Forrestal, for example, was against the resumption of civilian production "not merely from the standpoint of production itself, but from the indirect psychological results that would flow—namely, the assumption that the war was in the bag." [18] Furthermore, we do not believe that the Army's arguments were the decisive factor, because of the evidence which shows that civilians dominated the military even during World War II. As Janowitz concludes:

A small group of civilians operated at the top levels of the War and Navy Departments, with considerable influence in fashioning organizational and procurement decisions. Strategic decisions were formulated by the President and his immediate trusted advisers, and major figures in the Joint Chiefs of Staff.[19]

We agree, not with Mills's theory that the military rose to a place of prominence within the power elite, but with the view presented by Tristam Coffin in *The Armed Society*. According to Coffin, the military was co-opted by the corporate rich. For example, he notes that leading businessmen actively sought the cooperation of military leaders:

Hints were dropped that after the fighting is over, Colonel McDuff, we can use a good man like you. In 1944, the campaign had progressed so splendidly that the president of General Electric, Charles E. Wilson, advocated to the Army Ordnance Association a working arrangement between the military and industry and a "permanent war economy." [20]

Coffin's comments are especially relevant because the man he mentions as

* Byrnes was also aided by his good friend Bernard Baruch (SR, NY), who had held a similar position to Byrnes's during World War I. The reader is referred to Chapter 14 of Byrnes's *All in One Lifetime* and to Margaret Coit's *Mr. Baruch* for further insight into the reconversion decision. See especially page 513 of *Mr. Baruch.*

a potential threat to control of the war effort by leading businessmen was General Brehon Somervall, commander of the Services of Supply. After the war General Somervall became chairman and president of the Koppers Company of Pittsburgh, an important part of the Mellon interest group.

There were other important economic issues besides reconversion during the war years that were decided in favor of the corporate rich and their dollar-a-year men:[21]

1. Dollar-a-year men were not prohibited as had been suggested by the Truman Committee.

2. The War Department defeated a proposal to centralize scientific and technical research on production in an office of the War Production Board. The result was that 40 per cent of the $1 billion spent during the war for research went to the ten largest private laboratories, 67 per cent to the 68 largest. This helped further economic concentration because of the next point.

3. Ninety per cent of the government research contracts gave any new patents to the company involved. (Contracts were negotiated in the War Department.)* Senator Russell Long spoke out on this point in 1965:

"But that policy was changed during World War II. From that time forward the Department of Defense has been granting private patent rights on research contracts.

"To change that policy is beyond my power. It is beyond the power of any member of the Senate or any member of the House of Representatives to change. Why? Because both large political parties depend for financial support upon people connected with big business and such people are numerous in both parties.

"They have friends. They have votes. They are powerful and influential. . . . I make that statement because I know the realities of public life . . . we know that those elements will do anything within their power to fight to see that they preserve what they have in the Department of Defense, which is a $9 billion a year investment in research. Those industries and investors have control over that research." [23]

4. Small business was excluded from any significant role in the war effort. In 1941, 75 per cent of all the money spent for mobilization went to 56 corporations. Between 1940 and 1944, 33 per cent of the supply contracts went to the top ten corporations, 67 per cent to the top 100 corporations. These contracts, along with their favorable clauses such as five-year amortization, helped further economic concentration in the largest companies.*

---

* In 1963, 70 per cent of all research and development funds in the United States came from the government, with 80 per cent of this going for defense and space research.[22]

* The situation did not change later. In 1963, 24 companies did 70 per cent of the defense business.[24]

5. Labor was excluded from any significant role in the economic decision-making process.

The close relationship that developed between the corporate rich and the government during the war continued into the postwar years in various advisory committees and dollar-a-year consultants; this story has been told in detail by Grant McConnell in *Private Power and American Democracy*. Then too, to reciprocate the tie, retired military officers moved into the corporate hierarchy. A study in 1959 found that "more than 1400 retired officers of the rank of major or higher—including 261 of general or flag rank—were in the pay of the 100 largest defense contractors." [25] The intermingling was especially marked in the aerospace industry. However, as Janowitz notes, only a few of these men were in positions of great responsibility.

In summarizing our account of this all-important problem of economic reconversion and postwar military–business cooperation, we believe that our close look at the leading decision-makers shows the subordinate role played by the military. The decisive role played by upper-class civilians and the co-optation of the military are the most obvious features of this critical turning point in the shaping of the American power structure for the postwar years.

But the presence of military men in business and of corporation leaders at the head of the Defense Department are by no means the only evidence for a postwar power elite which intertwines the corporations and the military. Just as important in cementing the military–industrial complex were the formal ties that developed:

The special interest groups that best epitomize the military–industrial complex are the organizations of military service supporters, such as the Association of the United States Army, the Air Force Association, and the Navy League. . . . The members are active, reserve, and retired members of the Armed Forces, defense contractors, community leaders, and other supporters. The organizations are financed by membership fees and sums from contractors who pay for exhibits at conventions, subscribe to various dinner meetings and rallies, and place advertisements in the official publications. [26]

The membership of each association reflects the traditions and interests of the service it represents. The Air Force Association, founded in 1946, is much more closely tied to a single segment of industry than the other groups: Janowitz found that most civilian members of the Air Force Association were executives of the aerospace industry. While we believe such men are evidence for the influence of big business on the Air Force, Janowitz adds that there are within the group "few important financial figures or socially prominent leaders." [27] This may be true for the association, but we would add that the men who control the major defense industries are members of the upper class. Two of the top ten in defense and space spending, General Electric and Chrysler, are also leaders in other fields; they were among the 20 industrials studied in an earlier chapter. As to the eight leading specialists in defense and space contracts—Lockheed, General Dynamics, Grumman, United Aircraft, North American Aviation, Boeing, McDonnell, and Aerojet-General—we found that 47 per cent of their 95 directors are members of the upper class. These boards include such powerful members of the upper class as Courtland Gross (SR, Philadelphia; Lockheed); Artemus L. Gates (SR, NY; Boeing); Crawford Greenewalt (SR, Philadelphia; Boeing); G. H. Weyerhauser (Boeing); Henry B. du Pont (North American); Robert M. Lovett (North American); Henry T. Mudd (North American); George S. Moore (SR, NY; United); John L. Collyer (SR, Buffalo; Grumman); and Frank Pace (SR, Philadelphia; General Dynamics).

The Navy Association, as contrasted with the Air Force Association, has prewar origins and a board "composed mainly of important investment bankers, industrialists of considerable reputation, and men of upper-class social backgrounds." [28] Thus, we need say no more about it. The Army Association, developed in 1957-1958, is the most recent of the associations. In addition to retired generals, its board includes investment bankers, industrialists, foundation executives, and university presidents:

Affiliations with the older Eastern upper social stratum are symbolized by such men as the president of the Association, Anthony J. D. Biddle of Philadelphia, who during World War II served as General Eisenhower's military diplomat to the European governments in exile at SHAEF headquarters; Henry Cabot Lodge, Jr., of Boston, who holds the reserve rank of brigadier general; and Ogden R. Reid of New York City.* [29]

Even if it is hard to assess the effects of these associations, as we have seen to be the case for any lobby, it cannot be overemphasized that they create most of the stir that is mistaken for military dominance. Their publications, for example, are an important part of the lobbying effort by the services, and these publications are financed by the corporations. Julius Duscha summarizes the Army's attempt to overrule the Defense Department on the production of Nike-Zeus anti-missile missiles as follows:

* Janowitz reports the following comment from his research into the board of the Army Association: "When the list first appeared one public relations officer commented to the author that 'a colonel in the chief of staff's office must have read C. W. Mills's *The Power Elite* and thought it was a good idea to have one.'" [30]

The weapon had not been tested to the satisfaction of the Defense Department, but the Army and Western Electric, the prime contractor for the project, put pressure for production of the missile on both Congress and the new Kennedy Administration. . . . The campaign began with an issue of *Army* Magazine featuring articles by generals praising the Nike-Zeus and advertisements by Western Electric and eight of the subcontractors for the project. . . . The Nike-Zeus issue of *Army* contained a map showing that 37 states were already sharing in the work and would get even more defense dollars once production began on a project that might cost $20 billion before it was completed. Soon the Senate and the House rang with speeches for Nike-Zeus production to start immediately.[31]

Duscha is equally perceptive when he generalizes that "throughout the 1950's the Army, Navy, and Air Force were able to generate support on Capitol Hill by using the pressure of firms with which the services had contracts." [32] In short, even military lobbying and military publicity are not evidence for a military ascendancy within the power elite. Military leaders are subordinate to the corporate rich who finance their extracurricular activities and hire them upon retirement.

Despite corporate and associational ties, the social interaction between members of the upper class and the military elite remains minimal except possibly in Washington. Nor are a significant percentage of the military elite drawn from the upper class or assimilated into the *Social Register*. Defining upper-class status by evidence of considerable wealth or high social status, Janowitz found that in 1950, 4 per cent of Navy leadership, 3 per cent of Army leadership, and 0 per cent of Air Force leadership could be so indexed. The Navy men tended to be from the Eastern branch of the upper class, the Army men from the Southern branch. Janowitz also searched the *Social Registers* for several cities. Contrary to what we have noted in the case of successful businessmen, there was no evidence that the higher military was being assimilated into the upper class:

If the *Social Register* is taken as an indicator of integration with aristocratic families, the military is at best peripheral. This index demonstrates most sharply the different social position of the military in the United States, as compared with Germany, France, and even Great Britain. For 1951, in New York, Boston, and Chicago, the number of military officers listed in the *Social Register* is less than 1 per cent. In Philadelphia and San Francisco the percentage is between 1 and 2. Just as first-generation accumulation of wealth is no basis for listing in the *Social Register,* professional military achievement is insufficient by itself. This is demonstrated by the fact that there is no emphasis on higher rank in the *Social Register.* Instead, social pedigree—inheritance and social connections —is essential. The link between the military and the socialite elite is mainly centered in Washington, where 10 per cent of the names in the *Social Register* have professional military affiliations.[33]

Janowitz also points out that there is little intermarriage between members of the upper class and members of the military elite. Both Mills and Janowitz report studies on large numbers of military leaders which show that the marriages of the military elite involve other service families or other professional families. This marriage pattern is consistent with another finding by Mills and Janowitz—the typical military leader has upper-middle-class, rural, Protestant origins. This upper-middle-class bias, which was also tied to an overrepresentation of Southerners in the Army and Navy elites, is now changing to include a broader spectrum of the population, particularly in the Air Force.[34]

However, we agree with Mills that social background is not a primary consideration when trying to understand the American military establishment. The important factors are methods of selection and training, the military code, military etiquette, and the military way of life, all of which are discussed in considerable detail by Janowitz. Those who do not adapt to the system, as it is constructed from above, soon drop out or get lost by the wayside. Those who fit the system are encouraged and aided by their superiors. Perhaps the most important part of the whole system is the educational process, beginning at the service academy and culminating in the Industrial College of the Armed Forces, where the new members of the military elite are instructed in the ways of the corporate economy by its chief executives:

Industrial College students study manpower resources. . . . In ten months they hear lectures by such experts as Inland Steel's C. B. Randall, du Pont's C. H. Greenewalt, and 90-odd others. Meanwhile, in a sensible reciprocity, the college sends out teams from its own faculty to give two-week "field courses" in mobilization problems to businessmen (some of them reserve officers).[35] *

The schools are also important to young military men as places where they get to know other men who will some day be vying for positions in the military elite. As Janowitz demonstrates in the case of General Marshall, these informal associations are important when the military leader elevated to the top by his civilian superiors begins to put together his "team." [36]

The weight of the evidence presented so far suggests that the military is definitely subordinate to the corporate rich of the American upper class. Does it have any autonomy within the present-day American system? To

---

* It would be wrong to assume that the training process produces a completely monolithic military elite. Just as there are antagonisms within the upper class, so too are there differences of opinion within the military elite. Mills notes the existence of these cliques,[37] but Janowitz gives them considerable substance by distinguishing between the "pragmatic" and "absolutist" factions within the military elite.[38] The pragmatic clique has been favored by the dominant elements within the upper class over the past three decades, while the absolutist group has tended to join forces with what Baltzell calls "caste" elements of the upper class.

the degree that it does, it is because of its relationship to Congress, a relationship originally based in large measure upon what the Army Corps of Engineers could do for the congressman's state or district. The relationship developed considerably during the 1950's when many congressmen lost their traditional hostility to an enlarged military. This was especially the case with the sympathetic legislators who actively sought positions on the congressional committees which are concerned with the military. The military encouraged this relationship with the usual amenities offered by lobbyists, along with one unique benefit—a reserve commission. By 1963, there were 73 congressmen who were reserve officers, including Air Force General Barry Goldwater and Army General Strom Thurmond.[39] However, this friendly relationship gave the military very little freedom from its mentors in the Executive branch. Its primary value, until McNamara took steps to limit its usefulness, was in the military's attempts to receive a larger budget for a given service or project than was asked for by the Defense Department: as Janowitz notes, congressional supervision of the military is "essentially budgetary."[40] Both Janowitz and Cater refer to a paper by political scientist Lewis Dexter in which he reported the results of hundreds of interviews on Capitol Hill: "No one with whom I talked ever maintained that Congress has any significant role in the formulation of military policy. . . ."[41]

Our conclusion, then, is in agreement with that of Janowitz—the military does not have a predominant role within the all-important political decision-making process. However, we emphasize that control of the military by representatives of the upper class through the National Security Council, the Defense Department, and the service associations makes its highest-ranking officers members of the power elite. The situation is concisely summarized by Janowitz:

The military profession is not a monolithic power group. A deep split pervades its ranks in respect to its doctrine and viewpoints on foreign affairs, a split which mirrors civilian disagreements. Instead, the military profession and the military Establishment conform more to the pattern of an administrative pressure group, but one with a strong internal conflict of interest. It is a very special pressure group because of its immense reserves, and because of its grave problems of national security. The military have accumulated considerable power, and that power protrudes into the political fabric of contemporary society. It could not be otherwise. However, while they have no reluctance to press for larger budgets, they exercise their influence on political matters with considerable restraint and unease. Civilian control of military affairs remains intact and fundamentally acceptable to the military; any imbalance in military contributions to politico-military affairs—domestic or international—is therefore often the result of default by civilian political leadership.[42]

THE CENTRAL INTELLIGENCE AGENCY

Since it is still very young, the CIA can be treated historically to understand its control by members of the upper class and its function within the power elite. It was developed in 1947 from the wartime intelligence apparatus as part of the National Security Act, which began the reorganization of the civilian control of the military and created the National Security Council. The CIA is the major element in an "invisible government" within the Executive branch which Washington reporters David Wise and Tom Ross believe to be carrying out the policies of the United States in the Cold War.[43] It is the heart of an organization which includes nine other intelligence agencies as well as business firms, minor charitable foundations, and certain universities and university institutes. This "invisible government" is headed by the "Special Group," or "54/12 group," which is responsible for formulating its policy. The Special Group, with its headquarters in the "Situation Room" deep in the White House basement, does not even include the Vice-President. McGeorge Bundy (SR, Boston) was President Kennedy's personal link to the Special Group, and probably retained that function under President Johnson until he resigned to become president of the Ford Foundation. Four of the Special Group's five members during the Kennedy Administration were members of the innermost circles of the power elite—Bundy, McNamara, Gilpatric, and Los Angeles millionaire John McCone. The fifth, U. Alexis Johnson, is a career State Department employee of non-upper-class origins.

From its inception the CIA has been headed by members of the power elite. The first director was Rear Admiral Roscoe H. Hillenkoetter. The second was General Walter Bedell Smith, who had been President Eisenhower's Chief of Staff and an ambassador to the Soviet Union. Smith was followed by Allen Dulles (SR, NY), who had been deputy director for two years and a leading figure in the CIA from its beginning due to his outstanding record as wartime OSS chief in Switzerland. Dulles, like his brother John Foster, was a one-time lawyer with Sullivan and Cromwell, and was well acquainted with the political and industrial elite of Europe. Along with such members of the upper class as Paul Mellon, David K. E. Bruce, Alfred du Pont, Junius S. Morgan, Lester Armour, and Lloyd Cabot Briggs, he played a key role in organizing the postwar occupation of Germany, including the selection of many of its leaders.[44] The next head of the CIA, appointed by President Kennedy, was John McCone, a multimillionaire Catholic from Los Angeles who is a close associate of Stephen Bechtel of the Bechtel Corporation and the Bechtel-McCone Corporation. Previous to his appointment as CIA director, McCone had been a special deputy to Secretary of Defense Forrestal in 1948, an undersecretary of the

Air Force in 1950, and chairman of the Atomic Energy Commission from 1958 to 1960. When McCone resigned as CIA head, President Johnson replaced him with retired Admiral William Raborn, who was vice-president of Aerojet General Corporation of Los Angeles when he was tapped for service in still another outpost of the power elite.

We believe that the social backgrounds and previous institutional affiliations of these five directors, in conjunction with the sociological composition of the Special Group, is enough to establish the fact that members of the upper class control the CIA. An analysis of specific CIA operations makes this control even more likely, for we found by studying all the names mentioned in Wise and Ross's *The Invisible Government* that many of the leading figures in CIA intrigues are members of the upper class. On reflection this does not seem as unnatural as might be expected, for it is members of the upper class who are most likely to have the travel experience, the foreign language ability, and the all-around sophistication to be believable in such a role. Unfortunately, the secrecy of the CIA makes it impossible to provide systematic evidence concerning the percentage of CIA operatives who are members of the upper class.

The CIA's discovery of Russian missiles in Cuba in 1962, and the resulting crisis, occasioned a gathering of the innermost circle of the power elite during the Kennedy Administration. According to Wise and Ross,[45] the following men gathered to decide how to respond to the presence of these missiles:

John F. Kennedy, President, Boston branch of the upper class.

Robert F. Kennedy, Attorney-General, Boston branch of the upper class.

Lyndon Johnson, Vice-President, representative of Texas oil interests.[46]

Dean Rusk, Secretary of State, formerly president of the Rockefeller Foundation.

Robert McNamara, Secretary of Defense, formerly president of the Ford Motor Company.

Douglas Dillon, Secretary of the Treasury, New York branch of the upper class and former president of Dillon, Read.

Roswell Gilpatric, Deputy Secretary of Defense, New York branch of the upper class.

McGeorge Bundy, Presidential adviser, Boston branch of the upper class.

Adlai Stevenson, U. N. diplomat, Chicago branch of the upper class.

John McCone, CIA director, Los Angeles branch of the upper class.

Dean Acheson, former Secretary of State, Eastern branch of the upper class.

Robert Lovett, former Secretary of Defense, New York branch of the upper class and member of Brown Brothers, Harriman.

General Maxwell Taylor, Presidential military adviser, later Chairman of the Joint Chiefs of Staff.

Major General Marshall S. Carter, Deputy Director of the CIA.

George Ball, Undersecretary of State, long-time State Department employee of non-upper-class background.

Edwin M. Martin, Assistant Secretary of State for Latin American Affairs, not of the upper class, and present only because the crisis happened to be in Latin America.

Theodore C. Sorensen, Presidential speechwriter and adviser from Nebraska.

THE FBI

Unlike the CIA, the FBI is not headed by members of the upper class. It is also unlikely that any of its agents come from that group. However, as our brief glance at the agency's history will show, it did not grow to its present position of formidable power without the expressed consent of members of the power elite. Further, its seemingly autonomous director of so many decades, J. Edgar Hoover, has the closest of personal ties with members of the business aristocracy. He is in fact a member of the power elite, for he is a director of Acacia Mutual Assurance Company of Washington, D. C., the thirty-seventh largest insurance company in the country. His fellow board members include four *Social Register* listees as well as the chairman of the Greater Washington Individual Investments Corporation, the chairman of Peoples Drug Stores, the president of the Potomac Electric Power Company, and the president of the National Savings & Trust Bank. Nor is Hoover the only FBI man who is interlocked with the corporate hierarchy. Many FBI agents retire after 20 or more years of service to take important positions in the corporate world. Former FBI men serve as vice-presidents at Ford, American Airlines, Reynolds Metals, and Schenley Industries, to give four prominent examples.

From its inception the FBI has been a special project of one or another element in the national upper class. It was created and nurtured by progressives and liberals; after World War II it was championed by more conservative elements. As Fred Cook notes in his polemical *The FBI Nobody Knows,* "The FBI is indebted for its birth and its present stature to two of the strongest Presidents of the twentieth century," Theodore Roosevelt and Franklin D. Roosevelt.[47] The first Roosevelt created the agency by executive order in defiance of the will of Congress; the second Roosevelt gave it a liberal mandate to keep a close surveillance on left-wing politics. Although created by Teddy Roosevelt in 1908, the bureau first came to real prominence (along with J. Edgar Hoover) for its role in the World War I spy hysteria and the Red Scare, the latter of which crushed the Socialist Party and other left-wing groups.* Hoover became the bureau's No. 2 man in 1921 under chief William J. Burns, whose International Detective Agency had done a great amount of work for powerful business interests during the labor difficulties of the first decades of this century. He rose to the No. 1 spot in 1924 with the help of a strong recommendation from an important businessman who was then the Secretary of Commerce, Herbert Hoover. The two Hoovers were not related, J. Edgar coming from a family of government bureaucrats.

During the 1920's the bureau turned its attention to the extremists of the Right, the Ku Klux Klan, and played an important role in discrediting the hooded nativists. It was not until 1936, at the direct invitation of President Franklin D. Roosevelt, that Hoover and the FBI turned their attention once again to the Left. Cook summarizes Roosevelt's role as follows:

That Hoover has become the greatest untouchable in American history is not entirely by his own doing. He has been helped by many hands. One of the most important initially was Franklin Roosevelt, who took pride in Hoover's accomplishments and felt that they redounded to the credit of his Administration. It was Roosevelt, too, who made the cardinal mistake of violating Stone's wise dictum that the FBI should concern itself only with crime; it was Roosevelt who, in his concern with the problems of World War II, put the FBI back into the field of undercover work, back into the business of ferreting out potential dangers in men's ideas.[48]

The increased power and prominence of the FBI during the 1930's under President Roosevelt cannot be understood fully without a consideration of the National Crime Commission. Founded in 1925, the NCC was a nongovernmental committee dedicated to the development of a strong federal police force:

The NCC was organized at a meeting held in the director's room of the United States Steel Corporation. The first executive committee consisted of several prominent captains of industry, two brigadier generals, several educators, and a number of nationally prominent statesmen.[49]

The chairman of the NCC was Richard Washburn Child (SR, NY), a former ambassador to Italy. Among the members of this exclusive committee were Franklin Roosevelt, then the governor of New York, and

---

* Since the history of the bureau and Hoover's career are practically synonymous, we will discuss them at the same time.

Louis M. Howe, Roosevelt's personal secretary from 1905 until his death in 1935.* We believe that reporter William Seagle is right when he concludes that it was the pressure of big business through business associations which elevated the FBI to a new prominence.[50]

In conclusion, the military, the CIA, and the FBI play subservient roles within the power elite. They do not initiate policy but gather information for decision-makers and carry out directives from superiors in the Executive branch of the federal government. Except for the military in time of world war or limited war, none of the three has a direct impact on the day-to-day lives of most Americans. Nevertheless, they are a significant part of the power elite in time of crisis. They should not be overemphasized, nor should they be overlooked.

* Roosevelt's concern with crime also can be seen in the prominent role he gave to Raymond Moley as an adviser. As noted earlier, Moley was Roosevelt's adviser on penal reform in New York state before he became a Brain Truster.

Chapter Six . . . .
Control of State and
Local Governments.

No generalizations can be made about control of state and local governments by representatives of the American upper class. The situation is different from state to state and city to city, and would therefore have to be restudied for each locale that was of interest. That Delaware is a "caliphate" of the du Ponts does not imply upper-class control of the 17 states where organized labor is very influential in politics.[1] That Weirton, West Virginia, is the most obvious company town in the nation, a claim that was made before the president of Weirton Steel became its mayor in the mid-1950's, does not allow us to generalize to New Haven, Connecticut, which Dahl has shown to be governed by a variety of middle-class leadership groups.[2] Recognizing the diversity of control at state and local levels, this short chapter will have two important purposes:

1. To show that lack of control at the local level, such as in New Haven, is not incompatible with the thesis that the national upper class is a governing class.

2. To demonstrate the several means by which members of the power elite exert considerable influence on state and local politics even when they do not control them.

There have been a number of studies of local politics.[3] Perhaps the most detailed and methodologically sound of these was Dahl's. We will look at his findings and conclusions in some detail because they may be considered prototypical. If a careful analysis of Dahl's findings shows that they are not inconsistent with our thesis, we would assume that similar analyses would hold for other cities where the pluralistic model of a variety of leadership groups best describes the local power structure. In briefest summary, Dahl found that in the 1950's New Haven was governed by members of the middle class (pp. 229-230).[4] Further, different members of the middle class were influential in different issue-areas. There was no one group that made decisions on a wide variety of issues. On the other hand, blue-collar workers were almost totally excluded from decision-making groups (p. 230), and the local upper class was only represented in areas having to do with business prosperity (p. 84). Dahl demonstrated the unimportance of the local branch of the upper class in two different ways. (1) After defining "Social Notables" as those invited to the annual debutante Assemblies held at the New Haven Lawn Club, Dahl found that only two Social Notables were among 500 elective and party officials, only two were among 132 higher officers in public education, and only 24 were among 432 in important positions in urban redevelopment (p. 64). However, Dahl calls the last figure "large" (p. 64), because the number of Social Notables is 27 times greater than would be expected in terms of their percentage of the total population. (2) Since it could be argued that this handful of Social Notables may have all the power, Dahl did more refined studies of power on specific issues, determining which persons were the most influential in terms of initiating and vetoing proposals. These studies of the decision-making process showed that the few upper-class participants were not very powerful. Nor were they the same upper-class persons for the different issue-areas:

One could, no doubt, magnify these tiny proportions into great significance by assuming that the few Social Notables in public life are of extraordinary influence. Alas for such a hypothesis; the evidence to the contrary is devastating . . . their influence is evidently not very great.[5]

Political power in New Haven was not always as dispersed as Dahl's detailed study shows to be the case at the present time. According to Dahl, New Haven has gradually changed from oligarchy to pluralism (p. 11). We emphasize that Dahl reached this conclusion on the basis of a sociology-of-leadership study: "The main evidence for the shift from oligarchy to pluralism is found in changes in the social characteristics of elected officials in New Haven since 1784 . . ." (p. 11). Why did this change occur? Dahl suggests two complementary reasons: (1) The upper class withdrew from local politics because they did not like to deal with "alien stock" and a "new kind of politics" (p. 237); and (2) they would have lost out to the greater voting power of the lower classes anyhow (p. 84). It would seem that the local upper class made an expedient withdrawal that saved their reputations. However, as Dahl notes, the problem is not quite as simple as that. He gives what may be an equally important reason for their withdrawal in another chapter. In referring to financial support of political parties by "Economic Notables" (important businessmen in New Haven, including corporate executives of national corporations), he makes the following comment: "Because the policies acceptable to the many as well as to the wealthy few generally do not diverge much on the local level, the differences between the policies of leaders in the two parties are never very great" (p. 244). This would seem to imply that the interests of the Social Notables and the Economic Notables were not compromised by their withdrawal. Dahl also implies this in another context when he points out that Notables are influential on decisions that involve business prosperity: "Politicians are wary of their potential influence and avoid policies that might unite the Notables in bitter opposition" (p. 84).*

Dahl states that it is difficult to date the withdrawal of the Social Notables from local politics, "but it seems to have occurred between the beginning of this century and the end of the First World War" (p. 237). We would emphasize that this withdrawal very nearly coincides with the development of a national upper class which moved to the suburbs and sent its children to private schools. *Indeed, Dahl explains the Notables' lack of participation in New Haven affairs by the move to the suburbs and the entrance into private schools.* In discussing their lack of participation in local politics he says that "to hold office in the parties or in public education one must, with a few exceptions, have a residence in New Haven, and many of the Economic Notables live in the suburbs" (pp. 70-71). A little later he makes the same point for both the Social and Economic Notables: "Together with the descendants of the patricians and entrepreneurs [Social Notables], the managers and executives of New Haven's corporations [Economic Notables] generally live outside the city" (p. 76). The lack of participation in public education, the second of three issue-areas studied by Dahl, is explained by him as follows: "Most Social Notables and many Economic Notables living in New Haven send their children to private schools; as a consequence their interest in the public schools is ordinarily rather slight" (p. 70).

We believe that the state of affairs that Dahl describes for New Haven is not incompatible with the hypothesis that there is a national upper class that controls the federal government. His findings show that the Notables were not compromised by their withdrawal, which complements very well Baltzell's conclusion that the national upper class withdrew to the suburbs, attended private schools, and failed to live up to its political responsibilities. We would also note that Dahl's findings are not unique, nor are they unique to a decision-making methodology. For example, in 1951, after traveling

---

* Sociologists Scott Greer and Peter Orleans add further light as to why Economic Notables withdraw from local politics in all areas of the country: "The vulnerability of economic elites to purely local threats diminishes with merger in national systems; so does their commitment to the state of the local polity."[6] This point simply cannot be overemphasized in dealing with the objection that a national upper class must have local power as well as national power to be considered a governing class.

around the country talking to people from all walks of life, writer John Gunther summarized:

The Main Line and the aristocracy are factors largely through their absence, one might say. "The people who own the city," wrote George Sessions Perry, "have abandoned it." This phenomenon is not, of course, peculiar to Philadelphia; we have noted it in Boston and Chicago. In city after city, the ruling class moves out to escape the pressure of urban taxes.[7]

We do not wish to give the impression that all cities are necessarily as pluralistic as New Haven seems to be. Nor do we wish to imply that Dahl would generalize from New Haven to all other cities. Political scientist Dahl and sociologists Greer and Orleans agree that some cities may have tight-knit power structures while others may not.[8] Finally, we want to emphasize that Dahl is not necessarily in disagreement with our assertion that the American power elite has little interest in local politics. In commenting on such a claim by Mills, Dahl noted: "There is a considerable amount of suggestive evidence for this hypothesis."[9]

Turning now to our second purpose in this chapter, what influences do representatives of the American upper class have in the states and cities they do not control? At the state level, the three major influences possessed by the power elite are campaign finances, lobbying, and control of regulatory agencies. After pointing out that most campaign funds come from a few large contributors, political scientist Austin Ranney makes the following point about finances, a point which must be qualified by saying that local businesses and labor groups can often raise what would be considered "big money" at the state level:

Less widely discussed but probably more significant is the impact of money on nominations. Direct primaries make getting a nomination almost as expensive as winning an election; and there is little doubt that even an aspirant for nomination by a convention will receive substantial support if he has convinced the party's leaders that he and/or his backers are able and willing to contribute heavily to the party's war chest. It is these considerations rather than the ability to "buy" elections that increasingly favor the well-to-do and/or the well-backed in state politics.[10]

The second major influence of the power elite on state politics is through lobbying. Political scientist Harmon Zeigler states, "No matter what kind of economy enjoyed by the state, the businesses dominate the numerical structure of lobbying."[11] However, this does not necessarily mean that the lobbyists are always successful. Probably few state legislatures are as corrupt as that of Illinois during the 1950's, when a Republican lawmaker who was also a law school dean estimated that one-third of his fellow state legislators accepted payoffs.[12] Nor does it mean that all businesses are controlled by members of the national upper class. Small businesses, including farms, have a great amount of influence on state legislatures just as they do on the Congress in Washington.

The third influence of members of the power elite on state government is through close relationships with various state agencies, especially regulatory agencies. Political scientist Robert H. Simmons has shown in the case of the state of Washington, for instance, that these agencies develop effective ties with the "clientele group" they serve while at the same time seeking to escape gubernatorial control and supervision. These subsystems, which usually consist of agency, clientele group, and legislative subject-matter committee, are often able to obtain "dedicated revenue sources" which protect the programs desired by the agency and its clientele. In short, the governor and his staff are removed from the budgetary and decision-making processes except in time of "systemic crisis or extreme public need." The "pluralism" of the state government allows each interest group to protect and develop its interests whether or not it controls elective politics. The role of the governor within this system is quite ineffective:

He has few administrative controls of any quality over the fiscal system of the state. He is unable to manage the executive branch with any degree of effectiveness and comprehensiveness. Power, responsibility, and function are not fused, and are far more than divided. They are, rather, diffused throughout the entire fragmented executive system.[13]

It remains for Simmons and other political scientists to do detailed studies of other states to see how many of them have such independent subsystems dominated by powerful clientele groups. McConnell gives other examples in *Private Power and American Democracy,* and his quotation from a report published in 1942 is especially appropriate:

Some years ago a study of state regulatory agencies commented that banking and insurance-regulating agencies have been "to a significant degree creatures of the enterprise they regulate." [14]

We would conclude this third point by emphasizing that where this type of pluralism exists it works to the benefit of the entrenched interest groups in that such groups are able to remove themselves from a concern with elective politics. Even if the governor should be unsympathetic to the wishes of the members of the power elite in his state, he may not be able to do much about it if their business interests are part of one of these relatively autonomous subsystems within the state bureaucracy.

At the local level of government, the corporate rich have several means of influencing policy. The first of these, almost unique to that level of government, is the power to cut back production or to move the company to another location where the local government has expressed agreement with the interests of the corporation. Andrew Hacker has pointed out the ominous nature of such a power, for it can leave a broken city behind.[15] A second influence of the power elite on the local level is based on the assumption that corporate white-collar employees who hold elective or appointive office will not pass laws that are strenuously objected to by their corporate employers. If such an assumption is a tenuous one, it is at least one that is being made by the corporations, some of which encourage the practice with courses on politics, and by granting time off with pay for such activities:

Such companies as Alcoa, Ford, Chrysler, and the California Company grant time off for political work, and Chase Manhattan grants time off with full pay for employees who are elected to part-time political jobs. Chase now has 200 holding some kind of public office, from school committeeman to mayor. Last year 156 U. S. Steel employees went to the hustings and won election to local or state offices. Nine of 31 Ford workers running for office last month won, and 18 out of 42 won at Boeing. Detroit Edison's purchasing department alone boasts a Democratic mayor and a Republican city commissioner of nearby suburbs.[16]

As a third influence, members of the power elite often take a direct interest in one aspect of local politics, that aspect which concerns business prosperity. Dahl, for example, notes that in New Haven the mayor's finance committee is numerically dominated by big businessmen.[17] The final influence of representatives of the upper class on local government is through their control of various nongovernmental resources which partially shapes the general framework within which political decision-making takes place. This includes newspaper ownership, advertising in newspapers, civic associations, and charitable foundations. Specific examples of the importance of these nongovernmental influences would be the way in which Richard King Mellon almost singlehandedly mobilized the forces which cleaned up the city of Pittsburgh and the way in which Mrs. Norman Chandler's fund-raising efforts changed the skyline of downtown Los Angeles with various civic buildings.[18] A more general example can be taken from a study of Dallas, Texas, by Carol Thometz. Using Hunter's reputational method to locate top leaders, Thometz identified seven big businessmen whom she believed to be at the apex of power in Dallas. Even if her assumptions about political power are incorrect, due to all the weaknesses ascribed to this method by its critics, it is still the case that these men permeate all the major nongovernmental associations in that city.[19]

In summary, the national upper class, even if it is a governing class, does not control every aspect of American political life.

Chapter Seven . . . .
Is the American Upper Class
A Governing Class? . . . .

The preceding chapters led the reader through a jungle of names, agencies, and mechanisms with a minimum of digressions into definitions, methodology, and argumentation. It will be the function of this concluding chapter to make good this slight, to anticipate objections, and to summarize the findings of this inquiry. We begin with the concept "social class."

WHAT IS SOCIAL CLASS?

Most people seem to know what is meant by a "social class," but like many such terms it becomes problematical when a precise definition is needed. Kahl, in his textbook *The American Class Structure*, says, "If a large group of families are approximately equal to each other and clearly differentiated from other families, we call them a social class." [1] His book then gives a great deal of evidence for the existence of concrete, observable social groups which tend to be similar in income, education, and type of occupation. Kahl's definition is very similar to that given by Sweezy: "A social class, then, is made up of freely intermarrying families." [2] Equally appropriate is a definition by psychologists David Krech, Richard S. Crutchfield, and Egerton L. Ballachey: "A division of a society, made up of persons possessing certain common social characteristics which are taken to qualify them for intimate equal-status relations with one another, and which restrict their interaction with members of other social classes." [3] Sociologists Greer and Orleans place their emphasis on family and "class-endogamy" in a discussion of an "interlocking-elite system," by which they seem to mean a "ruling-class system," without actually using the term:

The interlocking-elite system is one in which the same class of persons produces leaders in the polity, the economy, the ecclesia, and the army. This class of persons . . . is typically hereditary, so family becomes the major transmission belt for the recruitment of the various elites. At the same time, control of the various command posts allows self-perpetuation of the class, while class-endogamy creates, from a set of elites in heterogeneous activity, a defensive social group with common norms and sanctions.[4]

If family, intermarriage, and similarity in income, wealth, and occupation are important elements in understanding what is meant by social class, they are not the only elements. Members of a given social class are likely to share similar values and attitudes, and to have a similar style of life. Then too, there are differences among social classes on a great many psychological variables.[5]

However, the similarity and insularity of people within a social class should not be overstated, particularly within the United States. Indeed, if we were to characterize criticisms of the concept "social class," we would say that they seem to be based upon models drawn from studies of caste and feudal social structures. As Kahl points out, however, our open-class system is almost the opposite of a caste system—there is no legal recognition of group inequality, there are a minimum of differences between the life styles of classes, and there is movement from one class to another.[6] None of this, he argues, means that social classes do not exist. Let us now turn to more specific criticisms.

One criticism based upon caste notions is that the concept "social class" is not meaningful unless the class has clear boundaries. On this point, we would first of all note that there are many important concepts which are not obviated because there is no clear definition of their boundaries. Second, we would point out that in the case of the *upper* class there are surprisingly definite boundaries; this may not be the case with lower social classes.[7] Another criticism of the concept "social class" based upon caste models concerns the relevance of social mobility, and a confusion of class *origins* with class membership. Hacker, for instance, seems to let this identification of origins with class membership lead him to reject the notion "ruling class." After stating his belief that the corporate rich are the leaders of the power elite, he says that there is no implication that "the corporate elite is a 'class,' any more than the corporate world is 'capitalist' in the traditional sense."[8] Hacker rejects the notion of a "ruling class" because members of the elite come from "at least every stratum of the middle class," because "birth and breeding are of negligible importance," because talent is more important than "manners or connections," and because the corporate chairs "have the power rather than their occupants."[9] However, as Sweezy points out, "class affiliation is not a question of social origins. One who is born a worker can become a capitalist and vice versa."[10] Furthermore, there is evidence to suggest that persons moving into a social class above their original one tend to take on the values and attitudes of the group they wish to join.[11] In short, the fact of social mobility is not antagonistic to the existence of social classes which are relatively static in their values and attitudes. We have stressed repeatedly the co-optive institutions and mechanisms which account for this phenomenon.

Finally, before turning to other problems, four minor points must be made about "social class." First, the notion does not imply that everyone in the group knows everyone else. In the case of the upper class, we have emphasized the importance of the "right" schools and clubs in establishing group membership, and others have noted the importance of clothes, language, and occupation in making the individual members recognizable to one another. Second, it is possible for antagonisms to exist within a social class, of both a personal and a political nature.[12] Third, a social class does not necessarily have a "center" or a "hub." The core of a social class is likely to be a number of overlapping social cliques with no one "innermost" circle. Fourth, class consciousness is not a criterion for the existence of a social class. If we observe that a given group of people tend to interact and intermarry with each other, we are justified in calling them a social class whether they are aware of the fact or not. However, as Mills notes, there is good reason to believe that members of the upper class are more class conscious than the members of other social groups.[13] Or, to quote Baltzell, "It is important to stress once again the fact that, while there are many middle and lower classes in America, and in Philadelphia, there exists one metropolitan upper class with a common cultural tradition, consciousness of kind, and 'we' feeling of solidarity which tends to be national in scope." [14]

IS THERE A NATIONAL UPPER CLASS?

Once the problems connected with the concept "social class" are clarified, the next step is to determine whether there is such a social upper class as a "national upper class" in the United States. We have relied on the works of Amory, Baltzell, Kavaler, and Wecter in answering the question in the affirmative. We also have presented evidence of our own to show that there is such a social class, made up of rich businessmen and their descendants, who interact at private schools, exclusive social clubs, exclusive summer resorts, and similar institutions. It seems unlikely that there are more than a few social scientists who would deny the existence of a "national upper class." Indeed, this is one of the few common grounds among the pluralist David Riesman, the power elitist C. Wright Mills, the Tocquevillian E. Digby Baltzell, and the Marxist Paul Sweezy, so we will not belabor it. The problem begins with the question of whether or not this national upper class is a "governing class."

IS THERE A GOVERNING CLASS?

Before looking at the term "governing class" in detail, it might be well to see how various theorists view the problem of power in the United States. For pluralists, the upper class is *no longer* a "ruling class." They argue that the upper class has lost its power over the past 30 or 35 years to a variety of "interest groups" or "veto groups" who contend for power on an almost equal footing. These veto groups include corporate managers (usually conceived of as a group apart from hereditary owners), technical–intellectual elites, organized farmers, organized laborers, consumers, and a strong federal government which has gained considerable autonomy from big business. Dahl summarizes the views of the pluralists as follows, contrasting them to the views of Mills and Hunter:

At the other extreme are neo-pluralists like Truman, Key, and Latham (and perhaps Berle) who suggest that there are a number of loci for arriving at political decisions; that businessmen, trade unions, politicians, consumers, farmers, voters, and many other aggregates all have an impact on policy outcomes; that none of these aggregates is homogeneous for all purposes; that each of them is highly influential over some scopes but weak over many others; and that the power to reject undesired alternatives is more common than the power to dominate over outcomes directly.[15]

On the other side of the fence from the pluralists are the Tocquevillian conservatives and the Marxist radicals. Both believe that the upper class remains an establishment or ruling class. Baltzell, speaking for the Tocquevillians, stresses the rise of a more ethnically representative establishment, while Sweezy stresses the increased importance of corporate executives at the expense of financiers. Standing between the pluralists and the ruling-class theorists are those who agree with C. Wright Mills. Mills was not impressed with the idea of distinguishing corporate executives from the hereditary rich who make up the national upper class. He lumped owners and managers together as "the corporate rich." However, Mills believed that the Depression, World War II, and the Cold War brought leading politicians and generals to the top levels of power. The importance of these two groups led Mills to say that the corporate rich are no longer a ruling class but, at best, first among equals in a power elite. His theoretical model is closer to the pluralists in abandoning a ruling-class model, closer to the ruling-class model in stressing the unequal power of a trio of closely knit veto groups.

There are few empirically testable definitions of "ruling class" or "governing class." Bell speaks of a power-holding group with a "continuity of interests" and "community of interests," but like so many others, he does not stress what they must hold power over to qualify as a "ruling class." [16] The definition given by Greer and Orleans at the start of this chapter stresses that the leaders holding command posts come from a hereditary social class with common norms and sanctions. Dahl presents the following definition of a ruling elite:

A ruling elite, then, is a controlling group less than a majority in size that is not a pure artifact of democratic rules. It is a minority of individuals whose preferences regularly prevail in cases of differences in preference on key political issues. If we are to avoid an infinite regress of explanations, the composition of the ruling elite must be more or less definitely specified.[17]

While Dahl's definition is valuable to us because it stresses that a ruling group must prevail on key political issues, it concerns a ruling-elite model, which is not quite the same as a governing-class model. A ruling-elite model implies that the same persons control a wide variety of issues, while a governing-class model implies only that the leaders are drawn from an upper class. There may or may not be more than one "ruling clique" within the "governing class," and as a matter of empirical fact, as has been shown, there are contending cliques within the American upper class of today. (Sometimes the cliques do not contend, but merely divide the labor.)

With the above definitions and the problems they imply uppermost in our minds, we developed the minimum definition of a "governing class" stated in the first chapter:

A governing class is a social upper class which receives a disproportionate amount of a country's income, owns a disproportionate amount of a country's wealth, and contributes a disproportionate number of its members to the controlling institutions and key decision-making groups in that country.

We recognize that this is a minimum definition. However, it is empirically testable, and it contains no value-laden assumptions.* By stressing disproportionate income and wealth, we are seeking an empirical base for the assumption that the members of the upper class have the community of interest and continuity of interest which Bell finds important. By stressing control over institutions, we are acknowledging the definition by Greer and Orleans, and by considering key decision-making groups we are taking cognizance of Dahl's concern with political issue-areas.

* We use disproportionate as a quantitative term. A proportionate amount of income, wealth, or leadership positions would be a percentage equal to the social class's percentage of the total population.

THE SOCIOLOGY-OF-LEADERSHIP METHOD

The definition of a governing class that we have given is closely related to the method we have used in our study, namely, the "sociology-of-leadership" method. This method studies the social backgrounds of the men who control institutions and make decisions. It has two drawbacks. The first is that it does not demonstrate "consequences" from upper-class control. Do upper-class leaders have "special interests"? Donald Matthews, in *The Social Background of Political Decision-Makers,* warns that even though most political leaders come from the higher social strata, they are not necessarily members of a "ruling class." Social class is not an automatic predictor of either ideology or political behavior:[18]

It is misleading to assume that a group must literally be represented among the political decision-makers to have influence or political power. The unrepresentative nature of America's political decision-makers no doubt has its consequences, but it does not free them from their ultimate accountability to the electorate at large. Thus the frequency with which members of certain groups are found among decision-makers should not be considered an infallible index of the distribution of power in a society. In America at least lower-status groups have political power far in excess of their number in Congress, the Cabinet, and so on.[19]

While this may sound farfetched, it is nonetheless plausible that the "real power" is in the masses, who let members of the upper class have the seats of honor as long as they make wise decisions. However, according to Dahl, this type of argument is usually used by ruling-class theorists who have not been able to find any members of the upper class in ruling positions.[20]

The second problem with the sociology-of-leadership methodology is to determine how much overrepresentation is necessary to support the hypothesis that the upper class is a governing class. If all the leaders were from the upper class, there would be little objection to this method. Dahl, for example, used it to conclude that aristocrats used to control New Haven. But not all present-day leaders are from the upper class. How significant is it that a social group which would contribute 0.5 per cent of the leaders in a completely open social system in fact contributes 100 or more times that number? * Statistically speaking, the findings are "significant." But statistical significance is not everything. When does the difference really make a difference? It could be argued that this overrepresentation does not have the consequences implied. Perhaps the non-upper-class leaders have the power, if not the wealth. We have tried to deal with

* Hypothesizing such a completely open social system for statistical reasons does not imply that one exists or that one will ever exist.

this second objection by understanding the backgrounds and training of the non-upper-class leaders. We have found in most instances that they were selected, trained, and employed in institutions which function to the benefit of members of the upper class and which are controlled by members of the upper class. From this we have argued that they are selected for advancement in terms of the interests of members of the upper class. We have thus introduced the "power elite" concept, which refers to high-level officials in institutions controlled by members of the upper class.[21] We have emphasized that members of the power elite may or may not be members of the upper class, but that the power elite is rooted in the upper class and serves the interests of members of the upper class.

The weaknesses of the sociology-of-leadership method are not present in the study of the political decision-making process that is advocated by Dahl. However, this method has its own limitations. The first comment to be made on this approach is that it is concerned only with key political issues. Unless the word "political" is given broad definition, such a limitation may be unjustified—economic, educational, and cultural decisions may be equally important from the point of view of members of the governing class, because such decisions determine the framework within which political decisions are made. However, this is a minor objection. The first real problem is in determining what are the "key political issues." Is it fair, for example, to expect members of the upper class to be interested in local politics, when it is known that these issues do not really concern them? Again, the problem is not insurmountable. Dahl has offered an excellent list of issues in an offhand fashion by way of example—"taxation and expenditures, subsidies, welfare programs, military policy. . . ."[22] If it could be shown that these casual suggestions are the ones that would be settled upon by lengthy deliberations, a governing-class theorist would be nine-tenths of the way home in an attempt to support his hypothesis by the decision-making method. Members of the upper class and their corporations benefit most from the tax structure and tax loopholes, large businesses receive most of the subsidies, welfare spending has dropped from $30 per citizen in 1939 when it made up 44 per cent of the budget to $16 per citizen in 1963 when it made up 7 per cent of the budget, and a group of *Social Register* listees and corporation executives make the key decisions on military policy.[23]

A second objection to Dahl's concept of the decision-making method is that it gives little importance to the situation where one group prevails over indifferent groups. Dahl emphasizes this because there is "a difference of some theoretical significance between a system in which a small group dominates over another that is opposed to it, and one in which a group dominates over an indifferent mass." [24] This is certainly true, but the difference in *systems* is not at issue. It may be that there are ruling elites or ruling classes in many different types of systems, and that they would use different techniques of control in the different systems. A third major objection to the decision-making method is that it is very difficult to find the "real interests" of the various groups that may be involved in a decision. Or it may be many years before such interests can be determined, just as it may be many years before it can be determined whether or not the "outcome" favored one group or another. Closely related to this objection is the fact that it is often difficult to determine what factors are involved in the making of any given decision. Many aspects of a situation may remain secret or be forgotten or repressed, and the participants themselves may not be able to assess correctly the roles of the various members of the group. Dahl agrees that such a determination is "enormously difficult." [25] We would stress that this is especially the case with corporations, the CIA, and the federal government, where a great deal of secrecy is the standard situation.

The final major difficulty with the decision-making model is that it does not specify how many decisions must be decided in favor of the upper class. Can members of the upper class occasionally lose, or make concessions, and still be considered part of a governing class? This is analogous to the problem of how much overrepresentation is necessary with the sociology-of-leadership methodology. Dahl offers a solution when he says: "We can say that a system approximates a true ruling elite system, to a greater or lesser degree, without insisting that it exemplify the extreme and limiting case." [26] In short, an upper class can be more or less a governing class depending upon how many decisions it controls.*

The differences between the sociology-of-leadership method and the decision-making method can be summarized as follows: The decision-making approach is concerned with issues and attempts to study the decision-making process and its outcome. The sociology-of-leadership methodology is concerned with sociological background and studies the sociological composition of institutional leadership and of decision-making groups. The decision-making method has trouble specifying key political issues, the real interests of the protagonists, the factors involved in the decision, and the long-run consequences of the outcome; the sociology-of-leadership method runs into trouble demonstrating that upper-class leaders have special interests and specifying how many of the decision-makers and institutional lead-

---

* Similarly, we can say with the sociology-of-leadership methodology that an upper class is more or less a governing class depending upon how much wealth it has and how many men it contributes to leadership positions.

ers must be members of the upper class. Recognizing the limitations of both methods, and of any and all methods, for that matter,[27] we have chosen to emphasize the sociology-of-leadership method for the following reasons:

1. There is more agreement about the major institutions of American society than about the true interests of various socioeconomic groups.

2. It is possible to determine the sociological composition of a leadership group, but it is seldom possible to know all the factors and arguments that went into a decision, much less who initiated and vetoed specific proposals. This is especially the case when decisions are made in complete privacy, such as corporate board meetings, National Security Council meetings, and Special Group meetings.

3. It is possible to determine in a short time whether or not the decision-makers are members of a given socioeconomic class or employees of a given institution, but it is seldom possible to determine immediately what will be the effect of a given decision; this is necessary to determine which group was favored by the decision.

4. In a governing-class study, as opposed to a ruling-elite study, it is ultimately necessary to determine social class membership to determine whether or not the opposing elites or political parties are from the same or different social classes.

5. It is possible to partially answer the objection to the sociology-of-leadership method concerning the special interests of upper-class leaders by showing that members of the upper class own a disproportionate amount of the country's wealth, particularly corporate wealth, and receive a disproportionate amount of the yearly income.

EMPIRICAL OBJECTIONS

So much, then, for the problems of definition and methodology. We have moved from a definition of "social class" to the fact of a "national upper class" to a definition of "governing class" and "power elite," and we have given our reasons for emphasizing the sociology-of-leadership methodology in attempting to test our hypothesis. Our next step is to anticipate objections. This can be accomplished from our detailed study of criticisms of *The Power Elite*.[28]

Scope and Magnitude of Power

The first question to be asked of a study emphasizing the sociology-of-leadership methodology concerns the specific powers that go with the various institutional positions held by members or representatives of the American upper class. Hacker points out that several of Mills's critics raised such a question about *The Power Elite*.[29] Dahl emphasizes that a study such as ours must, among other things, demonstrate the basis, technique, scope, and magnitude of the power of the hypothetical ruling group.[30] Our answer is as follows:

1. *The corporations.* The corporations are controlled by boards of directors. These boards have the final say-so on investment decisions. They can therefore influence the rate of national economic growth, the rise and fall of the stock market, and the number and type of jobs available. The corporate boards also choose the chief officers of the corporations, who in turn determine day-to-day operations and the advancement of lower-level managers.[31] Dahl, relying primarily upon a study by Gordon, would dispute these statements.[32] He believes that managers control the corporations, telling the directors which officers to advance to the very highest positions. Gordon, in turn, makes his claim because (a) 35 of 155 corporations had more "inside" than "outside" directors; (b) directors hold very little stock; and (c) the importance of interest groups has waned. We do not agree with Gordon's analysis for a number of reasons. First, we are inclined to accept the testimony of observers such as Berle who are closer to the day-to-day functioning of the corporate world.[33] Second, the small amount of stock held by directors may be explained in other ways, such as its being held by one's wife or a bank trust. Third, the greater number of inside directors in some corporations is not necessarily significant. We have seen, for example, that many private school graduates go to work in the corporate world and on Wall Street. Also, inside directors are not necessarily indicative of management control. Family-owned companies, which are dominated by a few persons, often have many employees on the board. Fourth, where the evidence is available, as in the case of the Cleveland interest group, the Mellon interest group, and the du Pont interest group, there is no reason to believe that the power of interest groups has declined. Finally, we mean by "control" the power to change management if the operation of the corporation does not suit its owners. That managers make day-to-day business decisions on technical matters is really irrelevant. As corporate spokesman after corporate spokesman makes clear, the primary goal is to make a profit, and that is what most concerns members of the upper class when it comes to their corporations.

2. *The corporation lawyers.* Corporate lawyers derive their power from their relationship to the corporate economy they helped to construct. They have the power of expertise on legal matters. They also have the power of persons who have a broader perspective of the system and can thereby give advice to those who function in narrower channels.[34]

3. *The foundation boards.* The foundation boards have the power to

accept or reject various scientific, educational, and cultural ventures. They therefore have the power to exert considerable influence over the noneconomic aspects of American life.

4. *The associations (CFR, FPA, BAC, CED, NAC, and NAM)*. The leaders of these associations, through their publications, seminars, and advertisements, have the power to influence public opinion. They also serve to educate persons who are going to be decision-makers in a given issue-area, such as economic development or foreign policy.

5. *The boards of trustees of universities*. The boards of trustees make long-term policy, thus setting the tone and orientation of the university. They also have the power to hire and fire university presidents and other top-level personnel.[35]

6. *The Executive branch of the federal government*. The Executive branch takes the initiative in matters of legislation and federal spending. It includes departments such as State, Treasury, and Defense which control the crucial issue-areas of foreign policy, financial policy, and military policy. The Executive branch also has appointive powers over the Judicial branch and the independent regulatory agencies. It can use its prestige to influence public opinion and its expertise to influence Congress.

7. *The military*. The military has the power to carry out whatever activity is called for by the National Security Council and the Defense Department. It has the power of expertise in giving advice on whether or not to undertake a given operation, how various operations should be carried out, and which branches of the military should be utilized in defense planning and military operations. Once a plan has been set, the military has the power to decide on operational details and to select personnel to carry out the task. The military has the power to influence public opinion through its large public relations apparatus.

The Managerial Revolution

The second major objection likely to be raised has to do with the decline of family capitalism and the rise of the managers (the managerial revolution). It is often argued that the owners no longer control and that the managers are a separate social group from the social upper class of stockholders. Sometimes it is argued that the rich have been diminished by inheritance taxes. Contrary to these arguments, it has been shown that successful managers become owners themselves with the help of stock options and stock tips, and that they are assimilated socially into the upper class. It also has been shown that a considerable number of corporate executives are of the upper class originally even when they are not majority owners in a given corporation. Finally, it has been shown that stock ownership is not so dispersed that it is meaningless. The rich have *not* lost in wealth, and may even be gaining because of easily avoided taxes. On the basis of these findings, it has been argued that the dispersal of stock ownership within the upper class makes members of this class concerned with the success of the system as a whole rather than with their own given company, as was the case with family capitalism. It was further argued that the dispersal of stock and the death of family capitalism freed the hereditary rich to go into government service, the professions, and the arts, contributing further to their control of the system and to its stability.

The Role of Expertise

A third major objection has to do with the importance of expertise in the modern world and the rise of the "meritocracy." This argument, which incorporates the rise of the corporate managers as one of its examples, claims that the upper-middle class of well-educated specialists, who are drawn before their training from all socioeconomic levels, has replaced the upper class of property owners as the wielders of power, as the makers of big decisions. There are several comments that can be made about this argument:

1. To advise a decision-maker is not to make a decision. As Mills was well aware, experts are often the "captains" of the power elite's higher thoughts, but as he also said of chief executives, "Theirs [is] the Judgment." [36] It is the function of the decision-maker to choose among the usually conflicting advice that he receives from his usually divided experts.

2. Final authority, or decision-making power, does not follow from the fact that one is necessary to the functioning of a system. Most parts of any system are necessary. It is perfectly possible for one part of a system to function for the benefit of another, which is the point we have argued by stressing the distribution of income and wealth.

3. We believe it is an *empirical* mistake to downgrade the amount of expertise located *within* the upper class. Too much is made of "café society," "the jet set," and the "functionless genteel" within the upper class. The fact is that most members of the upper class are hard-working and competent. We have demonstrated this in a number of ways:

a. Almost all graduates of private schools go on to college. Our study of one alumni bulletin showed that private school graduates go into a variety of activities that require a considerable amount of expertise.

b. Private school graduates go to the finest universities in the country, universities which are the major suppliers of American expertise.

c. Our study of the 1965 *Social Register Locater* showed that 8 per cent of a sample of 182 adult males have the title "doctor" before their names. Whether the degree is medical or academic, this percentage suggests a considerable amount of expertise within the upper class. Baltzell's study of Philadelphia suggests the same for medicine and architecture in that city.

d. Baltzell's study showed that one-fourth of the *Who's Who* listees from *Social Register* cities were in the *Social Register*.

e. Almost one third of the partners in the largest Wall Street law firms, a major source of American legal and political expertise, are listed in the *Social Register*. Baltzell's study of Philadelphia revealed several upper-class law firms in that city.

4. The major producers of expertise—*e.g.*, Harvard, Yale, Princeton, Columbia, Penn, and Stanford—are controlled by members of the American upper class. This implies at the very least the power to select and train those who will be experts.

5. Military experts are selected by the Department of Defense, which is dominated by members of the upper class and by high-level corporate executives.

6. Experts are advanced and acclaimed in accordance with their success in solving problems posed by a system which disproportionately benefits members of the upper class.

For all of these reasons, we do not believe that experts from the middle class have somehow displaced the American upper class as a governing class. They are well rewarded for their services to this group, however.

Conflict Within the Upper Class

Do the disagreements within the upper class contradict the notion that it is a governing class? Is such disagreement evidence for a pluralistic model? The answer is that it is very possible for members of a governing class to disagree as to what long-range strategies should be, not to mention short-range tactics. Indeed, Key's statement on page 2 makes such disagreement the prerequisite for democracy. Nor is the day-to-day reality of conflict, as depicted so beautifully in the case of the federal government by Cater in *Power in Washington,* necessarily in conflict with a governing-class theory. Sweezy believes that the pluralistic model integrates "a considerable body of observed fact" in a "tolerably satisfactory fashion." However, he also believes that "the state has a function in society which is prior to and more fundamental than any which present-day liberals attribute to it." [37] He is referring to the protection of private property as a system.

So What?

Another objection would run as follows. So what if the upper class controls a disproportionate amount of the wealth, and controls the corporations and the federal government? The important thing is whether or not their decisions are in the interests of the country as a whole. Would members of other classes make similar decisions on key issues? The answer to this question, above and beyond the special interests that are implied by disproportionate income and wealth, is that it is not really pertinent. This book has not tried to show that the rule of the American upper class has been a benevolent one or a malevolent one. Rather, it is concerned with the existence and the mechanics of the national upper class, not with an interpretation of the impact of its rule on American civilization for better or for worse. Whether decisions by members of the upper class are "good" for the whole country or only for themselves is difficult to answer in any case, but it is not relevant to the existence of a governing class by our definition. Such a criticism assumes that a study of social structure implies an attack on that social structure, but that is only the case, to quote Mills, under certain circumstances: "When little is known, or only trivial items publicized, or when myths prevail, then plain description becomes a radical fact—or at least is taken to be radically upsetting." [38]

Restraints

An objection closely related to the one immediately above could be formulated as follows. Even if it is true that one socioeconomic group owns a disproportionate share of the wealth and contributes a considerable percentage of national leaders, the fact remains that there are restraints on decision-makers. There are opposing interest groups and opposing socioeconomic classes, such as workers, farmers, small businessmen, and consumers, and there are restraining cultural values, as manifested in the Constitution, the Bill of Rights, civil rights laws, and the golden rule. Most of all, there is the right to vote, which means that the leaders are accountable to all the people. After showing that blue-collar workers are almost totally excluded from decision-making roles in New Haven, Dahl points to their restraining powers:

Nonetheless, it would be wrong to conclude that the activities and attitudes of people in these strata have no influence on the decisions of governmental officials. Though wage earners lack social standing, they are not without other resources, including the ballot, and what they lack as individuals they more than make up in collective resources. In short, although their direct influence is low, their indirect collective influence is high.[39]

We would agree, in Dahl's terms, that the underlying population's "potential for control" is infinitely greater than that of the upper class, but we would add that the "potential for unity" is much greater in the latter than it is in the former, which is hopelessly divided into income classes, religious groups, ethnic groups, and racial groups.[40] We also would agree that there are restraints on the power of the governing class, for the governing class is part of a system which includes other nation-states as well as other socioeconomic groups. We would even agree that members of the power elite often try to anticipate the reactions of other groups when they make their decisions. The potential power of angry, organized masses is well known in twentieth-century America thanks to foreign revolutions, the battle over women's suffrage, labor strikes, and the civil rights movement.

But Businessmen Hate Government

The final, and most important, objection that is usually raised against a governing-class model concerns the apparent autonomy of the federal government. Critics point to the New Deal, the Democratic Party, anti-business legislation, and the intense hostility of business to government in support of the idea that the federal government is a relatively autonomous institution that adjudicates disputes among various interest groups. Talcott Parsons finds business opposition to government "impossible to understand" unless we assume "genuine, and in some sense effective" governmental control of business.[41] Similarly, economist Edward S. Mason, an expert on corporations and a former president of the American Economic Association, was paraphrased as follows in *Business Week*: "Business' intense opposition to every proposed surrender of power to Washington is hardly consistent with the view that it itself dominates the U. S. government." [42]

In answer to these objections, this study has shown who controlled the New Deal—liberal elements of the American upper class, including many ex-Republicans. We have stressed that the New Deal created a split within the power elite which has not yet healed. Many members of the upper class remain unreconciled to the New Deal, believing that aristocrat Franklin Roosevelt ("Rosenfelt") was a traitor to his class who was part of an international Communist–Jewish conspiracy. However, this does not mean that other members of the upper class did not control the New Deal. As Baltzell documents, the New Deal was actually the beginning of a more ethnically representative establishment within the governing class which pushed aside the Protestant Establishment made up of heavy industrialists, fiscal conservatives, and prejudiced personalities. On a larger time scale, 1932–1964, this study has answered the claim that the federal government is autonomous by showing that the now-dominant Executive branch is honeycombed to an overwhelming degree by members of the power elite. This same evidence, buttressed by studies of campaign financing, also disposes of the myth that the Democratic Party is not controlled by elements of the American upper class. As to the charge that the upper class is not omnipotent, and therefore not a governing class, the fact remains that a very wealthy upper class which makes concessions remains a wealthy upper class. It stoops to conquer, taking the advice of its English counterparts rather than the foolhardy path of the French landlords. Perhaps Joseph P. Kennedy put this point as well as anybody could in discussing his reaction to the Depression, a time of genuine panic and confusion for many members of the upper class:

I am not ashamed to record that in those days I felt and said I would be willing to part with half of what I had if I could be sure of keeping, under law and order, the other half. Then it seemed that I should be able to hold nothing for the protection of my family.[43]

Why Businessmen Complain

There are several very good reasons why businessmen complain about the government, the first of which requires a slight detour into history. The original American political and economic system battled for many years against a centralized government in England. As Baltzell puts it, American institutions were "born in a revolt from the tyranny of a centralized government symbolized in the British monarchy and mercantilism. . . ."[44] We would add that this long and bitter struggle created an anti-government ideology, especially against a strong central government, and that this hostility has remained one of the most prominent features of American thought, if not of American practice. In short, there are historical and ideological reasons why businessmen would verbalize hostility toward the federal government. This ideological hostility, we would argue, does not answer the question of whether or not members of the American upper class of rich businessmen control the government they criticize. A second "historical" reason for hostility to the federal government has been noted in the previous paragraph; that is, many businessmen do not accept the New Deal. They remember the good old days before the Depression, and they deny the claim by some of their colleagues that changes were necessary in order to forestall more serious socioeconomic and political difficulties. However, on this point it is necessary to emphasize that not all businessmen are hostile to a strong central government and the innovations of the New Deal. Some even find labor unions a useful stabilizing influence.[45] We believe that these business liberals are coming to be the dominant influence within the upper class, as symbolized in the views of the CFR, FPA, CED, BAC, and NAC.

A third factor in understanding business hostility to the federal government is the fact that most businessmen are not part of the group that controls the government. The federal government is controlled by the corporate rich, and only a small percentage of American businesses are even incorporated, let alone large enough to sustain the owners as members of the national upper class. In short, it is necessary to specify *which* businessmen are complaining about the federal government. Small businessmen, for example, have good reason to complain. For them the government is largely an expensive nuisance which makes them keep annoying and costly records while doing very little for them. Needless to say, some of these small businessmen line up with the anti-New Deal members of the upper class to form the conservative wing of the Republican Party, which is very vocal in its hostility to a strong federal government. We suspect that this coalition would be the origin of most of the examples that Parsons and Mason could give in supporting their claim that businessmen are hostile to the federal government.

Other factors must be considered in explaining business hostility toward the federal government. First, much of this hostility is really hostility toward other businessmen, especially in the case of the regulatory agencies. For example, we have cited the case of the fight over an increase in natural gas prices, which was opposed by the other elements of the business community who would pay most of the increase in higher production costs. The FPC nonetheless took the brunt of the hostility. Along this same line, McConnell points out that "some industries, including the radio industry, the airlines, the railroad and trucking industries, and the oil companies, have actively sought regulation." [46] Then too, many businessmen are temperamentally unsuited for the give-and-take of the political world. Nor are they comfortable with the hoopla of electioneering. They see government as a bureaucratic tangle opposed to the orderly, efficient atmosphere of the corporate world. Osborn Elliott (SR, NY) goes so far as to call the corporate structure "authoritarian" in making this point.[47] This would suggest that members of the upper class with temperaments and interests different from those of most businessmen would be more successful as political leaders. Neither President Roosevelt nor President Kennedy, for example, could get very enthusiastic about business careers.

As still another factor in considering business hostility to the federal government, it must be realized that even a government controlled by the corporate rich will often take measures which are distasteful to many corporations and corporate executives. Good examples from the mid-1960's would be the need to curtail overseas spending to halt the outflow of gold to other countries, and the need to curtail investment spending to discourage the inflationary tendencies which developed in an economy that was spending increasing sums on national defense. While both of these measures were in the interests of the system as a whole, they were not in the interests of the individual corporations, and many seemed to ignore the pleas of Secretary of Commerce John T. Connor, the former president of Merck and Company, and Secretary of Defense Robert McNamara, the former president of the Ford Motor Company.

Finally, there are good reasons why businessmen well aware of their power would pretend that they did not control the government. This is such a charged point, impugning as it does the motives of our corporate leaders, that we would not make it ourselves. Instead, we will let a respectable political scientist, Grant McConnell, and a highly regarded reporter, Bernard Nossiter, speak for themselves. After pointing to business antagonisms as the first element in explaining hostility to government, McConnell goes on as follows:

Second, whether the issue is understood explicitly, intuitively, or not at all, the denunciations serve to establish and maintain the subservience of governmental units to the business constituencies to which they are actually held responsible. Attacks upon government in general place continuing pressure on governmental officers to accommodate their activities to the groups from which support is most reliable. Third, and probably most important, is that business attacks upon government are directed at any tendency toward the development of larger constituencies for the government units.[48]

After noting that "some businessmen believe the myths cultivated by the image-makers of both major parties," and that pressure on President Kennedy brought the best results for business interests, Nossiter makes this important point:

A second and related reason has to do with business sensitivity about its own power. To proclaim the triumph of business doctrine on the New Frontier might invite retaliation and counterpressure by organized labor, farmers, and other interest groups. Overt display of power in the corporate world is not only vulgar, it is unprofitable.[49]

We believe the above arguments are an adequate explanation as to why many businessmen would express hostility toward the federal government. However, even if they were not, we would still argue that a decision about business domination of the government cannot be based upon the subjective feelings of the corporate executives, corporate lawyers, and aristocrats who provide the leadership of the State Department, Defense Department, and Treasury Department. We thus conclude from our empirical evidence that many social scientists are mistaken in their respective emphases on the New Deal, the Democratic Party, and business hostility as considerations which are contrary to the notion of a governing class.

CONCLUSION

Now the reader has been introduced to the main arguments raised in the past when the upper reaches of society have been studied with the sociology-of-leadership methodology. He must re-assess these arguments in the light of the empirical evidence presented in the previous chapters. For ourselves, we conclude that the income, wealth, and institutional leadership of what Baltzell calls the "American business aristocracy" are more than sufficient to earn it the designation "governing class." As Sweezy would say, this "ruling class" is based upon the national corporate economy and the institutions that economy nourishes. It manifests itself through what the late C. Wright Mills called the power elite.

Notes . . . . . | I have used these notes for two purposes: to provide documentation and to make comments that are peripheral to the ongoing argument of the book. In cases where I have named the author and title of a book as part of the text, I have not redundantly footnoted it here.

INTRODUCTION

(*1*) *An American Business Aristocracy* was originally titled *The Philadelphia Gentleman* when it was first published by the Free Press of Glencoe in 1958. The reader is advised to use the paperback edition, *An American Business Aristocracy*, because it reprints as an appendix a paper Baltzell published in the interim between his first and second books.

(*2*) For Mills's ambivalent attitudes toward the United States, and for excellent portraits of Mills as well, see Ralph Miliband's articles "C. Wright Mills," *Monthly Review*, September 1962, pp. 260-266, and "Mills and Politics," in *The New Sociology*, edited by Irving L. Horowitz, New York: Oxford University Press, 1964. See also Saul Landau's "The Last Six Months of C. Wright Mills," *Ramparts*, August 1965, pp. 46-54. (*3*) For Mills's attitude toward Marxism, see his *The Marxists*, New York: Dell Publishing Co., 1962, and Landau, 1965. (*4*) Seymour Martin Lipset, "Aristocracy in America," *Commentary*, 26, 1958, pp. 534-537. This is a favorable review of Baltzell's first book. Lipset agrees that "There can be little doubt that America is developing something like an elite Establishment resembling Great Britain; but it is an Establishment which resembles the new, more open British one rather than the old aristocratic institution that died between 1940 and 1950" (page 537).

(*5*) Mills called Sweezy a "plain Marxist" on page 98 of *The Marxists*, 1962. (*6*) V. O. Key, *Southern Politics*, New York: Vintage Books, 1949, p. 180. At least when commenting on the higher reaches of society and money in politics, Key has a wry style. (*7*) See T. B. Bottomore, *Elites and Society*, New York: Basic Books, 1964, for an excellent discussion of Pareto, and of Mills too for that matter. (*8*) Irving L. Horowitz, "The Sociological Imagination of C. Wright Mills: In Memorium," *International Journal of Comparative Sociology*, IV, 1 (March 1963), p. 75.

(*9*) The footnote appeared on page 277 of *The Power Elite*, New York: Oxford University Press, 1956. See also pp. 11, 13, 15, 27, and 170 to understand how equivocal Mills is on this problem. On pp. 11, 13, and 15 he talks of the power elite as if it were a social class, but on page 27 he rejects the idea of a "ruling class." On page 170 he says that the federal government is not "merely" an extension of the corporate world, nor is it "in any simple way" a committee of the "ruling class." On Mills's narrow conception of "class," see the review of *The Power Elite* by Robert Lynd entitled "Power in the United States" in *The Nation*, May 12, 1956, pp. 408-411.

(*10*) Baltzell, 1958, p. 78. Baltzell is quoting from page 59 of A. Davis, B. B. Gardner, and M. R. Gardner, *Deep South: Social Anthropological Study of Caste and Class*, Chicago: University of Chicago Press, 1941. (*11*) Paul Sweezy, "The American Ruling Class," in *The Present As History*, New York: Monthly Review Press, 1953, p. 124. (*12*) Joseph A. Kahl, *The American Class Structure*, New York: Rinehart & Co., 1957, p. 12. Kahl then comments: "Here, obviously, we depart from the terminology of Weber in favor of ordinary English."

(*13*) Robert A. Dahl, *Who Governs?* New Haven: Yale University Press, 1961, p. 229. For further discussions of social class, see the essays by a wide variety of experts in Reinhard Bendix and Seymour Martin Lipset, eds., *Class, Status and Power,* Second Edition, New York: The Free Press, 1966.

(*14*) William Kornhauser, "Power Elite or Veto Groups?" in *Culture and Social Character*, edited by S. M. Lipset and Leo Lowenthal, New York: The Free Press, 1961, p. 265. This essay is especially important because it compares and contrasts the views of Mills and the pluralist David Riesman. Riesman states in the same book that contains Kornhauser's essay that it "clearly analyzed" the arguments between his position and that of Mills (p. 449).

(*15*) See Seymour Martin Lipset and Reinhard Bendix, *Social Mobility in Industrial Society*, Berkeley: University of California Press, 1959. See also the more recent essays in the already-cited volume edited by Bendix and Lipset, 1966. (*16*) E. Digby Baltzell, *The Protestant Establishment*, New York: Random House, 1964, pp. 3-4.

(*17*) According to sociologists Scott Greer and Peter Orleans in an article on "Political Sociology" in the *Handbook of Modern Sociolgy*, edited by Robert Feris, Chicago: Rand McNally, 1964, p. 830, the term "co-optation" was first used as a research term by Philip Selznick in his study of the TVA. Greer and Orleans define co-optation as the mechanism of committing necessary subgroups to the dominant group; this does not differ greatly from my emphasis on the commitment of individuals to the dominant group. I will refer to this article several times throughout this book because it is a summary of views and findings on "political sociology" as of the mid-1960's.

(*18*) Robert A. Dahl, "A Critique of the Ruling Elite Model," *American Political Science Review*, LII (1958), 468. (*19*) Dahl, 1958; Nelson Polsby, *Community Power and Political Theory*, New Haven: Yale University Press, 1963, pp. 42-44. Dahl's article, "A Critique of the Ruling Elite Model," is one of the best reviews of Mills's *The Power Elite*. It has only limited relevance for this study because I am concerned with a governing *class* model rather than a ruling *elite* model.

(*20*)Dahl, 1961, p. 331. (*21*) The phrase "sociology of leadership" is based upon a sentence on page 304 of Baltzell's *The Protestant Establishment*: ". . .

it is the sociological composition of its leadership which is my main concern."
(*22*) Dahl, 1961, p. 66. (*23*) Dahl, 1961, p. 334. (*24*) Baltzell, 1958, p. 424,
and especially Raymond Bauer, "Social Psychology and the Study of Policy
Formation," *American Psychologist*, XXI (1966), 933-942.

(*25*) Nelson Polsby, "How to Study Community Power: The Pluralist Alterna-
tive," *Journal of Politics*, XXII (1960), 482-483. (*26*) Polsby, 1963, p. 119.
(*27*) Dixon Wecter, *The Saga of American Society*, New York: Charles
Scribner's and Sons; Harold M. Hodges, Jr., *Peninsula People: Social Stratifi-
cation in a Metropolitan Complex*, San Jose State College, 1962, mimeographed.

(*28*) Baltzell, 1964, pp. 141-142. (*29*) Baltzell, 1964, p. 8. (*30*) I learned about
Rusk's "severance pay" arrangements on page 4 of *I. F. Stone's Weekly* for
September 20, 1965.

CHAPTER ONE

(*1*) Wecter, 1937, pp. 103-104. (*2*) Wecter, 1937, p. 473. (*3*) Harvey W.
Zorbaugh, *The Gold Coast and the Slum*, Chicago: University of Chicago Press,
1929; Lucy Kavaler, *The Private World of High Society*, New York: Douglas
McKay, 1960. On the *Social Register* in general, see Cleveland Amory, *Who
Killed Society?*, New York: Harper & Bros., 1960, Chapter 1; Baltzell, 1958;
and *The New York Times*, April 7, 1963, E-120. (*4*) E. Digby Baltzell, "Who's
Who in America" and "The Social Register," 1953, p. 272, in Bendix and Lipset,
1966.

(*5*) Cleveland Amory, unlike his 31 Proper Bostonian relatives who also are
descended from the wealthy eighteenth-century merchant of the same name,
chooses not to be listed in the *Social Register*. This is to his credit, perhaps, for
he dislikes its ethnic bias and its exclusion of men of talent and achievement.
But when he pooh-poohs its value as an index and implies that its vogue is
passing, he is simply mistaken, as a cross-checking of his excellent books with
the 1965 *Social Register Locater* shows. There are other members of the "old
guard" who disparage the *Social Register* as an index, but they do so for a
different reason. Namely, they claim that "anybody" can get in. However, as
Kavaler notes, there is usually a copy handy in the homes of such people. If
the *Social Register* is just a telephone book, it is nonetheless supported by
38,000 families in 12 cities, who faithfully return the forms which keep their
names in its pages. See Amory, 1960.

(*6*) Baltzell, 1958, pp. 36-37. (*7*) Mills, 1956, p. 117. Mills does not develop
this finding. In fact, he only checked four volumes, Philadelphia, Boston,
Chicago, and New York. It should be noted that Mills was aware of Baltzell's
findings when he wrote. He footnotes Baltzell's dissertation in his chapter on
the "Metropolitan 400." (*8*) *The New York Times*, April 7, 1963, E-120.

(*9*) Baltzell, 1958, p. 37. See also Jacob Brackman, "The Gospel According to
St Paul's," *Esquire*, June 1966, pp. 92-94, 135-136. (*10*) The quote from Sweezy
and the quote from Baltzell are both to be found in Baltzell, 1964, p. 344. The
comment by Sweezy is in his review of Mills's *The Power Elite*, "Power Elite
or Ruling Class?" *Monthly Review*, September, 1956, p. 148.

(*11*) *Newsweek*, February 9, 1959, pp. 53-56. (*12*) I tabulated these schools from the Lawrenceville alumni journal, the *Lawrentian*, XXX, No. 1 (Autumn, 1965), 33-34. (*13*) Gene Hawes, "The Colleges of America's Upper Class," *Saturday Review of Literature*, November 16, 1963, pp. 68-71.

(*14*) Baltzell, 1964, p. 135. (*15*) See Mills, 1956, pp. 400-402. The quote is on page 402. (*16*) Baltzell, 1964, p. 340. (*17*) *Congressional Record* (Senate), July 19, 1965, A3870. (*18*) Baltzell, 1964, p. 19. (*19*) Baltzell, 1958, p. 380. (*20*) Baltzell, 1958, p. 26. (*21*) Wecter, 1937, p. 137. (*22*) Baltzell, 1964, p. 300. The remark by Morgan is on page 36.

(*23*) *Look*, April 6, 1965, p. 41. (*24*) Time, December 4, 1964, pp. 54-67. For the tremendous importance of big businessmen in charity fund raising, see the article on that topic in the January, 1966, *Fortune*, "The Fund Raising Businessmen—Eight Billion Dollars," by Robert Sheehan. (*25*) *Time*, December 11, 1964, p. 56. (*26*) Baltzell, 1958, p. 379.

(*27*) J. W. Moore, "Exclusiveness and Ethnocentrism in a Metropolitan Upper Class Agency." *Pacific Sociological Review*, V (1962), 16-20.

(*28*) On tuition, expenses, and sheltering a horse, see Kavaler, 1960; on the right connections, see *Time*, July 30, 1965, p. 41; and on the style inculcated at these schools, see Kavaler, 1960, and Brackman, 1966. (*29*) Sweezy, 1953, p. 124. (*30*) See Roger Brown's *Social Psychology*, New York: The Free Press, 1966, for an excellent chapter on social class which abandons the concept.

(*31*) St. Paul's *Alumni Horae*, Spring, 1965, pp. 30-31. Baltzell's (St. Paul's, 1935) *The Protestant Establishment* is reviewed in this issue by another prominent sociologist, George Homans (St. Paul's, 1928; SR, Boston), who hardly believes a word of it. Homans, an expert on small groups, does not see how symptomatic it is that Jews are excluded from clubs. He thinks Baltzell "obsessed" with club membership. Homans is a member of the Society of the Cincinnati, the Colonial Society of Massachusetts, and the Tavern Club. (*32*) St. Paul's *Alumni Horae*, Spring, 1965, p. 68.

(*33*) Kavaler, 1960, p. 285. (*34*) Kavaler, 1960, p. 289. (*35*) *Time*, July 2, 1965, pp. 38-50. (*36*) Kavaler, 1960, p. 37. (*37*) *Time*, July 2, 1965, pp. 38-50. (*38*) *Time*, July 2, 1965, pp. 38-50. (*39*) Santa Cruz *Sentinel*, April 18, 1965, p. 16A. (*40*) Baltzell, 1958, pp. 250-251. (*41*) Ann Bicknell, "The Directors of the 20 Largest Industrials for 1963," a student project for my course on the upper class at California State College at Los Angeles, Spring, 1965. It should be mentioned that James Morrison and I re-analyzed and supplemented all student-collected information.

(*42*) Baltzell, 1964, p. 371. (*43*) *Time*, August 7, 1964, p. 21. (*44*) The details of these studies for my course on the American upper class at the University of California, Santa Cruz, Winter, 1966, will be published as a single paper. That they are separate studies accounts for the fact that there were 25 people from San Francisco and only 20 from Los Angeles.

(*45*) James W. Gerard, *My first 83 Years in America*, Garden City, New York: Doubleday, 1951, p. 317. (*46*) *Forbes*, August 15, 1965, p. 15. The article went on: "Why is the federal government insisting on setting natural gas prices? Largely because a good segment of private industry wants it to." (*47*) Mills, 1956, p. 122.

(*48*) See Baltzell, 1964, for details on the depth of this chasm between the two religious groups. I think his account justifies the word "incredible" in describing the behavior of some WASPs. See especially the incredible letter written by then-President Herbert Hoover on page 30 of Baltzell's account. (*49*) Baltzell, 1964, p. 63.

(*50*) For a detailed study of the problems of the ethnic rich, see Richard Whalen's *The Founding Father*, New York: New American Library, 1964, which tells the story of the Kennedy family's rise to a position of importance within the national upper class. (*51*) Amory, 1960. (*52*) Stewart Alsop, "America's New Big Rich," *Saturday Evening Post*, July 17, 1965, pp. 23-46. (*53*) See John Bainbridge, *The Super-Americans*, New York: Doubleday & Co., 1961.

(*54*) Baltzell's *The Protestant Establishment* is concerned primarily with this split as it manifested itself throughout the first 60 years of this century, while Sweezy acknowledges its existence on the second to last page of his article on "The American Ruling Class," in *The Present as History*, 1953.

(*55*) The paper I am referring to is "Characteristics of Political Liberals and Conservatives" by Jack E. Rossmann (Macalester College) and David P. Campbell (University of Minnesota), which was read at the Midwestern Psychological Association meeting in Chicago, Ill., May 1, 1965. I would also refer the reader to "Left and Right: A Basic Dimension of Ideology and Personality," by Silvan Tomkins, published in *The Study of Lives*, ed. Robert W. White, New York: Atherton Press, 1963. In a study I did with psychologist Henry Minton, it was found that Tomkins's Left-Right personality test correlated highly with political liberalism and political conservatism, both by *self-ratings* of political attitude (obviating criticisms of previous studies that selected their conservatives by poorly-worded ideological tests) *and* by group identification (our subjects were college students who were Goldwater Republicans, Young Democrats, Young Trotskyists, and members of the DuBois Club, as well as the usual classroom of introductory psychology students). The correlation between self-rated conservatism (7-point scale) and the Right Score on Tomkins's test was .46, the correlation between self-rated liberalism and Tomkins's Left Score was .42.

(*56*) Mills, 1956, p. 108. (*57*) Herman Miller, *Rich Man Poor Man*, New York: Signet Books, 1964, p. 138. Here Miller tells us that only 3 per cent of the top 1 per cent lived entirely on unearned income. This translates to 13,500 families if the top 1 per cent is 450,000 families, to 15,000 families if the top 1 per cent is "about one-half million."

(*58*) Mills, 1956, p. 74; Kavaler, 1960, p. 231. For the raw data for a study of the "jet set" of the mid-Sixties, see *The International Nomads*, New York: G. P. Putnam's Sons, 1966, by Lanfranco Rasponi, especially pp. 238-436. (*59*) Mills, 1956, p. 60. Mills is probably following Baltzell's dissertation at this point. (*60*) Baltzell, 1958, p. 45. (*61*) Mervin B. Freedman, "The Post-Industrial Generation: Roots of Student Discontent," *The Nation*, June 14, 1965, p. 642. (*62*) Baltzell, 1958, p. 59. (*63*) Baltzell, 1964, pp. 80-81. (*64*) Baltzell, 1958, pp. 330, 439-440.

(*65*) With one exception, the clubs on this list are said by either Baltzell or Kavaler to be "very exclusive." For some, membership is supposedly hereditary. The one exception is the Rainier Club, which I learned to be the most exclusive club in Seattle from one of the investigators of "Pacific City." See Delbert C. Miller's "Decision-Making Cliques in Community Power Structures: A Comparative Study of an American and an English City," *The American Journal of Sociology*, LXIV, No. 3 (November, 1958), 229-310. Nine of Miller's 12 Seattle "Key Influentials" were in this club (p. 304). Careful studies are needed to determine the clubs in all parts of the country which have as their members private school graduates who interact and intermarry with *Social Register* listees and members of the clubs on our list.

(*66*) Baltzell, 1964, pp. 370-373. (*67*) Kavaler, 1960, pp. 8-9. (*68*) Baltzell, 1953, p. 271.

CHAPTER TWO

(*1*) See especially A. A. Berle Jr.'s *Power Without Property*, New York: Harcourt, Brace, 1959. However, for a detailed technical consideration of the problem of concentration in the modern corporate economy, see the testimony by various experts before the Hart Committee, published by the U. S. Government Printing Office in 1964 under the title *Economic Concentration, Part 1, Overall and Conglomerate Aspects*. See especially the testimony of Gardner Means on pp. 9-19. For a summary of the TNEC hearings of the 1930's, see David Lynch, *The Concentration of Economic Power*, New York: Columbia University Press, 1946. For a readable summary of the Hart Committee findings as of the mid-Sixties, see David Michaels' article, "Monopoly in the United States," in the *Monthly Review* for April, 1966.

(*2*) F. G. Clark and S. Ramonaczy, *Where the Money Comes From*, New York: D. Van Nostrand, 1961, p. 42. (*3*) Economist Robert Gordon's *Business Leadership in the Large Corporation*, first published in 1945 by the Brookings Institution, and reissued as a paperback with a new preface by the University of California Press in 1966, makes much of the existence of a great many inside directors. As shall be seen, especially in the last chapter, I am at odds with Gordon on this point.

(*4*) See Andrew Hacker, "Power to Do What?", *The New Sociology*, edited by Irving Horowitz, New York: Oxford University Press, 1964, for an excellent discussion of the powers of corporation directors. Hacker considered this paper a partial answer to those critics of Mills who said that he did not spell out the powers of his power elite. See also *Forbes*, November 15, 1965, p. 11.

(*5*) A. A. Berle, Jr., *Economic Power and the Free Society: A Preliminary Discussion of the Corporation*, New York: The Fund for the Republic, 1958, p. 10. After selecting this quote, I later discovered in my study of the relevant works of Robert A. Dahl that he too found it appropriate. See Dahl, "Business and Politics: A Critical Appraisal of Political Science," *Social Science Research on Business: Product and Potential*, New York: Columbia University Press, 1959, pp. 9-10. (*6*) This is of course the title of Berle's 1959 book, already cited. It neatly summarizes the theory held by Berle.

(*7*) See Robert Heilbroner, "The View from the Top," *The Business Establishment*, edited by Earl F. Cheit, New York: John Wiley & Sons, 1964; Benjamin Smith, "Economic Ideologies and the Political System," *Government and Society*, edited by Ake Sandler and Robert H. Simmons, Dubuque, Iowa: Wm. C. Brown, 1965; and most especially, Victor Perlo's article, "People's Capitalism and Stock Ownership," in the *American Economic Review*, XLVIII, 3, June,

1958. Perlo is a Marxist, but the staid old *American Economic Review* apparently found the information developed in this article to be of a quality suitable for its unmarxist pages.

(*8*) Talcott Parsons, *Structure and Process in Modern Societies*, New York: The Free Press, 1960, pp. 199-225. This is a detailed review of Mills's *The Power Elite*. (*9*) Daniel Bell, *The End of Ideology*, New York: The Free Press, 1960, p. 42. (*10*) *Wall Street Journal*, May 6, 1966, p. 1, Pacific Coast Edition. (*11*) Floyd Hunter, *The Big Rich and the Little Rich*, Garden City, New York: Doubleday, 1965, pp. 131-133.

(*12*) Hodges, 1962. There are no page numbers on this mimeographed research report. (*13*) Miller, 1964, p. 24. The information on the top .1 per cent comes from Jean Crockett and Irwin Friend, "Characteristics of Stock Ownership," 1963 *Proceedings* of the Business and Economic Statistics Section, American Statistical Association, Washington, D. C. (*14*) Miller, 1964, p. 233. In 1959, the OBE estimate of "income other than earnings" was $60.1 billion, the Census estimate was $37.3 billion.

(*15*) Gabriel Kolko, *Wealth and Power in America*, New York: Praeger, 1962; George Lent, *Ownership and Tax Exempt Securities 1913-1953*, New York: National Bureau of Economic Research, 1953. According to Lent, in 1940-41, one of the last years taxpayers with incomes in excess of $5,000 were asked but not required to report income from tax-exempt securities, only 40 per cent—about $3 billion out of $8 billion—was actually reported for state and local securities held by individuals (p. 94). Furthermore, "somewhat smaller fractions were reported on other tax-exempt securities (p. 96)." Lent adds that for the same year, 1941, and the same over-$5,000 income group, only 53.1 per cent of net total dividends were reported. Even including an estimate of the dividend component of fiduciary income raises the total to only 61.1 per cent (p. 96).

(*16*) Miller, 1964, p. 53. (*17*) Leon Keyserling, "Taxes From Whom, For What?" *The New Republic*, April 23, 1966, p. 18. (*18*) Mills, 1956, pp. 152-154. The phrase "soak the high salaried" comes from a column by Eric Sevareid, *Los Angeles Times*, April 18, 1965, G-3. On avoiding inheritance taxes, see *Time*, July 8, 1966, pp. 65-67. (*19*) See the table prepared by the Office of Tax Analysis, *Congressional Record* (Senate), November 1, 1963, p. 19872. The tax rate for income groups over $1 million averaged from 23.7 per cent to 24.6 per cent.

(*20*) William A. Williams, *The Great Evasion*, Chicago: Quadrangle Books, 1964, p. 159; Bernard D. Nossiter, *The Mythmakers*, Boston: Houghton, Mifflin, 1964, p. 24. (*21*) Robert J. Lampman, *The Share of Top Wealth-Holders in National Wealth*, Princeton: Princeton University Press, 1962, p. 2.

(*22*) R. M. Titmus, "Poverty vs. Inequality: Diagnosis," *The Nation*, February 8, 1965, p. 132. (*23*) Robert Heilbroner, *The Future as History*, New York: Harper & Bros., 1959, p. 125; Keith Butters, Lawrence E. Thompson and Lynn L. Bollinger, *Effect of Taxation on Investments by Individuals*, Cambridge: The Riverside Press, 1953, p. 400, but see all of their chapter 16 for a detailed discussion of this complex problem. (*24*) Mills, 1956, p. 122. (*25*) John Brooks, *The Seven Fat Years*, New York: Harper & Bros., 1958, p. 49.

(*26*) Mills, 1956, pp. 149-150. Butters et al., 1953, p. 25, estimated that the .1

per cent of families who had incomes over $50,000 in 1949 held 35 per cent of all outstanding stock held by individuals, that the .5 per cent who made over $25,000 had 50 per cent of the stock, and that the 1 per cent who made over $15,000 had 65 per cent of the stock.

(*27*) Cleveland Amory, *The Proper Bostonians,* New York: E. P. Dutton & Co., 1947; Baltzell, 1958. (*28*) Don Villarejo, "Stock Ownership and Control of Corporations," *New University Thought,* II Autumn, 1961 and Winter, 1962, 33-77, 47-65. (*29*) Paul Sweezy, "Interest Groups in the American Economy," reprinted in *The Present as History,* New York: Monthly Review Press, 1953.

(*30*) Victor Perlo, *The Empire of High Finance,* New York: International Publishers, 1957, pp. 47-49. And as Villarejo points out, 1961, p. 56, Firestone Tire and Rubber was listed as management controlled when even today the Firestone family owns 25 per cent of the stock. (*31*) Ferdinand Lundberg, *America's Sixty Families,* New York: The Citadel Press, 1937, p. 507. (*32*) Lundberg, 1937, pp. 504-505. (*33*) *Congressional Record* (House), July 29, 1965, pp. 18040-18041. Also March 15, 1966, pp. 5590-5594. (*34*) Gordon, 1945, pp. 43, 154.

(*35*) *Forbes,* May 1, 1964, p. 22. According to TNEC monograph No. 29, p. xvi, during the 1930's the du Ponts, Mellons and Rockefellers controlled 15 of the then-largest 200 nonfinancial corporations—11 per cent of the total assets of the top 200 were theirs. (*36*) Cheit, 1964, p. 172. (*37*) Cheit, 1964, p. 173.

(*38*) Cheit, 1964, p. 174. (*39*) Villarejo, 1961, p. 59. This study explores all the issues of stock ownership in detail. By "control" Villarejo means the power to change management when necessary. (*40*) Cheit, 1964, p. 175; Villarejo, 1961, p. 50. (*41*) Villarejo, 1962, pp. 47-61, has an excellent discussion of directors with a slightly different classification scheme.

(*42*) C. V. Parkinson, "The Web of the Giant Banks," *The Minority of One,* February, 1963, p. 4; Perlo, 1957. (*43*) For a summary of studies on interlocks, see *Interlocks in Corporate Management,* a staff report to the House Antitrust Subcommittee, March 12, 1965, U. S. Government Printing Office. See also Gordon, 1945.

(*44*) Fred Nuss, "The Directors of the Top 15 Banks," a student project for my course on the upper class at California State College at Los Angeles, Spring, 1965. (*45*) Peter F. Drucker, "The New Tycoons," *Harper's Magazine,* May, 1955, p. 40. (*46*) Drucker, 1955, p. 39. (*47*) Ronald Schaffer, "The Directors of the Top 15 Insurance Companies," a student project for my course on the upper class at California State College at Los Angeles, Spring, 1965.

(*48*) Berle, 1959. (*49*) Parkinson, 1963. (*50*) For my course on the upper class at California State College at Los Angeles, Spring, 1965. This student studied only outside directors because she went into great detail on their careers. (*51*) The information for the analysis of transportation, utilities, and merchandising was gathered by Katherine Casey, one of my undergraduate research assistants at the University of California, Santa Cruz.

(*52*) *Time,* January 21, 1966, p. 69A, in an article on a takeover attempt by multi-millionaire Norton Simon. (*53*) Perlo, 1957, p. 93. (*54*) Perlo, 1957, p. 93. (*55*) All information on power companies comes from *Top Stockholders of*

Private Power Companies, mimeographed by the Electric Consumers Information Service (ECIC), 2000 Florida Avenue N. W., Washington 9, D. C.

(56) Perlo, 1957, pp. 182-186. *(57)* C. Wright Mills, "The American Business Elite: A Collective Portrait," in *Power, Politics, and People,* New York: Ballantine, 1963, p. 122.

(58) W. Lloyd Warner and James C. Abegglin, *Big Business Leaders in America,* New York: Harper & Bros., 1955, p. 156. See their chapter 8 for a comparison of the leaders originally from the upper class and those who have risen. *(59)* Here I am following psychologists David Krech, Richard S. Crutchfield and Egerton L. Ballachey on page 327 of their best-selling social psychology textbook, *Individual in Society,* New York, McGraw-Hill Book Company, 1962. For an economist who thinks the managerial revolution is fantasy because of the psychology of managers, see Sumner Slichter, "The Power Holders in the American Economy," *Saturday Evening Post,* December 13, 1958, p. 99, who says that "Burnham badly misjudged the psychology of managers . . . Managers, on the whole, are a cautious and conventional group, well suited to run going concerns according to accepted rules and tradition, but far from fitted to grab power."

(60) Cheit, 1964; Kolko, 1962. *(61)* Gordon, 1945, p. 158. *(62) Time,* April 16, 1965, p. 42 *(63)* On the "managerial revolution," see also C. Wright Mills, "A Marx for the Managers," 1942, reprinted in *Power, Politics, and People,* New York: Ballantine Books, 1963, and Paul M. Sweezy, 1942, "The Illusion of the Managerial Revolution," reprinted in *The Present as History,* 1953.

(64) Gordon, 1945, pp. 264-265. On the importance of the law firms Gordon and I are in complete accord. He also agrees with Mills and Berle, to be quoted later in this section, that these firms are tied closely to—"really a part of"—the financial community.

(65) Erwin O. Smigel, *The Wall Street Lawyer,* New York: The Free Press, 1964, p. 74. *(66)* Smigel, 1964, p. 9. *(67)* Donald Matthews, *The Social Background of Political Decision-Makers,* New York: Random House, 1954, p. 30. The percentages on lawyers are from Suzanne Keller, *Beyond the Ruling Class,* New York: Random House, 1963, p. 325. *(68)* Baltzell, 1958, p. 55. *(69)* Mills, 1956, p. 289.

(70) A. A. Berle, Jr., *Encyclopedia of the Social Sciences,* IX New York: Macmillan, 1948, p. 341. The use of this and the preceding quote were suggested to me by a reading of Smigel, 1964. They can be found on pages 12 and 13 of Smigel's book. There is a wonderful Freudian slip in Smigel's quote from Mills in which he says the military "squanders" rather than "ponders," as Mills said.

(71) Richard Kronish, "The House of Delegates of the American Bar Association," a student paper for my course on the upper class at the University of California, Santa Cruz, Winter, 1966. This is my interpretation of Kronish's basic data. *(72)* Smigel, 1964, p. 4. *(73)* D. C. Blaisdell, *Economic Power and Political Pressures,* TNEC Monograph No. 26, Washington, D. C.: U. S. Government Printing Office, 1941, p. 37. *(74)* Mills, 1956, pp. 147-148.

CHAPTER THREE

(1) Richard Rovere, *The American Establishment,* New York: Harcourt,

Brace & World, 1962, p. 9. (*2*) Richard Rovere, "The Interlocking Overlappers," *The American Establishment,* 1962, p. 268. Only Rovere will notice that I omitted the word "unhappy" between "the" and "influence." (*3*) See *The Foundation Directory,* New York: Russell Sage Foundation, 1964.

(*4*) See Fred Cook's "Foundations as a Tax Dodge," *The Nation,* April 20, 1963, pp. 321-324. However, there is much that is not covered in Cook's early article. I have benefited greatly from a reading of the relevant prose in Congressman Wright Patman's hearings. See *Tax-Exempt Foundations and Charitable Trusts: Their Impact on Our Economy,* December 31, 1962, October 16, 1963, and March 20, 1964, U. S. Government Printing Office. The first installment tells about size, the second installment discusses shady dealings, and the third installment tells about the great power in Florida of one branch of the du Pont family through a charitable foundation. See also *Tax-Exempt Foundations: Their Impact on Small Business,* Hearings Before Subcommittee No. 1 on Foundations, July, August, September, 1964, Washington, D. C.: U. S. Government Printing Office. See especially pp. 4-5, 125 (where it is stated that 11 large foundations have 56 per cent of foundation assets), and p. 136 (where it reveals the large sums paid to trustees for a few days of meetings).

(*5*) *Virginia Law Review,* XXXIV, February, 1948, 182-201. The quote is from page 188. (*6*) The information on the foundation trustees was gathered and analyzed by Patricia Allen as a student report for my course on the upper class at California State College at Los Angeles, Spring, 1965. James Morrison and I re-analyzed the data to determine the percentage who were members of the upper class and power elite.

(*7*) Richard Elman, "The Timid Crusaders," *The Nation,* March 1, 1965, p. 217. (*8*) "Study of Soviet Union Rewarding, Frustrating," Los Angeles *Times,* February 14, 1965, E-8. (*9*) Cook, 1963. (*10*) Dan Smoot, *The Invisible Government,* 1962, published by the Dan Smoot Report, Inc., P. O. Box 9538, Dallas, Texas. See first, however, Joseph Kraft's "School for Statesmen," *Harper's Magazine,* July, 1958, pp. 64-68, and Paul Rowen's "America's Most Powerful Club," *Harper's Magazine,* September, 1960, pp. 79-84.

(*11*) Smoot, 1962, pp. 14-16. (*12*) Smoot, 1962, p. 21. Smoot is quoting from a booklet entitled "Committees on Foreign Relations: Directory of Members," January, 1961, available from CFR. A list of the members of these committees for the early 1960's also can be found in Mary M. Davison's *The Secret Government of the United States,* Omaha, Neb.: The Greater Nebraskan, 1962, and available in any American Opinion Bookstore. Mary Davison is secretary of the Council on American Relations. (*13*) Smoot, 1962, pp. 168-171.

(*14*) The information on FPA's Great Decisions was obtained from one of its pamphlets advertising the 1965 program. On the FPA and its relation to CFR, see Joseph Kraft, "School for Statesmen," *Harper's Magazine,* July, 1958. (*15*) For information on the CED, see Smoot, 1962; and Joseph Monsen and Mark Cannon, *The Makers of Public Policy,* New York: McGraw-Hill Book Company, 1965, and CED pamphlets.

(*16*) Hobart Rowen, *The Free Enterprisers,* New York: G. P. Putnam's Sons, 1964, p. 77. See also the excellent scholarly article by Norman F. Keiser, "Public Responsibility and Federal Advisory Groups: A Case Study," *Western Po-*

litical Science Quarterly, June, 1958, pp. 251-264, which gives details on the origins of the BAC, attempts to investigate its activities, and the nature of its meetings. (*17*) Hobart Rowen, "America's Most Powerful Private Club," *Harper's Magazine,* September, 1960, p. 84. Quoted in Smoot, 1962, p. 84.

(*18*) *Time,* January 8, 1965, pp. 40-41. (*19*) David Wise and Thomas B. Ross, *The Invisible Government,* New York: Random House, 1964, p. 321. (*20*) See the excellent analysis by David S. McLellan and Charles Woodhouse, "The Business Elite and Foreign Policy," *Western Political Science Quarterly,* XIII March, 1960. (*21*) R. W. Gable, "NAM: Influential Lobby or Kiss of Death?" *Journal of Politics,* XV (May, 1953), 271. (*22*) *Forbes,* October 1, 1965, p. 37. On corporate fund raising for the universities see Sheehan, 1966. (*23*) Gerard, 1951, p. 320. Gerard believes his list was the starting point for *America's Sixty Families,* but Lundberg, 1937, p. xi, denies this.

(*24*) Irving Janowitz, *The Professional Soldier,* New York: The Free Press, 1960, pp. 401-402. (*25*) Douglass Cater, *Power in Washington,* New York: Random House, 1964, pp. 14-15. Emmet Hughes, *The Ordeal of Power,* New York: Atheneum, 1963, p. 157, tells of at least one ambassador who relied on air mail editions of the New York papers for information on policy. (*26*) William Rivers, *The Opinionmakers,* Boston: Beacon Press, 1965, chapter 3.

(*27*) On this more important, more subtle control by advertising, see the excellent article by Howard Gossage, an advertising executive, in the August, 1965, issue of *Ramparts,* pp. 31-36. The article is titled "The Fictitious Freedom of the Press." (*28*) *Time,* March 4, 1966, p. 64. (*29*) *Time,* June 28, 1963, p. 58; *Time,* January 1, 1965, p. 49; *Saturday Evening Post,* October 9, 1965, pp. 33-60.

(*30*) On *Time,* see the *Saturday Evening Post,* January 16, 1965, pp. 28-45. For my information on newspaper and magazine chains in general, I relied primarily on Edwin Emery's *The Press and America,* 2nd Edition, New Jersey: Prentice-Hall, 1962. (*31*) Rivers, 1965, p. 31.

(*32*) "The flaw in the pluralist heaven is that the heavenly chorus sings with a strong upper-class accent." E. E. Schattschneider, *The Semisovereign People,* New York: Holt, Rinehart & Winston, 1960, p. 35. I am grateful to Terry Ball and his paper on shaping public opinion for my course on the upper class at the University of California, Santa Cruz, Winter, 1966, for this reference and several other details in this chapter. (*33*) Cater, 1964, p. 247.

CHAPTER FOUR

(*1*) See Brogan's Introduction to the revised edition of Joseph S. Clark's *Congress: The Sapless Branch,* New York: Harper & Row, 1965. (*2*) See Alan Cranston, "A Million-Dollar Loser Looks at Campaigning," *Fortune,* November, 1964, for a candidate's tale of woe. See also Mills, 1956, chapter 11. (*3*) Cater, 1964, p. 7.

(*4*) Alexander Heard, *The Costs of Democracy,* New York: Doubleday, 1962.

(*5*) Daniel M. Ogden and Arthur L. Peterson, *Electing the President 1964,* San Francisco: Chandler Publishing Co., 1965, p. 207. (*6*) See, for example, Parsons, 1960, p. 214. (*7*) Cater, 1964, p. 182. (*8*) Cater, 1964, p. 193.

(*9*) On 1952, see Mills, 1956, p. 166. For 1952 and 1956, see *Hearings on 1956 Presidential and Senatorial Campaign Practice* (1956) and *1956 General Elec-*

tion Campaigns, U. S. Senate, 84th Congress, Second Session (known as Gore Committee). (*10*) V. O. Key, *Politics, Parties, and Pressure Groups,* New York: Thomas Y. Crowell, 1958, p. 543. My understanding of political party finances in general owes much to Chapter 18 of this book. (*11*) Herbert Alexander, *Financing the 1960 Election,* Princeton: Citizens' Research Foundation, 1962, p. 61; Herbert E. Alexander, *Financing the 1964 Election,* Princeton: Citizens' Research Foundation, 1966, p. 89, (*12*) Key 1958, p. 548. (*13*) *U. S. World News & Report,* July 20, 1964, p. 41.

(*14*) I found this quote on pp. 276-277 of an article by Paul Sweezy and Leo Huberman on "Goldwaterism" in the *Monthly Review,* September, 1964. It is from a column by the syndicated columnists Allen and Scott, which Sweezy and Huberman read in the *Daily Times,* Mamoroneck, N. Y., July 15, 1964. (*15*) "Goldwater Diggins," *The Nation,* August 24, 1964. I am indebted to a paper for my course on the upper class at California State College at Los Angeles, Spring, 1965, by Richard Valdez, entitled "Goldwater Funds," for a detailed study of newspaper and magazine accounts of Goldwater funding. (*16*) Heilbronner, 1964, p. 18.

(*17*) Stephen Shaddegg, New York: Holt, Rinehart & Winston, 1965, p. 91. This is an amusing book on *What Happened to Goldwater?* What happened was he abandoned Shaddegg and other "true conservatives" for the likes of Kitchel, *et al.* See also, Walter Pincus, "The Fight Over Money," *Atlantic,* April, 1966.

(*18*) Alexander, 1966. This source shows the slight changes in 1964 Republican giving, but it also shows the continued importance of New York, Pennsylvania, and other Eastern states, and the continued reliance on big givers (12 per cent of Republican national income came from 15,000 people who gave $1,000 or more—p. 84). (*19*) Lundberg, 1937, p. 450.

(*20*) Key, 1958, p. 544. (*21*) Baltzell, 1958, p. 502. (*22*) Whalen, 1964, p. 119. (*23*) Baltzell, 1958, pp. 162-163, 438-440, 464-465. (*24*) Baltzell, 1964, pp. 239-240. (*25*) Whalen, 1964, p. 119. This is an example of co-optation. (*26*) Gerard, 1951, p. 324. Gerard's assistant was Walter J. Cummings (SR, Chicago), head of the Continental Illinois National Bank and Trust Company. (*27*) Gerard, 1951, p. 325.

(*28*) For Daly and Bryan, see Gerard, 1951, p. 92. For the fact that Gerard lived next door to the ex-Democrat Willkie, whom Gerard met at the 1924 Democratic National Convention, see Gerard, 1951, p. 308. (*29*) Baltzell, 1964, p. 253. (*30*) Robert Engler, *The Politics of Oil,* New York: Macmillan, 1961, p. 353.

(*31*)On Pauley, see Engler, 1961, pp. 341-343; the quote in the main text is on p. 341, the quote that is the footnote is on p. 342. (*32*) Engler, 1961, p. 345. (*33*) This information was compiled for me by Terry Ball from the Gore Committee lists. See note 9 above.

(*34*) As a matter of fact, social interactions within the Democratic Party may lead to assimilation, but this point needs further study. See Baltzell, 1964, pp. 307-312, and Lipset's hopeful comment in his review of Baltzell's first book (*Commentary,* 1958, p. 537) that "young scions of the *Social Register* mingle at social, political, and intellectual gatherings with minority group, especially Jewish, professionals whom they have met at the meetings of ADA or other community welfare-minded organizations."

(35) Alexander, 1962, 1966. *(36)* Baltzell, 1964, pp. 305-306. *(37)* *Forbes,* August 1, 1965, pp. 20-25. See also Rasponi, 1966, pp. 274-277. *(38)* Nick Thimmesch and William Johnson, *Robert Kennedy at 40,* New York: W. W. Norton & Co., 1965, p. 42. *(39)* Allan Potter, "The American Governing Class," *British Journal of Sociology,* 13, 1962, p. 314. *(40)* Much of the data in this section comes from a student paper at California State College at Los Angeles by Mary Ann Ross, "The Cabinet," which, of course, drew on Richard F. Fenno, *The President's Cabinet,* Cambridge: Harvard University Press, 1959, and John F. Carter, *The New Dealers,* New York: Simon and Schuster, 1934, to a great extent. See also Lester Tanzer, *The Kennedy Circle,* New York: David McKay, 1961.

(41) See Katherine Marshall, *Together: Annals of an Army Wife,* Atlanta, Georgia: Tupper & Love, 1946, for an account of her life with Marshall. Both of Mrs. Marshall's sons went to Woodberry Forest Preparatory School. The Marshalls had homes at Fire Island, N. Y.; Leesburg, Va.; and Pinehurst, N. C.

(42) Quoted in Lloyd C. Gardner, *Economic Aspects of New Deal Diplomacy,* Madison: University of Wisconsin Press, 1964, p. 22. *(43)* Joseph M. Jones, *The Fifteen Weeks,* New York: Viking Press, 1955, p. 93.

(44) Forrestal, the first person to be called Secretary of Defense, first came into government service from the presidency of Dillon, Read. Along with Stimson, Patterson, McCloy, Harriman, Marshall, George Earle, and William Bullitt, he was one of eight *Social Register* listees in the inner circle around President Roosevelt during the war years. He was also a key adviser to President Truman during the early postwar years. On Forrestal see the excellent book by Arnold A. Rogow, *James Forrestal,* New York: Macmillan, 1963, which has a wealth of interesting information on the Democrats of the 1940's. Dillon, Read and other Wall Street firms figure very prominently in Rogow's account. Mills, 1956, p. 289, knew of the tie between Dillon, Read and the Democrats, but he did not integrate it into his analysis. For that matter, he did not deal at all with the political parties, one of the most serious lacks of his book. This is in keeping with the weakness of the chapter on "The Political Directorate," which makes only three points: (1) the rise of the Executive branch and the political outsider (pp. 228-231); (2) the big business character of the Eisenhower Administration (pp. 231-235); and (3) the lack of a civil service because neither corporate executives nor party politicians want one (pp. 235-241).

(45) Grant McConnell, *Private Power and American Democracy,* New York: Alfred A. Knopf, 1966, pp. 273-274. *(46)* See Cater, 1964, pp. 192-193, for the opinion that foreign policy, defense, and economic policy are the most important issues. *(47)* Mills, 1956, p. 228. *(48)* *Forbes,* July 15, 1965, p. 33. *(49)* On Frankfurter, see *Time,* March 5, 1965, p. 68. I have relied on Carter, 1934, and Gardner, 1964, for information on the men around President Roosevelt. *(50)* Carter, 1934, p. 315. *(51)* Gerard, 1951, p. 317. *(52)* Gardner, 1964. This is a "must" book for understanding that the foreign trade policy of the business aristocracy has not changed in many decades, especially in conjunction with Jones, 1955, McLellan and Woodhouse, 1960, and Williams, 1964.

(53) James P. Warburg, *The Long Road Home,* Garden City, New York: Doubleday, 1964. This autobiography gives insight into one aspect of upper-class life and the thinking of at least one liberal member of the upper class. *(54)* See

Charles B. Seib and Alan L. Otten, "Abe, Help!—LBJ," *Esquire,* June, 1965, p. 86.

(55) "LBJ and the Drug Industry," *I. F. Stone's Weekly,* April 26, 1965. Among Johnson's cabinet appointments were Secretary of Commerce John T. Connor, president of Merck & Company, and Secretary of the Treasury Henry Fowler, chief Washington lobbyist for Merck when appointed. (56) *I. F. Stone's Weekly,* July 26, 1965, p. 3. See also *Congressional Record* (Senate) May 26, 1965, pp. 11399-11403.

(57) Charles Roberts, *LBJ's Inner Circle,* New York: Delacorte Press, 1965, p. 168. My original understanding of the men around Johnson was based upon "The 'inner inner' circle around Johnson," *The New York Times,* February 28, 1965, p. 21; a book review by I. F. Stone in *The New York Review of Books,* July 30, 1965; *Newsweek,* July 13, 1964, pp. 65-66; and *Time,* December 11, 1964, p. 31-32. (58) Keller, 1963, p. 297.

(59) Mills, 1956, p. 207. (60) Potter, 1962, points out that most of these men do not like the idea of a government career and hence do nothing that would compromise their chance of returning to the more lucrative corporate world. (61) Seymour Harris, *The Economics of the Political Parties,* New York: Macmillan, 1962, p. 15. The first two examples are paraphrases, the third is a direct quote. (62) Richard Harris, *The Real Voice,* New York: Macmillan, 1964, p. 145.

(63) See Henry J. Abraham and Edward M. Goldberg, "A Note on the Appointment of Justices of the Supreme Court of the United States," *American Bar Association Journal,* February, 1960, for details on delay and rejection of confirmations for Supreme Court justices. The only person rejected in the twentieth century was Southern conservative John J. Parker in 1930. My special thanks to Professor Goldberg for his comments and suggestions on my discussion of the federal judiciary. (64) Joel B. Grossman, "Federal Judicial Selection: The Work of the ABA Committee," *Midwest Journal of Political Science,* VIII, 3 August, 1964. The first two sentences are on pp. 222-223, the next sentence is in footnote 5 on p. 223, and the last sentence is on page 235.

(65) Grossman, 1964, pp. 225-233. (66) James Moore, "The Power Elite and Federal Judges," a paper for my course on the upper class at California State College at Los Angeles. I reanalyzed the data collected by Moore, who also gathered the information on judges reported in the next paragraphs of the narrative. (67) John R. Schmidhauser, *The Supreme Court: Its Politics, Personalities, and Procedures,* New York: Holt Rinehart & Winston, 1960, p. 55. The quote is as it was in Keller, 1963, p. 300.

(68) Joseph S. Clark, *The Senate Establishment,* New York: Hill & Wang, 1963, p. 22.

(69) Donald Matthews, *U. S. Senators and Their World,* Chapel Hill: University of North Carolina Press, 1960, p. 61; the information that follows on the patricians is on pp. 61-62, 132-133, 158, 163, and 240. (70) Matthews, 1960, p. 61. (71) Other senators who are members of the upper class besides those mentioned in the text are liberals Joseph Clark (SR, Philadelphia), Ernest Gruening (Hotchkiss, Harvard); Claiborne Pell (SR, New York), and William Proxmire (Hill School, Yale, and Harvard); middle-of-the-roader Hugh Scott

(SR, Philadelphia); and conservatives Harry Byrd and Peter Dominick (SR, NY).

(*72*) My understanding of the literature on lobbying was greatly enhanced by discussions with political scientist Murray Frost and by "The Lobbyists," a student paper by Douglas Eddy which summarized the relevant literature. Eddy also studied 124 registered lobbyists and found no members of the upper class in that game.

(*73*) *I. F. Stone's Weekly*, June 21, 1965, p. 2. (*74*) Larry L. King, "Washington's Money Birds," *Harper's Magazine*, August, 1965. (*75*) Elinor Langer, "Crusade and After," *The Nation*, September 28, 1964, p. 166. (*76*) See Andrew Hacker, "The Corporation and Campaign Politics" (mimeographed), 1961, for examples of these techniques. See also Lee Metcalf and Vic Reinemer, *Overcharge: How Electric Utilities Exploit and Mislead the Public, and What You Can Do About It.* New York: David McKay, 1967. (*77*) For why the committee is in action, see "The Money Never Leaves Home," *Forbes*, May 1, 1965, pp. 15-16. (*78*) *The Nation*, October 11, 1965, editorial entitled "A Presidential Front."

(*79*) Desmond Smith, "American Radio Today," *Harper's Magazine*, September, 1964. (*80*) Mills, 1956, p. 275. (*81*) Engler, 1961, p. 492, and all of Chapter 16. (*82*) "Once a proposition has been confirmed by two or more independent measurement processes, the uncertainty of its interpretation is greatly reduced." Eugene Webb, Donald Campbell, Richard Schwartz, and Lee Sechrest, *Unobtrusive Measures: Nonreactive Research in the Social Sciences.* Chicago: Rand McNally, 1966, p. 3.

CHAPTER FIVE

(*1*) Contrary to the claims of some critics, one of whom, Dennis Wrong (*Commentary*, September, 1956, p. 278-280), said that Mills implied that defense spending was primarily an attempt to prop up the economy, Mills in fact agreed that the military ascendancy was based upon the technological advances which placed the United States in a "military neighborhood." His views can be found on pp. 183-184 and 275 of *The Power Elite*. It is certainly the case that he was not very explicit about the matter, however. The closest Mills comes to an economic theory of defense spending is when he quotes New York *Times* columnist Arthur Krock (SR, NY) to the effect that "the stock market selling that followed the sudden conciliatory overtures from the Kremlin supports the thesis that immediate prosperity in this country is linked to a war economy and suggests desperate economic problems that may arise on the home front" (p. 216, but see also pp. 149 and 167). Few would disagree with Mills and Krock on the possible economic difficulties that could be caused by a decline in defense spending. One eminent economist, Murray L. Weidenbaum, senior economist of the Stanford Research Institute and formerly with the Budget Bureau and Boeing Aircraft, warned in a government report that a drop-off of 1 per cent in such spending would have to be managed with great care to avoid a serious slowdown. Weidenbaum's opinions can be found on p. 8650 of the *Congressional Record* (Senate), April 23, 1964. See also Jack Raymond, *Power at the Pentagon*, New York: Harper & Row, 1964, for further information and excellent references.

(2) Janowitz, 1960, p. 378. See pp. 374-382 for a detailed empirical discussion of the second careers of military men. *(3)* Janowitz, 1960, p. 375. This was Hunter's first list. Earlier I reported an analysis of the 100 top ("starred") names on Hunter's second list. I added the information on Doolittle. One name more that perhaps should be counted is retired Admiral Ben Moreell, who is on both Hunter lists. *(4)* Mills, 1956, p. 196; Janowitz, 1960, p. viii. *(5)* Robert G. Sherrill, "The Brass Pyramid," *The Nation,* July 11, 1966, pp. 49-51; Janowitz, 1960, p. 382.

(6) Janowitz, 1960, pp. 347-348; on the subordination of the military by Mc-Namara, see Raymond, 1964, chapter 16. *(7)* Raymond, 1964, p. 286. *(8)* Raymond, 1964, pp. 287-288 *(9)* Bruce Catton, *The War Lords of Washington,* New York: Harcourt, Brace, 1948, pp. 302-303, 308, 311. *(10)* Mills, 1956, p. 275. *(11)* Catton, 1948, p. 246; see also p. 46. *(12)* Catton, 1948, p. 281; the information on two of these "blue book" executives, Searls and Weinberg, came from James Byrnes's *All in One Lifetime,* New York: Harper & Bros., 1958, pp. 171 and 243. *(13)* Catton, 1948, pp. 117-118. Nelson agreed vehemently that the dollar-a-year men were necessary. See his account of the war production effort, *Arsenal of Democracy,* New York: Harcourt, Brace, 1946.

(14) Rogow, 1963, pp. 102-103. *(15)* Catton, 1948, pp. 231-236. *(16)* Raymond, 1964, p. 82. *(17)* Catton, 1948, pp. 290-292. *(18)* Rogow, 1963, p. 122. *(19)* Janowitz, 1960, p. 347. *(20)* Tristam Coffin, *The Armed Society,* Baltimore: Penguin Books, 1964, p. 169. *(21)* These points are summarized by Catton, 1948, pp. 310-311. But see also pp. 114-115, 118, 120, 135-136, and 138. *(22)* Julius Duscha, *Arms, Money and Politics,* New York: Ives Washburn, Inc., 1964, p. 67, p. 178. *(23)* *Congressional Record* (Senate), June 25, 1965, p. 14291. *(24)* Coffin, 1964, p. 165. *(25)* Cater, 1964, p. 36 *(26)* Raymond, 1964, p. 192.

(27) Janowitz, 1960, p. 384. *(28)* Janowitz, 1960, p. 385. *(29)* Janowitz, 1960, p. 387. *(30)* Janowitz, 1960, p. 387. *(31)* Duscha, 1964, p. 95. *(32)* Duscha, 1964, p. 87; see Coffin, 1964, pp. 172-182, for further information on the associations and their activities. *(33)* Janowitz, 1960, p. 209. *(34)* Janowitz, 1960, chapter 5 and p. 209 ff. In Mills, 1956, see p. 393, note 20 and note 29. *(35)* *Fortune,* February 15, 1952, p. 208. *(36)* Janowitz, 1960, pp. 296-297. *(37)* Mills, 1956, pp. 187-188. *(38)* Janowitz, 1960, p. 312.

(39) Coffin, 1964, pp. 270-272, gives a complete list of solons with uniforms. *(40)* Janowitz, 1960, p. 349. *(41)* Cater, 1964, p. 135. *(42)* Janowitz, 1960, p. viii. *(43)* Wise and Ross, *The Invisible Government,* 1964. This is not quite the same "invisible government" that Smoot sees. *(44)* I. F. Stone, *The Truman Era,* New York: Monthly Review Press, 1953, pp. 21-24. *(45)* Wise and Ross, 1964, p. 293. I added the sociological information.

(46) Robert G. Sherrill, "Johnson and the Oil Men," *Ramparts,* January, 1967. *(47)* Fred Cook, *The FBI Nobody Knows,* New York: Macmillan, 1964, p. 49. *(48)* Cook, 1964, p. 420, but see also pp. 240-242. *(49)* William Seagle, "The American National Police," *Harper's Magazine,* November, 1934, p. 753. *(50)* Seagle, 1934.

CHAPTER SIX

(1) See John Gunther, *Inside U.S.A.,* New York: Harper & Bros., 1951, p. 678, for the "caliphate" remark about Delaware. It would not be overly facetious to

say that control of the state of Delaware is all that is needed at this level from the point of view of members of the upper class, for that state has virtually no tax on corporations. To avoid the taxes imposed by other states, nearly 44,000 businesses are incorporated there. One-third of the companies listed on the New York Stock Exchange do this, including such well-known companies as General Motors, Bethlehem Steel, General Dynamics, du Pont, General Foods, RCA, and Ford. U. S. Steel joined the ranks in 1965 when it merged with one of its subsidiaries. See *Time*, August 27, 1965, p. 74, and the *San Francisco Chronicle*, September 2, 1965, p. 54.

See Harmon Zeigler, "Interest Groups in the States," *Politics in the American States*, eds. Herbert Jacob and Kenneth Vines, Boston: Little, Brown & Co., 1965, p. 133, for the fact that 17 states have an important labor contingent. Michigan is supposedly the best example of a labor state, but then there is the following quote from aristocrat G. Mennen (Soapy) Williams about the nature of the Democratic Party in that state: "people associated with business outnumbered those identified with labor in the roster of delegates and alternates to the 1956 Democratic National Convention. Nor is this an isolated phenomenon; business and professional men and women make up the majority of our county chairmen." Quoted by Heard, 1962, p. 106. Williams, a member of the upper class, is a leading figure in the Democratic Party in Michigan. See also John P. White and John R. Owens, *Parties, Group Interests, and Campaign Finance: Michigan '56*. Princeton: Citizens' Research Foundation, 1960.

(*2*) Gunther, 1951, p. 785; Dahl, 1961. (*3*) I am grateful to political scientist Murray Frost for his concise summaries of most of these studies. See Polsby, 1963, for a detailed account. (*4*) Dahl, 1961. All subsequent page numbers in parentheses in this chapter refer to this 1961 work by Dahl, *Who Governs?* (*5*) Dahl, 1961, p. 66. (*6*) Greer and Orleans, 1964, p. 827. (*7*) Gunther, 1951, p. 650.

(*8*) Dahl, 1959, p. 33; Greer and Orleans, 1964. (*9*) Dahl, 1959, p. 32. (*10*) Austin Ranney, "Parties in State Politics," in Jacob and Vines, 1965, p. 80. (*11*) Zeigler, 1965, p. 109. (*12*) Paul Simon, "The Illinois State Legislature," *Harper's Magazine*, September, 1964, p. 74. (*13*) Robert H. Simmons, "The Washington State Plural Executive: An Initial Effort in Interaction Analysis," *The Western Political Science Quarterly*, XVIII, 2, part 1 (June 1965), p. 381. The words "clientele," "dedicated revenue sources," and "systemic crisis" are also from this article. Since I shared an office for three years with this excellent political scientist, I borrow his words at will.

(*14*) McConnell, 1966, p. 188, quoting a study by James W. Fesler, *The Independence of State Regulatory Agencies*, Chicago: Public Administration Service, 1942. There is, of course, a vast literature on this subject, all of which says about the same thing except for the case where the agency has several "clients" and can play one against the other to gain some autonomy. My knowledge of this literature is based upon discussions with political scientists Robert H. Simmons and Benjamin Smith.

(*15*) Hacker, 1964, p. 138. (*16*) *Time*, October 9, 1964, p. 100; for details on the courses on politics given by corporations, see Hacker, "The Corporation and Campaign Politics," 1961, pp. 8-9. At that time Hacker thought the program a failure. (*17*) Dahl, 1961, p. 82. (*18*) See Arnold Auerbach, "Power and Progress in Pittsburgh," *Trans-action*, II, 6 (1965), 15-20, on Mellon. See

Time, December 18, 1964, pp. 56-58, on Mrs. Chandler. (*19*) Carol Estes Thometz, *The Decision-Makers: The Power Structure of Dallas,* Dallas: Southern Methodist University Press, 1963, p. 56.

CHAPTER SEVEN

(*1*) Kahl, 1957, p. 12. (*2*) Sweezy, 1953, p. 124. (*3*) Krech, Crutchfield, and Ballachey, 1962, p. 338. (*4*) Greer and Orleans, 1964, p. 833.

(*5*) See Kahl, 1957; Krech, Crutchfield, and Ballachey, 1962; and Paul Mussen, John Conger, and Jerome Kagan, *Child Development and Personality,* New York: Harper & Row, 1963. Most studies demonstrating psychological differences between social classes compare the "middle" and "working" classes, but for one that found the interesting differences that had been predicted between upper and middle-class boys at Harvard, see Charles McArthur, "Personality Differences Between Middle and Upper Classes," *Journal of Abnormal and Social Psychology,* L (1955), 247-254. (*6*) Kahl, 1957, p. 14.

(*7*) See W. S. Landecker, "Class Boundaries," *American Sociological Review,* XXV (1960), 868-877, for the suggestion that the continuum hypothesis may be appropriate to one part of the social ladder, the class hypothesis to other parts. I believe the suggestion has merit, for the club-like institutions and property-holding interests of the upper class give it a definiteness and cohesiveness that does not appear to exist in the "income classes" at the middle levels. See C. Wright Mills, *White Collar,* New York: Oxford University Press, 1952, and *The Marxists,* 1962, for excellent discussions of the middle and lower levels of society.

(*8*) Hacker, 1964, p. 141. (*9*) Hacker, 1964, p. 142. (*10*) Sweezy, 1953, p. 57. (*11*) Krech, et al., 1962, pp. 334-336. (*12*) See Dahl, 1961, p. 229; and Paul Sweezy, "Has Capitalism Changed?" in *Has Capitalism Changed,* ed. Shigeto Tsuru, Tokyo: Twanami Shotin, 1961, pp. 87-90. (*13*) Mills, 1956, p. 30. (*14*) Baltzell, 1958, p. 435. (*15*) Dahl, 1959, p. 36. (*16*) Bell, 1960, p. 42. (*17*) Dahl, 1958, p. 464. (*18*) Greer and Orleans, 1964, pp. 824-825. (*19*) Matthews, 1954, p. 32.

(*20*) Dahl, 1958, p. 463. (*21*) See the discussion of this concept in the Introduction. (*22*) Dahl, 1958, p. 469. (*23*) On taxes, see Nossiter, 1964; Rowen, 1964; and Philip Stern, *The Great Treasury Raid,* New York: Random House, 1964. On subsidies, see all of the above, plus Engler, 1961, Chapter 7, especially pp. 161-162. On welfare spending, see Morris Udall, "Where's the Welfare State?" *New Republic,* October 1, 1962, p. 13. On the military, see Chapter 5 of this book; Wise and Ross, 1964; and Raymond, 1964. (*24*) Dahl, 1958, p. 467. (*25*) Dahl, 1959, p. 36. See especially, Bauer, 1966. (*26*) Dahl, 1958, p. 468.

(*27*) See Webb, Campbell, Schwartz, and Sechrest, 1966, especially chapter 1. "No research method is without bias" (p. 1). (*28*) Needless to say, many criticisms of Mills are not relevant to this book. For example, I did not overemphasize the military or neglect the political parties. For a selection of the most representative criticisms of *The Power Elite* and Mills's answer to them, as well as my own attempt to adjudicate the dispute, see *C. Wright Mills and The Power Elite,* edited by G. William Domhoff and Hoyt B. Ballard, Boston:

Beacon Press, 1968. (*29*) Hacker, 1964. (*30*) Dahl, 1959. (*31*) See Hacker, 1964, for details and references. (*32*) Dahl, 1959; Gordon, 1945.

(*33*) Berle is himself a corporate director. (*34*) See Smigel, 1964, for details and references. (*35*) See Hubert Beck, *Men Who Control Our Universities*, Morningside Heights, New York: King's Crown Press, 1947, for further details. (*36*) Mills, 1956, p. 4, p. 134. (*37*) Paul Sweezy, *The Theory of Capitalist Development*, New York: Monthly Review Press, 1942, pp. 240–241; see also Sweezy, 1962, pp. 87–90.

(*38*) C. Wright Mills, "Comments on Criticism," *Dissent*, V, 1 (1957), 33. (*39*) Dahl, 1961, p. 233. (*40*) Dahl, 1958, p. 465. (*41*) Parsons, 1960, pp. 213–214. (*42*) "Viewing U. S. Economy With a Marxist Glass," *Business Week*, April 13, 1963. (*43*) Whalen, 1964, p. 112. This is the difference between a New Dealer and a member of the old guard. (*44*) Baltzell, 1958, p. 429. (*45*) Osborn Elliott, *Men at the Top*, New York: Harper & Bros., 1960.

(*46*) McConnell, 1966, p. 284. What the businessman objects to in regulation is that it clashes with his ideology (Dahl, 1959, p. 38, quoting R. E. Lane's *The Regulation of Businessmen*. (*47*) Elliott, 1960. (*48*) McConnell, 1966, p. 294. (*49*) Nossiter, 1964, pp. 40-41.

Index